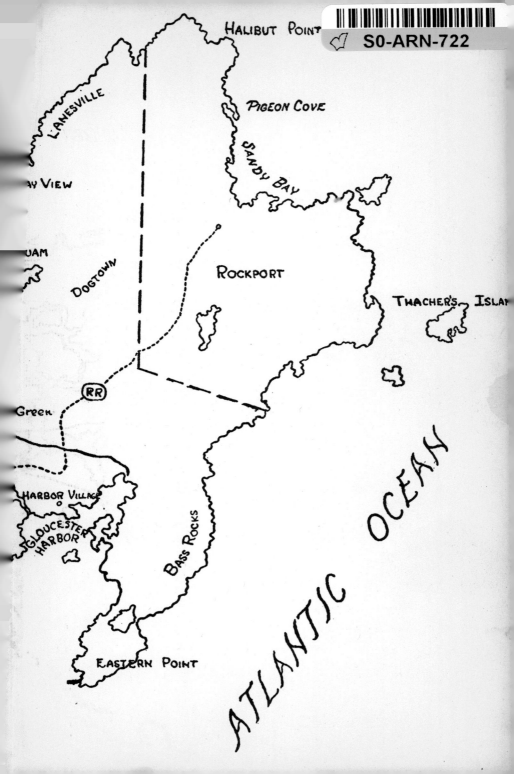

The Saga of Cape Ann

BANKERS IN GLOUCESTER HARBOR

The Saga of Cape Ann

Melvin T. Copeland
&
Elliott C. Rogers

THE BOND WHEELWRIGHT CO.
PORTER'S LANDING, FREEPORT, MAINE.

THEY THAT GO
DOWN TO THE SEA
IN SHIPS
1623 — 1923

Preface

THE IDEA OF our writing a book about Cape Ann originated with Mr. Rogers. He offered to dig up material for such a volume if Mr. Copeland would do the writing. That, by and large, has been the working arrangement.

Mr. Rogers was born in Gloucester and his family has lived there for seven generations. Mr. Copeland is a native of Maine but he began to spend his summers in Gloucester thirty-five years ago and has been a year-round resident for about ten years. Thus both authors have a firsthand acquaintance with the Cape.

This volume does not pretend to be exhaustive; its preparation was not undertaken with that end in view. Rather the purpose has been to depict the landmarks of the Cape, with their historical setting, and to record some of the local folklore. On some points discrepancies and inaccuracies have been found in the published material examined. In such cases we have weighed the conflicting evidence and then stated what seems to us to be the best substantiated conclusions, without going into all the details.

The material utilized in preparing the volume has come from numerous books, brochures, and pamphlets published about Cape Ann and its various features; from numerous scrapbooks of old newspaper clippings; from several unpublished memoranda; from inquiries among long-time residents of the Cape; from the personal experiences of the authors; and by no means least, from their firsthand observations on frequent tramps over all parts of the Cape.

The illustrations in this volume were reproduced from photographs taken by Mr. and Mrs. George W. Harvey about sixty or seventy years ago. The local area maps were prepared by George E. Hodsdon and the end-page map by Christopher Brown.

We are indebted to many people who have supplied us with information and helpful leads. The list is much too long to publish here, but we are indeed grateful to all of them. We appreciate most of all the careful assistance of Mrs. Helen G. Rogers in patiently typing the manuscript and in offering numerous helpful suggestions.

MELVIN T. COPELAND
ELLIOTT C. ROGERS

Annisquam, Massachusetts
  March, 1959

Contents

Illustrations and Maps

I

Planting the Settlement

ON THE SHORE of Gloucester Harbor, looking eastward to the sea, stands a bronze old fishing captain, alert and ready, come what may. For over three centuries the men whom the old captain symbolizes have been watching that same horizon. They have seen many ships come and go—fishing craft and foreign traders, sleek bankers and tubby pinkies, pirate ships and war vessels, lobster boats and pleasure craft, in infinite variety. On the land, wives and children also have watched, sometimes with fear in their hearts and lumps in their throats. And around them farmers and ship carpenters, granite cutters and fish lumpers, and flocks of summer vacationers have followed their trades and pursued their pleasures.

Salty old Cape Ann has had a rugged, adventuresome, and at times, a turbulent history. Much of that history has left its landmarks as well as its sea tales. They are to be found along the shores of the Cape, on the river and its creeks, and on the old paths across the moors and through the woods. In this volume we are attempting to point out some of those landmarks and to note the historical events associated with them. In addition to its marine and topographical features with which legends and traditions are associated, Cape Ann also has numerous items of geological, botanical, and biological interest which merit occasional comment.

The white man's history of Cape Ann began early in the seventeenth century. In 1605 and 1606 Champlain, the great French explorer, made trips along the coast of what soon was to be known as New England, and landed on a

1

beach on the northeastern shore of Gloucester Harbor. On his visit in 1606, Champlain found about two hundred Indians on the Cape and one of their encampments was on the upland back of the beach where he came ashore. The Indians, under their chief Quiouhamenec, were friendly, but Champlain did not tarry long with them.

In 1614 Captain John Smith, that lively adventurer and romantic storyteller, sailed along the shores of the Cape on an exploratory trip, but he did not land, perhaps because he spied no Indian maidens to be charmed.

The first settlement on the Cape was a transitory one, and like various other settlements of that era, came about somewhat accidentally. In 1623 a small ship sailed from Dorchester, England, for a summer fishing trip on the banks off the northern coast of North America, with the intention also of founding a colony. The ship did not secure a full cargo at the usual fishing grounds, so it proceeded southward to Massachusetts Bay where it found an abundance of cod. That circumstance led to the first attempt at settlement on Cape Ann.

Since a larger crew was needed for fishing than for working the ship, the expedition had been planned with a view to leaving some of the men in the new country while the remainder returned to Europe with the cargo of fish. It was expected that during the winter, the men left behind could erect dwellings and lay in a store of meat and fish for the next year's fishing expedition. Consequently, after the ship had filled its holds with fish, fourteen members of its crew were put ashore with provisions for the winter. They were landed at the harbor on the south side of "Cape Anne," the name which already had been assigned to this piece of land in honor of the mother of King Charles I of England.

Thus the first temporary settlement resulted from the finding of a good supply of codfish in the vicinity of the Cape in the summer of 1623, and for better or for worse, much of

2

the history of the Cape thereafter was linked to the fishing industry and subject to its frustrations.

The Dorchester ship took its first cargo to Spain, hoping for a better price than could be obtained in England, but the price was low also in Spain, and the proceeds of the trip did not cover the ship's expenses. Hopeful of better luck next time, the owners of the Dorchester ship sent it forth again in the spring of 1624. That year they also sent a second boat, considerably larger in size. The boats reached Cape Ann, picked up the men who had spent the winter there, and devoted the summer to fishing. Again, however, the fishermen suffered disappointment. The catch that summer was very poor, and the proceeds were barely sufficient to cover the cost of the wages and provisions for the men who remained for the winter. When the ships sailed for England that fall, they left thirty-two men to spend the winter on the Cape.

In the spring of 1625 the Dorchester Company made a third attempt to prove that its venture could be successful. That year the company sent three ships, but the largest vessel was damaged soon after it put to sea, and had to return to England. The results of the third summer expedition also turned out to be unprofitable, and that ended the Dorchester venture. Most of the members of the crew returned to England when the ships sailed for home in the fall of 1625. A few did remain in the new, wild country, however, and joined with several men, who had been cast out of the young Plymouth colony, to start a temporary settlement on Cape Ann and a year later to lay the foundations for the Puritan settlement at Naumkeag (Salem) out of which the dominant Massachusetts Bay Colony eventually emerged.

Here on Cape Ann, furthermore, a series of events occurred in 1624 and 1625 which were of deep significance in the history of New England.

While Edward Winslow of the Plymouth Colony had been in England in the fall of 1623, he and Robert Cushman,

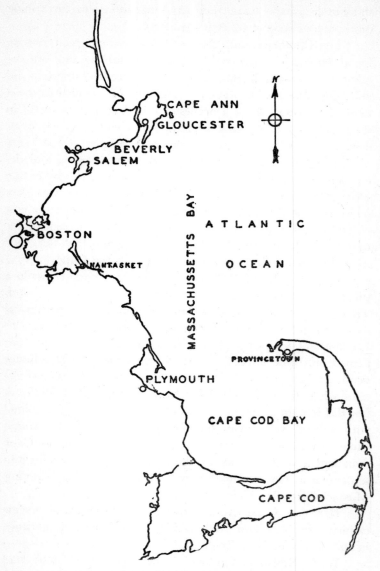

MASSACHUSETTS BAY
Where the Pilgrim and Puritan colonies were planted.

another Pilgrim, obtained a grant nominally giving them title to the American region known as "Cape Anne." In the following spring, after she had discharged her cargo of supplies at Plymouth, the Pilgrims sent their ship, the *Charity*, forty miles across Massachusetts Bay to their new domain. Along the shore of Cape Ann, of course, they found the men sent over by the Dorchester Company, but no friction appears to have arisen between the two groups at that time. The men from Plymouth built a fishing stage—a frame for drying fish—and set up salt pans on Fisherman's Field, now Stage Fort Park, just to the southwest of where the bronze statue of the old fishing captain stands on the shore of Gloucester Harbor. The *Charity*'s fishing trip in 1624, however, was not a profitable one, and its lack of success was attributed to the lateness of its arrival and the habitual drunkenness of its guzzling skipper.

In 1625 the Pilgrims sent another fishing expedition from Plymouth to Cape Ann, but before recounting what happened on its arrival in Gloucester Harbor, it is necessary to go back and relate certain events which had transpired in Plymouth during the preceding year.

First it should be pointed out, perhaps, that when the Pilgrims sailed from England in the *Mayflower* in 1620 only slightly more than half their number were members of the Pilgrim church.[1] The remainder had been recruited by the Merchant Adventurers, who were financing the expedition, without regard to the recruits' religious beliefs. The Pilgrims were known as "Saints," the nonmembers as "Strangers." Some of the Strangers played an important part, of course, in the new settlement; Captain Myles Standish and John Alden, for example, were Strangers.

In the years following 1620 more Strangers were sent over by the promoters of the colony. They generally were under contract to share in the work for the benefit of the pro-

---

1 George F. Willison, *Saints and Strangers* (New York, Reynal and Hitchcock, 1945), pp. 437-42.

5

moters and in return were furnished subsistence, such as it was. In 1623, however, a third distinct group arrived. This group, the only one of its kind sent to Plymouth, consisted of ten persons. Its leader was John Oldham and one of the other men in the group was Roger Conant. The members of the group were "on their perticuler. . . . They made no contributions to the common store and had no rights in the joint stock, enjoying an independent economic status on the lands assigned to them."[2] Both Oldham and Conant were to figure in subsequent events on Cape Ann.

A third person who was to share in those events, along with Oldham and Conant, was the Reverend John Lyford, who arrived at Plymouth in the spring of 1624. The Reverend Lyford was accompanied by his wife and five children. He was a graduate of Magdalen College, Oxford, and had served as minister in several small parishes in England and Ireland. He was the first clergyman to arrive at Plymouth, and although he was a member of the Church of England, he soon requested, with great humility, that he be admitted to the Pilgrim church. His request was granted and he began to share the pulpit each Sunday with William Brewster, the patriarch of the Pilgrims.

Within a few weeks after the Reverend Lyford's arrival, the Saints discovered that he and John Oldham were fomenting discontent in the colony. Roger Conant also was one of the malcontents.[3] The *Charity* had returned from her first fishing trip to Cape Ann and was preparing to sail again for England when Governor Bradford of the Plymouth Colony learned that the Reverend Lyford was sending letters home which were derogatory of the conduct of the colony. Consequently, on the evening after the *Charity* sailed, Governor Bradford followed her offshore in a shallop. He boarded the

---

2 *Ibid.*, p. 236.

3 William Bradford, *Of Plymouth Plantation 1620-1647*, Samuel Eliot Morrison, ed. (New York, Alfred Knopf, 1952), p. 169.

Charity and demanded the letters written by Lyford, and the passengers and crew were searched to obtain them. Over twenty letters by Lyford and several written by Oldham were found. Lyford's letters were "full of slanders and false accusations," and in one of them he wrote: "This Captain Standish looks like a silly boy and is in utter contempt."[4]

Governor Bradford made copies of some of the letters and kept the originals of others, but when he returned to the shore he made no mention of the evidence he had obtained. He merely bided his time. Several weeks later Oldham and Lyford became insolent and undertook to set up a separate meeting on the Lord's Day. Then the Governor put them on trial and produced the letters which he had intercepted. Oldham raged and made mutinous threats, but Lyford humbly confessed. Oldham was sentenced to be expelled from the colony immediately, but Lyford was to be permitted to remain for six months.

Nevertheless, after a month or two Lyford wrote another letter to England in which he alleged that his previous accusations were true. That letter also was intercepted. At about the same time it was learned by the Pilgrims that Lyford had committed several moral offenses in England and Ireland before coming to Plymouth, and his wife sorrowfully made a statement to one of the deacons that she "could keep no maids but he would be meddling with them."[5] As a result of all his perfidy, the Reverend Lyford was banished, and he went to Nantasket to join John Oldham and Roger Conant.

In the spring of 1625 Oldham returned to Plymouth, without first having obtained permission, and resumed his violent verbal attacks upon those who were not on his side. He was committed to the guardhouse for a time and then ordered to depart. On the way to the boat on which he was to leave, he was forced to pass through a guard of Captain Stan-

---

4 *Ibid.*, p. 150.
5 *Ibid.*, p. 167.

dish's musketeers, each of whom "was ordered to give him a thump on the breech with the butt end of his musket"[6] as he passed down the line. He returned to Nantasket.

Now we revert to Cape Ann. When the second Pilgrim fishing expedition arrived at Fisherman's Field in Gloucester Harbor in the summer of 1625, who should they find in possession of the fishing stage which they had built the previous year but John Oldham, Roger Conant, and the Reverend Lyford.[7] When Captain Standish, who had accompanied the expedition, demanded surrender of the stage, Oldham and his associates merely laughed and jeered at him and told him that the Pilgrims' grant to the Cape Ann territory was worthless, as in fact it was. The fiery captain naturally was enraged at this seeming impudence of men he had helped to drive out of Plymouth. Bloodshed was narrowly averted, but on Governor Bradford's advice, the outcasts were permitted to keep the old stage and the Pilgrims built a new one.

It appears that Conant and Oldham had moved from Nantasket to Cape Ann at the suggestion of Reverend John White of England, one of the founders of the Dorchester Company and a critic of the Pilgrims.[8] The Reverend White subsequently was one of the promoters of the Puritan Massachusetts Bay Colony. Thus the clash at Fisherman's Field in 1625 marked the opening of the strife between the separatist Pilgrims and the nonconformist Puritans.[9]

The Plymouth ship is reported to have made a good catch of fish that summer, but that was the last attempt by the Pilgrims to operate a fishing stage on the Cape Ann shore.

6 *Ibid.*, p. 165.
7 *Ibid.*, p. 170.
8 Willison, *op. cit.*, p. 252.
9 Both sects were ardently Protestant—the Pilgrims desiring to worship as a separate church while the more well-to-do Puritans opposed the traditional and formal usages in the established church and advocated simpler forms of faith and worship than those then required by law. The Pilgrims were a small sect, the Puritans a large one. The Puritans were more tightly strait-laced in demanding sober observance of the Sabbath and in various other matters of personal conduct.

Thus both the Dorchester Company and the Plymouth Colony ended their operations at Cape Ann in the summer of 1625. But out of those operations came the nucleus of a permanent settlement on the Cape and the base for a founding of the Massachusetts Bay Colony.

Roger Conant, John Oldham, the Reverend Lyford, a few of their friends from Nantasket, and several members of the Dorchester crew remained on Cape Ann when the fishing boats sailed away in the fall of 1625. In the following year, under the leadership of Roger Conant, most of that group moved from Cape Ann to Naumkeag, where they started a new settlement. It was from that settlement that the Puritan Massachusetts Bay Colony developed.

The first Puritans migrated from England to Naumkeag in 1628 and settled with Roger Conant's little group. By having a few white men and not merely Indians on hand to receive them, they were much more fortunate than the Pilgrims had been at Plymouth eight years earlier. There were 60 persons in that first party of Puritan settlers and their leader was John Endicott. As the restrictions on freedom of religious worship were tightened in England under Charles I and as the persecution of the Puritans became more severe, a great exodus took place. In 1629 about 350 more Puritans arrived at Naumkeag, soon renamed Salem; in 1630 about 1000 came; between 1631 and 1634 about 2500; and between 1634 and 1640 at least 16,000. That was a grand total of about 20,000 persons arriving on the northern shore of Massachusetts Bay within a period of a dozen years.

The significance to Cape Ann of that influx of Puritans into Salem, only fifteen miles away, will be pointed out in a moment, but first it may be of some interest for us to recount, very briefly, what happened to Roger Conant, John Oldham, and the Reverend Lyford after the Puritans arrived. Soon after they came, the Reverend Lyford departed. He went to Virginia, where he died a couple of years later. In 1630

Roger Conant quarreled with John Winthrop, who had succeeded John Endicott as Governor of Salem, and Conant and his group then moved across the North River to start a new settlement in Beverly. In 1630 also John Oldham moved to Watertown, where he engaged in Indian and coastal trade and became wealthy. He apparently learned to control his temper and his tongue and became an influential member of the Massachusetts Bay Colony.

There is a legend that the Dorchester men brought with them in 1623 the materials for building a house which was erected on Fisherman's Field and that the house was moved to Naumkeag by Roger Conant and his party. At the time of the 250th anniversary of Gloucester in 1892 a picture was published of what purported to be that house. The inscription read: "First House erected in Gloucester, 1623-24. Trading House of the Dorchester Company. Brought from England and located at Stage Fort Park. Removed to Salem in 1628." The picture shows a house with a two and a half story frame and two gables in front. It had ten double windows on the front and end, a brick chimney, boarded sides, shingled roof, and a stone foundation.

That picture must have been the product of the imagination of some local latter-day enthusiast with no historical acumen. The materials for such a structure could not have been brought across the ocean on a small fishing vessel. Glass was not in use for windows till a much later date. And even if they had been competent carpenters and masons, the Dorchester fishermen would not have had the time to lay bricks and erect such a structure. The portrayal presumably was instigated by some zealous resident of Cape Ann to support the claim that the first permanent settlement in the Massachusetts Bay Colony was located at Fisherman's Field. Cape Ann has enough interesting and famous landmarks, however, without our being gullible enough to swallow that house.

10

The heavy influx of Puritans into Salem between 1628 and 1640 resulted in a population too large to be supported by the supply of food available there. Consequently the new-comers spread out, establishing new settlements at Charles-town, Cambridge, Watertown, Dorchester, Roxbury, and later Boston. A few of those Puritans also moved northward to Cape Ann. There is no clear record of settlers coming to Cape Ann between 1628 and 1642, but that lack of evidence is understandable. Many of the colonists could not read and write and they were much more interested, furthermore, in keeping body and soul together in a wild country than in keeping records for posterity.

One of the generally accepted stories about the early settlement of the Cape is that in 1631 a band of Pilgrims came across Massachusetts Bay and settled at Planters Neck, where they set up a fishing stage. Planters Neck was on the north-erly side of Cape Ann, on a cove near where the river flows into Ipswich Bay. It was where the village of Annisquam now stands. The leader of that band is said to have been Abraham Robinson, and it also has been generally accepted that he was the son of Reverend John Robinson who had been pastor of the Pilgrims in Holland before they migrated to Plymouth.

That legend is subject to considerable revision. We accept as valid the tradition that settlers came to Planters Neck about 1631, and they may have come from Plymouth. But if so, they were Strangers, not Pilgrims. Willison gives the names[10] of the Pilgrims who landed at Plymouth and tells where they settled. There is no mention of any of them coming to Cape Ann. Abraham Robinson, furthermore, was not a son of the Reverend John Robinson. The only child of the Reverend John Robinson who came to America was his son Isaac,[11] who did not arrive in Plymouth until 1632. He then settled in Scituate and in 1639 moved to Barnstable.

---

10 Willison, *op. cit.*, pp. 437-453.
11 *Ibid.*, p. 452.

The top men in the young Puritan colony at Salem, however, did take an early interest in having a settlement planted on Cape Ann. In friendly hands, the Cape could serve as a bulwark against marauders and unwelcome intruders from the sea. The Cape also was in a position to dominate the local fishing grounds. And attention early was given to the possibility of cutting through the marsh at the southern end of the Annisquam River, so as to connect the river with Gloucester Harbor and thereby facilitate coastwise travel to such points as Ipswich where some of the Puritans also had settled. In 1638, in fact, the colonial legislative assembly at Salem, known as the General Court, authorized Deputy Governor Endicott to send three men to Cape Ann to determine whether a cut could be made through the marsh.

At a meeting of the General Court in 1641, Deputy Governor Endicott, Mr. Downing, and Mr. Hathorne, deputies from Salem, were appointed commissioners to settle the boundaries of Ipswich, Cape Ann, and Jeffries Creek (now Manchester) and to dispose of all land "and other things" at Cape Ann. In accordance with that authorization, Mr. Endicott and Mr. Downing made the first assignment of titles to land to settlers on Cape Ann, in February 1642.

The next steps were to obtain a minister, build a meetinghouse, and charter a town. All three steps were necessary in order that the residents of the plantation might participate in the government of the Massachusetts Bay Colony. Under a rule adopted by the General Court, only church members could be admitted as "freemen," and only freemen could hold public office. Hence ministers were a political as well as a spiritual necessity.

Employable ministers were hard to find in Massachusetts in those days, but in order to have a church, the people of Cape Ann had to have a minister. It presumably was the task of the commissioners to find a minister for the new town which they were planning to charter, and they engaged the

Reverend Richard Blynman, who had resigned his pastorate at Marshfield, near Plymouth, where he was having trouble with his congregation. The Reverend Blynman and a small group of loyal adherents came to Cape Ann in 1642. Then the meetinghouse was built and the town incorporated. The town was given the name of "Gloucester," in memory of Gloucester, England, whence some of the settlers had come.

To manage the affairs of the plantation until the first town meeting could be held, the commissioners appointed eight men, William Stevens, John Sadler, Obadiah Bruen, George Norton, William Addes, Thomas Milward, Thomas Fryer, and Walter Tybbot. Messrs. Sadler, Bruen, Addes, and Tybbot were members of the Blynman party. The others had come to Cape Ann from Salem, either in 1642 or in earlier years. In 1643 the first town meeting was held, and the voters elected five selectmen to manage the town's affairs. They were Messrs. Stevens, Tybbot, Norton, Bruen, and Hugh Calkins, another member of the Blynman party. Perhaps it should be added that while the Reverend Blynman and his group came from the Plymouth Colony, none of them were Pilgrims.

Thus in 1642, through the auspices of the Deputy Governor of the Massachusetts Bay Colony, a permanent settlement was planted on Cape Ann.

The houses of those early settlers were scattered, wherever tillable land for farming could be found among the ledges and boulder-strewn hills of the Cape. But the center of the new town was "The Green," situated near where Route 128 now circles its traffic into Washington Street. The Green was about a mile from Gloucester Harbor and about three miles, by land, from Planters Neck. There at The Green were located the meetinghouse and a tavern, and later a schoolhouse.

Those early settlers, however, were a restless lot. In his classic history of Gloucester,[12] John J. Babson states that be-

---

12 *History of the Town of Gloucester* (Gloucester, Procter Bros., 1860), pp. 52-53.

tween 1642 and 1650 eighty-two men settled in the new plantation, and presumably many of them had families. But some of the newcomers soon moved on, perhaps hoping to find more fertile land elsewhere, perhaps because of social frictions, or perhaps because of mere wanderlust. This was the start of the American frontier, of course, and for the next two hundred and fifty years the same sort of restless settlement featured the westward movement until the continent had been conquered. Here on Cape Ann thirteen of the men and their families followed the Reverend Blynman when he departed to New London, Connecticut, about 1650. Six later moved to Falmouth, Maine, and over thirty left for other places, with the result that only twenty-eight of the first eighty-two settlers became permanent residents of the new community.

Fishing was not much of a commercial enterprise on the Cape during the first sixty years after the settlements were made there. Fish were caught for food, and some were sold, but the major industries in those years were farming and wood-coasting. The Cape was heavily forested and cordwood was cut and shipped by boat to Boston and Salem to be sold for fuel. Structural timbers and lumber also were shipped. And sometimes the wood coasters smuggled merchandise into Boston which had been landed at Cape Ann from foreign ports. John J. Babson states that in 1706 at least thirty sloops were employed in carrying wood to market from the Annisquam River section, and about twenty others were engaged in the trade at other points on the Cape. Five years later in one three-week period over five hundred cords of wood were shipped from Cape Ann to Boston. That business gave a start to the boatbuilding industry.

Around 1700 a major change began to take place in the Cape's industry, and its population increased more rapidly. In 1704 the Cape had a population of about seven hundred people. By 1755 that number had increased to about twenty-eight hundred. The fishing industry became active; foreign

14

trade expanded; and smuggling was not uncommon. Fish and other provisions were shipped to the West Indies, where the slave population provided a growing market. Fish also were shipped to Europe. And as the number of slaves increased in our southern colonies, a market developed there for the Gloucester traders. From Europe salt, fruit, and wine were brought back; from the West Indies, sugar, molasses, rum, and coffee; and from the southern colonies, corn, beans, bacon, live hogs, and other products. Much of the rum, sugar, molasses, and other goods obtained in trade were re-sold in other markets, and Gloucester vessels also engaged in a general carrying trade. In the pre-Revolutionary days, the logbook of Captain Moses Low of Gloucester,[13] for example, recorded trips to the following ports in sequence: Havana, Rotterdam, Hellevoetluys, Boston, Charleston, Liverpool, Havana, Matanzas, Cowes, London, Boston, Charleston, New York, New Orleans, Glasgow, and New York. In the eighteenth century the Gloucester merchants and seafarers were an enterprising and resourceful lot.

As the fishing industry and foreign trade prospered, the center of the community shifted from The Green to the neighborhood of the harbor. In 1700 there were only about twenty families living at the harbor in scattered spots, but soon thereafter, that number substantially increased. In 1698 the shore path had been laid out as a public highway, the first in that vicinity. It was twenty-one feet wide and was named Front Street, a name which many years later was changed to Main Street. Presently other streets were laid out; taverns were opened; and other commercial facilities became available to the public. On the other side of the Cape, the settlement at Planters Neck also was thriving. And on the outer end of the Cape at Sandy Bay, the early name for Rockport, another settlement was growing up.

---

13 Babson, *op. cit.*, p. 380.

The residents of Cape Ann were hard hit by the Revolutionary War and by the War of 1812. The British warships destroyed many fishing vessels and thoroughly disrupted the activities of the Gloucester traders. Soon after 1820, however, a new period of prosperity began for Cape Ann which lasted, with only occasional temporary setbacks, for nearly a hundred years. The fishing industry revived and expanded. The shipbuilding business became active. In 1823 the granite quarrying industry began to develop on a large scale. And in the middle of the nineteenth century, the Cape began to attract summer vacationers.

Before the white people arrived, and for some time thereafter, Cape Ann apparently was a popular summer resort for Indians, as evidenced by great piles of clam shells found at Annisquam, Rust Island, and Coffin's Beach by the early English settlers. It likewise attracted white folks from out of town when they acquired adequate means of transportation and sufficient leisure time. By the latter half of the nineteenth century, the entertainment of summer visitors became one of the major industries of the Cape, and it has far outlasted some of the other industries.

The industrial and commercial developments of the late eighteenth and nineteenth centuries were accompanied and facilitated by new means of land transportation. The first public transportation from Gloucester to Boston was provided by Jonathan Lowe, who began to operate a two-horse open carriage over that route twice a week in 1788. The trip, one way, took all day, and the traveling was not very comfortable. In 1805 daily service was inaugurated over the route, and soon thereafter four-horse coaches took the place of the open carriages. The stagecoaches averaged two or three passengers per trip out of Gloucester, but of course others were picked up en route. The time was four and a half to five hours to Salem, where drivers and horses were changed, and about the same

16

from Salem to Boston. The fare was $1.75 from Gloucester to Salem, and $1.00 from Salem to Boston.

The railroad from Gloucester to Boston was opened in November 1847, and of course that stimulated more travel.

For local transportation, horsecars began running between the center of the town and East Gloucester in June 1886, and in 1889 a horsecar line to Riverdale was opened. In 1890 electric cars were introduced and soon thereafter one not only could take an excursion all around the Cape by electric car but also could travel by the same means to Essex and Salem. Thus the recreation business was stimulated.

Until the middle of the nineteenth century the population of Cape Ann consisted largely of persons of English origin or descent. About that time, however, newcomers from Ireland arrived in considerable numbers, to work in the local industries and to man the fishing fleets. Later came Portuguese fishermen, from the Azores, and Italians to engage in the fishing industry. And a large colony of Finns settled in Lanesville to work in the quarries. The population of Cape Ann was 6,384 in 1820; 12,433 in 1855; and 29,398 in 1950.

Because of the nature of the terrain, the settlements on Cape Ann have been located chiefly on its outer perimeter, and each of those settlements has its own individual characteristics and its own historical episodes and traditions, some saltier than others.

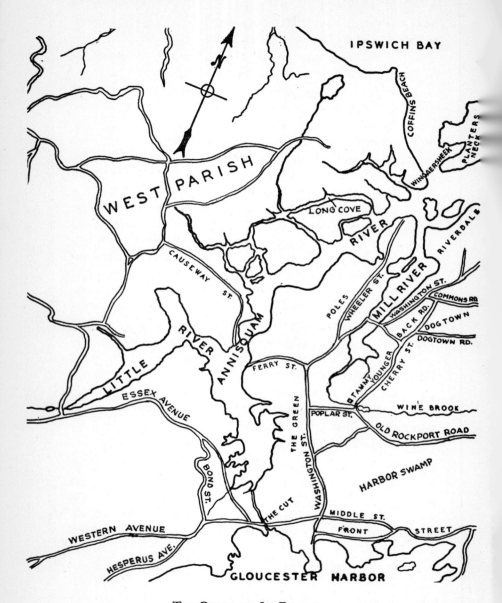

IPSWICH BAY

WEST PARISH

COFFINS BEACH

WINGAERSHEEK

PLANTERS NECK

LONG COVE

RIVER

CAUSEWAY ST.

POLES

WHEELER ST.

MILL RIVER

RIVERDALE

WASHINGTON ST.

COMMONS RD.

BACK RD.

DOGTOWN

CHERRY ST.

DOGTOWN RD.

LITTLE

RIVER

ANNISQUAM

TAMMY

YOUNGER

FERRY ST.

THE GREEN

ESSEX AVENUE

POPLAR ST.

WINE BROOK

OLD ROCKPORT ROAD

WASHINGTON ST.

BOND ST.

HARBOR SWAMP

WESTERN AVENUE

THE CUT

MIDDLE ST.

FRONT

STREET

HESPERUS AVE.

GLOUCESTER HARBOR

THE GREEN AND ITS ENVIRONS

The Green

IN A PURITAN COLONY, the meetinghouse was the community center, and in 1642, the Cape Ann colonists decided to erect their meetinghouse on what they then called The Green. They did not build it near the harbor, because at that time they were not primarily concerned with fishing. In fact, it was not until half a century later that commercial fishing came to be of any real importance to the residents of the new town of Gloucester. In 1642 their primary interest was in growing grain and other products for food, and in providing shelters in which to live.

For the colonists, The Green had several advantages as the center of their settlement. In the first place, it was a relatively sheltered area and around it were stretches of level land more suitable for farming than much of the rocky, boulder-covered soil and brier-filled swamps so prevalent elsewhere on the Cape. A large portion of the area nearer the harbor, for example, was either too hilly or too swampy to be useful for farming at that time.

The site of The Green also was close to the Annisquam River and not far distant from the head of the tidal inlet which came to be known as Mill River. Thus the settlers could travel from The Green by water in one direction nearly to Gloucester Harbor, and in the other direction to Planters Neck and Ipswich Bay. Soon after the meetinghouse was built, furthermore, a canal was cut through the marsh at the harbor end of the Annisquam River to permit the small boats of the settlers a means of egress to the sea in that direction.

19

To the families who settled on the west side of the Annisquam River, in what was to become the West Parish, The Green was accessible by a short boat ride and later by means of a ferry.

Near The Green, too, was a brook of fresh water which flowed down from the hills into Mill River. The brook provided the settlers with sites for building mills to grind their grain, saw their lumber, and full their cloth. Although the brook never has been accorded special emphasis in the historical writings about the Cape, it was one of the major resources of the early settlers.

There seems to be no record as to what name, if any, was attached to it by the early colonists, but in later years it was referred to variously as Cape Pond Brook, Brier Brook, Stony Brook, Wine Brook, and Alewife Brook. For convenience we call it Wine Brook.

In present-day geographical terms, Wine Brook has its origin in Brier Swamp at the eastern end of Dogtown, just over the Rockport line. From the swamp it flows in a southerly direction, across wild, rugged country, through the gigantic glacial boulders of the terminal moraine, to the vicinity of Beaver Dam, near where Eastern Avenue now passes an old stone house on the main road to Rockport. At Beaver Dam, Wine Brook turns westward, at right angles, and flows for about two miles through a valley between a rocky ridge to the south and the Dogtown moors to the north. For the latter half of that distance, the brook is now submerged in the Babson Reservoir, one of the units of the water supply for the City of Gloucester. To the west, beyond the reservoir dam, the brook runs by the end of Fox Hill, close to where Tammy Younger lived, to the Mill Pond at Riverdale.

The name "Wine Brook" derived from its port-wine color. In Brier Swamp, where the brook has its source, there is a deposit of bog iron ore, and the leachings from that ore cause discoloration of the water in the brook in spite of a

20

concrete dam, built as a WPA project in the thirties, to keep the "red water" of the swamp out of Wine Brook and thus out of Babson's Reservoir and the city water supply. Housewives in Gloucester nowadays frequently are annoyed by the color of the water flowing from their taps when the city is pumping from the Babson Reservoir, but the color comes in part, at least, from the bog iron ore in Brier Swamp.

In the various books and articles on the history of Gloucester, conflicting statements have been made as to the location and precedence of the early mills. After giving careful consideration to all the evidence available, including numerous firsthand investigations of the topography of the area, we have come to the conclusion that the first sawmill probably was erected in 1642 on Wine Brook, roughly a mile and a half east of Fox Hill. At that point the terrain was favorable for constructing a dam and a millpond. Near that location, furthermore, there were heavy stands of oak and pine timber, and after the trees had been felled, the logs readily could be floated or hauled to the mill. Remnants of the dam and the site where the old mill stood are still clearly discernible among the trees and brush by the side of Wine Brook.

From the mill a road was opened up, along the crest of the ridge south of the brook, for hauling lumber to the neighborhood of The Green. That road became a section of what a couple of hundred years later was known as the Old Rockport Road. From the neighborhood of the mill, it appears that another road led to the south—to Joppa, where homes also were being built. At a later date lumber apparently was hauled over that road from the mill to Little Good Harbor for shipment to other points by water.

A couple of years after the sawmill was erected, a gristmill was built farther down Wine Brook, at Fox Hill. It was operated for only a few years, however, presumably because the millpond on the side of the hill could not store a large quantity of water. That mill was supplanted by another mill located at the point where the brook flowed into Mill River. A dam was built at that point, and the meadow above the dam became a large millpond. A sawmill that sawed timber cut on Dogtown and at other nearby points was located at that dam. It was from this mill that Mill River got its name; in fact, in the early days it was known as Sawmill River. Washington Street now crosses the dam and the millpond is still there. The mill located at that point continued in operation until 1925.

The records of the builders and owners of those early mills are so incomplete and confused that it does not seem possible at this time to reconstruct an accurate historical account of them. One of the traditional statements, for example, attributes the construction of the first mill on Wine Brook to the Reverend John Emerson, who was the parish minister for nearly forty years. That tradition, however, cannot be true. The Reverend Emerson, who graduated from Harvard College in 1656, did not arrive in Gloucester until 1661, nearly twenty years after the mill was built.

The Reverend Emerson, nevertheless, eventually did become owner of that mill, as well as of other mills, and he was responsible, according to another tradition, for having a ditch dug from Cape Pond, half a mile to the east, to the Wine Brook millpond near Beaver Dam. The purpose of the ditch, which incidentally is still open, was to augment the supply of water for the mill, but the calculations were in error and water from Cape Pond flowed through the ditch only in periods of extra high-water levels. At such times the additional supply of water from Cape Pond was not needed.

The Reverend Emerson, however, apparently did not make many mistakes. His initial salary as minister was only sixty pounds a year, payable in produce. Nevertheless, in his later years he was reported to be the wealthiest man in Gloucester.

In addition to a sawmill and a gristmill, the settlers also needed a fulling mill, a primitive labor-saving device for pre-shrinking homespun woolen cloth. Consequently a little fulling mill was built on a small brook which flowed down to the millpond from the Dogtown area, across the upper end of what is now Reynard Street.

Thus The Green became a sort of primitive industrial center.

Inasmuch as the river and its coves and the ocean waters around the Cape afforded means of travel by boat from The Green to practically all the inhabited districts on the Cape, the early residents did not spend much time and effort in building roads. Footpaths and bridle paths must have been tracked out as soon as the settlers began to build their homes. Then came rough roads for ox teams, rutty and uneven, with corduroy laid down in swampy or marshy spots to prevent the carts from miring in the mud. As rocks were cleared from the land to make plowing and mowing easier, they commonly were piled into stone walls along the roadsides. There the rocks were out of the way and they also served as markers and rough property lines. Some of the old roads on the Cape, as elsewhere in New England, can still be traced, in part at least, by the stone walls piled up by the settlers who cleared the land.

The early roads were altogether primitive and not for pleasure travel. In fact, John J. Babson states that at the time of the Revolutionary War, nearly one hundred and fifty years after the first settlers arrived on the Cape, there were only thirty-one pleasure carriages on Cape Ann, including "chairs, sulkies and chaises."

From The Green in the early days, roads radiated to the harbor (Washington Street), to Meeting House Neck, later named Wheeler's Point (Washington Street and Wheeler Street), and to Fox Hill, at the head of the millpond (Poplar

Street). After the ferry from Biskie Island to Trynall Cove (Wolf Hill) went into operation in 1694, a road connected the ferry landing with the Meeting House Neck road.

At Fox Hill, near where the gristmill was erected, there was firm ground for constructing a bridge over the brook, and from the bridge a road was built which wound up over the hill and proceeded along the high land on the eastern side of the millpond (Cherry Street) to a junction with a road from the milldam (Reynard Street). From that junction another road (The Back Road) skirted the southwestern borders of Dogtown, then wound downhill to the 'Squam Willows. From the Willows a road went up over Pilgrim Hill, where Holly Street now runs, to the head of Goose Cove. From Goose Cove it climbed another sharp hill and followed what became Bennett Street, now partly overgrown and passable only on foot or by jeep, to the head of Lobster Cove in Annisquam.

It was a long trip by land from The Green to Planters Neck in those days.

From the head of Lobster Cove another road followed what is now Revere Street up over another hill and then proceeded through the woods to Sandy Bay on the outer end of the Cape. That was known as "the old road through the woods to Sandy Bay."

Reference already has been made to the early road from the sawmill on Wine Brook to Fox Hill, which eventually became part of the Old Rockport Road. With the construction of a traffic circle on the extension of Route 128 to East Gloucester, the old sawmill road is now passing into oblivion, but there are a few landmarks along its way which should not be forgotten. One of these landmarks is the keystone bridge over the railroad track. The old road was built, of course, long before the railroad. But when the Rockport branch of the railroad was constructed, it was necessary to make a cut about forty feet deep through the solid ledge of the ridge half a mile to the northeast of the Gloucester railroad station. The old

24

sawmill road which ran along the crest of that ridge was still in active use as one of the main thoroughfares to Rockport. Hence, a bridge had to be built over the railroad cut. The bridge was built of stone, without cement or any other binder; it was held solidly together by the keystone wedged in at the top of the arch. It is a notable example of that type of bridge construction and it appears to be just as solid today as when it was built nearly one hundred years ago.

So much for the brook and the early mills and some of the old roads. Let us return to The Green.

When the town of Gloucester was chartered, a meeting-house was built on The Green, and for nearly seventy-five years—until 1716—that was the only meetinghouse on the Cape. Attendance at Sunday services was obligatory for all members of the parish, unless they could furnish substantial reasons for being absent. Families came from scattered farms to gather once a week at the meetinghouse on The Green, where they not only could worship but presumably exchange information and perhaps gossip a bit. In those early days the meetinghouse on The Green thus provided a social center for the community.

With the growth of commercial activity around the harbor after 1700, and the consequent shifting of population to that area, complaints arose among the people residing there about their having to travel so far to attend Sunday services. To a younger generation it seemed a much longer distance than it had been for their elders. Those complaints led to a divisive controversy, which started in 1733 and continued for ten years.

In 1738 a self-constituted committee of persons living at the harbor erected a new meetinghouse on Middle Street, and after its completion they offered it to the parish on condition that the committee should be reimbursed for their expenditures from money to be collected from a sale of pews in the meetinghouse. The offer was accepted and the minister who had preached at the meetinghouse on The Green was transferred to the new one. The parishioners who lived on the other side of The Green objected, however, to having services at the old meetinghouse discontinued, and they petitioned the General Court in Boston to have the district set off as a separate parish. Some of them living at Wheeler's Point, Riverdale, and Dogtown, who formerly had had to travel a mile and a half to church, now would have to travel more than two and a half miles, and that was a long distance, they said, for those too poor to own conveyances.

The separation of the parish finally was agreed to in December 1742, by a vote of the parishioners, 50 to 35. Thereby the district around the old meetinghouse became the Fourth Parish, a second parish already having been set up on the west side of the river, and a third parish in Annisquam. The Fourth Parish included the homes in the vicinity of The Green, all of Riverdale as far as the 'Squam Willows, Dogtown, Wheeler's Point, and Thurston's Point.

In 1752 the old meetinghouse on The Green was replaced by a new structure, but regular services continued there for only thirty years. The meetinghouse remained standing, however, until 1840, and in its later years frequently was used by itinerant Methodist preachers.

The only landmark at The Green itself which still survives is the old Ellery House. It formerly was located on the south side of The Green, but when traffic Route 128 was constructed in 1953 the old house was moved to the other side of Washington Street, north of the traffic circle, where it still stands. It was built for the Reverend Mr. White, who was chosen minister of the parish in 1702. A few years later it was sold to James Stevens, who converted it into a tavern. In 1740 it was sold to Capt. William Ellery, who continued to operate it as a tavern for some years, presumably until the patronage had largely shifted to other taverns in the village at the harbor. If that old house could talk, it undoubtedly could

26

tell some interesting tales about the convivialities which took place there. The Stevens Tavern, incidentally, was one of the places where the selectmen met to transact the town's business in the early eighteenth century. The town paid for the food and liquor served at those meetings, but the expenses eventually became so high that a limit was placed on them by vote at the annual town meeting.

The first public school on Cape Ann was opened in the meetinghouse on The Green in 1698. In that year one of the citizens, Thomas Riggs, Sr., was elected schoolmaster with an arrangement whereby he was to receive a salary of one shilling sixpence per day while teaching. But controversy arose, as it still does so frequently about public schools, and Mr. Riggs served for only one year. Then public schooling lapsed until 1703, when a new teacher was obtained. In 1708 a new schoolhouse was built on The Green.

Until the public school was opened, such schooling as the children had received had been given them at home. In other words, for over fifty years after the people settled on the Cape, there was no public school for the children. The opening of the school is one of the indications of a new awakening all over Cape Ann. By 1698 the intensification of religious and political discussions in the colony and the widening of the local interest in both domestic and foreign trade stimulated the effort to provide better schooling for the children.

To shoe their oxen and their horses and to repair their carts and tools, the colonists eventually felt the need for a blacksmith. Consequently in 1674 they persuaded one Joseph Allen to settle in Gloucester and set up a blacksmith shop on the road at the top of Fox Hill. As an inducement to settle here, he received a grant of land and certain common rights. That was the first blacksmith shop on Cape Ann. Joseph Allen, incidentally, was the father of seventeen children.

By the crossroads at the foot of Fox Hill, which became something of a primitive traffic center, stood the house where

27

old "Luce" George, and her niece, Tammy Younger, dwelt. Old Luce was one of the famous witches of Cape Ann, and she is reputed to have collected tolls from teams crossing the bridge by her house as her price for not putting her curse on the oxen. When a driver with a load of corn was dilatory about coming across with his toll, old Luce would keep the oxen standing at the foot of the hill, with their tongues hanging out. When a driver with a load of wood came by, if she was in need of fuel, old Luce could so bewitch the load, it was said, that the wood would roll off the ox cart unless several sticks were deposited at her door. She also went to the harbor to collect tolls of fish from the vessels coming in, those tolls likewise being paid to forestall her curse. When old Luce passed on, Tammy Younger continued to live in her aunt's house until she died in 1829. Tammy acquired a reputation of her own and the building came to be known for many years as the "Tammy Younger house."

Tammy Younger, who was born in 1753, was sometimes referred to as the "queen of the witches," but it appears that she attained her ends by use of her sharp tongue rather than by black magic. There was a square window in the rear of her house which looked out on the bridge over Wine Brook near where the early gristmill had stood. When she heard a team or a person crossing the bridge, Tammy would throw open her window and cajole or curse the traveler into making whatever contribution she sought at the time. There also was a tradition that she entertained buccaneers and other lawless men in her house, with fortunetelling, card playing, and other amusements. There also was a rumor that after her death money was found in the cellar of her house, and for many years the boys of the neighborhood were wont to dig around in that cellar, looking for treasure. One boy did turn up a highly ornamental snuffbox, on the cover of which was a model of a full-rigged ship. There was some uncertainty as to whether the box had belonged to Tammy—she was a snuff taker—or to some British sea captain who had been visiting her. At all events, Tammy Younger's house long was one of the landmarks of Cape Ann.

After 1800, or thereabouts, the neighborhood of The Green had few experiences of any particular historical significance. One exception, however, was the alewife fishing which gave Wine Brook one of its nicknames. Alewives are a type of herring which run up into fresh-water streams in the spring to deposit their eggs. At some earlier date, alewives had been placed in Cape Pond. But they could not readily get back and forth between the pond and the sea through the dam at Riverdale. Consequently in 1816, as a result of a petition, the Massachusetts legislature passed an act regulating the taking of alewives in that Gloucester brook. The town then purchased from Zachariah Stevens the right to open a passageway for alewives through his milldam at Riverdale. A committee of five persons was chosen annually at town meeting to catch the alewives in the brook or to arrange to have them caught. The fish were to be sold at the rate of fifty cents per hundred pounds, and the proceeds, after the expenses had been deducted, went into the town treasury.

The fish were caught in nets and sometimes as many as two hundred barrels were taken in a single day. They were sold for bait for the offshore fishing vessels and also to be smoked and marketed for food. In an article in the *Gloucester Daily Times,* January 1, 1889, from which the foregoing information was obtained, it was stated that the alewife fishery on the brook which flowed into Mill River "was prosecuted many years, but finally failed to receive that attention from the town that was necessary for its protection and successful prosecution, and of late years but few have been caught." Thus, like many another Gloucester enterprise, the alewife business languished.

After The Green gradually had ceased to be the religious and social center of the Cape, it still was used for certain other purposes.

When the population of the Cape had grown to a size where militia companies could be manned, for example, The Green served them as a training ground and review ground. In the early nineteenth century there were eight such companies, with headquarters in the various sections of the Cape, and "General Training," which usually occurred in October, became a great holiday. On that day, the soldiers, in full uniform of course, marched from their various headquarters to The Green, where they were reviewed. Eatables and drinkables, such as egg pop at a cent a glass, were sold at booths around The Green, and the pomp and excitement attracted a large crowd. In fact, contemporary reports indicate that the crowd at General Training was as great as that at a circus when it came to town. General Training days were held annually for over forty years prior to the Civil War.

They eventually went out of vogue, and now a circus seldom visits Cape Ann. During the last twenty-five years the chief gatherings of crowds such as the ones which attended General Training a century and more ago, have been at the carnivals sponsored by various fraternal and social organizations and they have been held at Stage Fort Park, not at The Green.

After electric streetcars came into use in Gloucester, a carbarn was built on the edge of the marsh by The Green. Thirty years later the streetcars were supplanted by private automobiles and buses. The carbarn then fell into disuse, and presently was demolished. Then came the opening of traffic Route 128, with a circle where The Green had been. Thus The Green had run the gamut from being the center of the early settlement of the Cape to becoming a major dispersion point for the ever-increasing automobile traffic flowing into the Cape.

30

Dogtown

THE DESERTED VILLAGE of Dogtown lies in the heart of Cape Ann. It is located around a quadrangle formed by the Back Road, Dogtown Road, the Commons Road, and Wharf Road, now a path which connects Dogtown Road and the Commons Road about a mile and a half in from the Back Road.

The Back Road, as stated previously, was part of the main thoroughfare from The Green to Annisquam for many years after the settlement was started. Dogtown Road branches off from the Back Road at Gravel Hill, a few hundred yards beyond Reynard Street. The Commons Road runs practically parallel to Dogtown Road, about a mile to the westward, and is essentially a continuation of what is now Gee Avenue.

When the settlement was established at The Green, much of the Dogtown area was common land in which each settler had certain rights for cutting wood and pasturing cattle and sheep. Hence it was known as the "Commons." It was heavily wooded, and a road was opened in 1646 and formally laid out in 1707, to permit the transportation of cordwood and timber from the Commons to tidewater and to the mill at the head of Mill River. That road later was named Reynard Street.

In 1719, when much of the timber on the Commons had been cut off and little free farming land remained available elsewhere on the Cape, most of the common land was divided for allocation to individual settlers, and a village started to grow on the Commons. A century later, when the village had become largely deserted, it acquired the name of Dogtown, the name being derived, according to tradition, from the dogs kept by the poor old women who then eked out an existence there.

Dogtown was settled by just the same sort of people as were filling the vacant spaces elsewhere around the Cape in the first half of the eighteenth century—sons and daughters of earlier settlers, newcomers from elsewhere in New England, and migrants from overseas.

Charles E. Mann, whose history of Dogtown[14] provides most of the authentic information now available about the old village, states that in 1741-42 there were about twenty-five houses in the village. He also states that when the village reached its peak, over one hundred families lived there, but that number must have included some who resided far on the outskirts. After the end of the Revolutionary War the population of the village gradually declined. In 1814 there were only seven houses still occupied in the village and in 1830 the last inhabitant was taken to the poorhouse.

The desertion of the village was brought about by several factors. The soil was too poor and too dry for profitable farming. Furthermore, after a new road nearer the shore was opened up through Riverdale to the Willows (Washington Street) the Back Road fell more and more into disuse. And the fishing and trading activities at the harbor drew many of the able-bodied people away from the rather barren village at Dogtown. In other words, life on the moors became less attractive to the second and third generations than it had appeared to be to the settlers.

The fame of Dogtown has come, therefore, not so much from its eighteenth-century residents as from the features of its landscape and from the legends about some of the persons who lived there during the final stages of its decadence.

Dogtown is located on high land. It abounds in boulders, large and small. In and near Dogtown are several swamps,

---

14 Charles E. Mann, *The Story of Dogtown* (Gloucester, The Procter Bros. Co., 1896). A second edition was published in 1906 which has a supplement on "The Beginnings of Dogtown."

ELLERY HOUSE

Built in 1702: first a parsonage, then a tavern.

A DOGTOWN LANDSCAPE

but otherwise the soil is gravelly and arid. It is a land where blueberries, huckleberries, blackberries, bayberries, sweet fern, and red cedar flourish. Many birds nest there in the summer; and in the autumn, when the open areas are carpeted with blue asters and the bushes are clothed in brilliant red and purple, it is a popular overnight stop for great flocks of birds migrating to the south.

In the setting of Dogtown it is not difficult to believe in witches. For example, in the summer of 1955 a small group of us were walking along the Commons Road a short distance beyond the Wharf Road, when around a bend in the path an old berry picker came stivering toward us. She had straight, straggly, disheveled hair, a grim and grimy face, a soiled dress, a piece of rope for a belt, clumsy, ragged shoes, and a ten-quart pail full of blueberries. Whence she came or where she was going we did not know; she was there one moment and gone the next; but we could not avoid a suspicion that Judy Rhines or Molly Jakups had come out of a cellar, where she lived one hundred and fifty years ago, to have another feast on Dogtown blueberries. We did know that it probably was not Easter Carter, because she aristocratically scorned her neighbors who lived on berries in the summer with the remark: "I eats no trash."

Many of the cellars on which the houses of Dogtown stood in its days of respectability are still to be seen by the roadside amid clumps of barberry bushes.

Inasmuch as a list of the families who once lived in Dogtown would be of interest chiefly to genealogists, we shall not repeat all their names here. We merely will pick out a few of the celebrities, as we pass the cellars of their erstwhile homes in a walk around the village, starting at Gravel Hill. For this tour we have used a map prepared over seventy-five years ago by Isaac F. Day, of Riverdale, but never published.[15]

---

15 The original map was loaned to us by Mr. Herbert Montgomery of Riverdale, kin to Isaac F. Day.

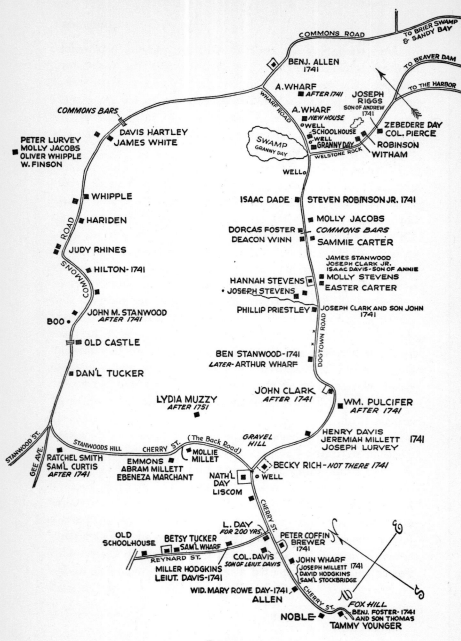

COMMONS ROAD

TO BRIER SWAMP
& SANDY BAY

BENJ. ALLEN
1741

TO BEAVER DAM

A. WHARF
AFTER 1741

TO THE HARBOR

JOSEPH
RIGGS
SON OF ANDREW
1741

A. WHARF
NEW HOUSE
WELL

SCHOOLHOUSE

WELL

ZEBEDERE DAY
COL. PIERCE

COMMONS BARS

DAVIS HARTLEY
JAMES WHITE

PETER LURVEY
MOLLY JACOBS
OLIVER WHIPPLE
W. FINSON

WHARF ROAD

SWAMP
GRANNY DAY

GRANNY DAY

WELSTONE ROCK

ROBINSON
WITHAM

WELL

WHIPPLE

ISAAC DADE

STEVEN ROBINSON JR. 1741

HARIDEN

MOLLY JACOBS

DORCAS FOSTER
DEACON WINN

COMMONS BARS

JUDY RHINES

SAMMIE CARTER

HILTON- 1741

JAMES STANWOOD
JOSEPH CLARK JR.
ISAAC DAVIS - SON OF ANNIE

HANNAH STEVENS

MOLLY STEVENS

COMMONS ROAD

JOSEPH STEVENS

EASTER CARTER

JOHN M. STANWOOD
AFTER 1741

PHILLIP PRIESTLEY

JOSEPH CLARK AND SON JOHN
1741

BOO

OLD CASTLE

DOGTOWN ROAD

DAN'L TUCKER

BEN STANWOOD-1741
LATER- ARTHUR WHARF

LYDIA MUZZY
AFTER 1751

JOHN CLARK
AFTER 1741

WM. PULCIFER
AFTER 1741

STANWOOD ST.

STANWOODS HILL

CHERRY ST.

(The Back Road)

*GRAVEL
HILL*

HENRY DAVIS
JEREMIAH MILLETT
JOSEPH LURVEY

1741

GEE AVE.

RATCHEL SMITH
SAM'L CURTIS
AFTER 1741

EMMONS
ABRAM MILLETT
EBENEZA MARCHANT

MOLLIE
MILLET

BECKY RICH - *NOT THERE 1741*

NATH'L
DAY
LISCOM

WELL

CHERRY ST.

L. DAY
FOR 200 YRS.

OLD
SCHOOLHOUSE

BETSY TUCKER
SAM'L WHARF

PETER COFFIN
BREWER
1741

REYNARD ST.

COL. DAVIS
SON OF LEIUT. DAVIS

JOHN WHARF
JOSEPH MILLETT 1741
DAVID HODGKINS
SAM'L STOCKBRIDGE

MILLER HODGKINS
LEIUT. DAVIS-1741

WID. MARY ROWE DAY-1741
ALLEN

CHERRY ST.

FOX HILL

NOBLE

BENJ. FOSTER- 1741
AND SON THOMAS

TAMMY YOUNGER

DOGTOWN

Near the foot of Gravel Hill stood the house of Nathaniel Day. His chief distinction was that he was the father of seventeen children, including three pairs of twins. His dwelling, moreover, was less than a mile distant from that of Joseph Allen, the blacksmith, who it will be recalled also had seventeen children.

On the right-hand side of Dogtown Road, about a mile from Gravel Hill, stood the house where Easter (Esther) Carter lived in the decadent years of Dogtown. She is supposed to have come from England with her brother about 1741 and eventually she arrived in Dogtown. She was a spinster who went out nursing. She was very poor, but she was kind and hospitable and widely known. Her house was the only two-story house in Dogtown, at least at the time she lived there, and it was clapboarded, the clapboards being fastened with wooden pegs.

After she moved to the village at the harbor, her dwelling continued to be known as "the Easter Carter house." The next tenant was Becky Rich, who previously had lived at the foot of Gravel Hill. When her house there became so dilapidated as to be untenable, Becky was moved to Easter Carter's house. She also was known as Granny Rich and she had a daughter, Rachel Smith, who made a "dire drink" brewed from foxberry leaves, spruce tops, and other herbs, which she peddled in the village, to make her customers feel "springish."

"Aunt Rachel" often entertained parties of young people from Riverdale and Annisquam who visited her at the Easter Carter house on picnic excursions. She boiled cabbage and baked johnnycakes for them, told their fortunes from coffee grounds, and generally helped them to have a good time. The Easter Carter house was "somewhere to go" for the young people of the neighboring villages a century and a half ago, and it is easy to imagine that the spectral shadows of the boulders and cedars along the Dogtown paths gave a romantic setting for such excursions, especially on the long walks home in the moonlight.

On the upper floor of Easter Carter's house "Old Ruth" lived for some years. She was a mulatto who presumably once had been a slave. She also was known as "John Woodman." She usually was employed for building stone walls and other heavy outdoor work to which she had become accustomed when she was young. Since she did a man's work, she dressed accordingly. It was only when she went to the poorhouse to spend her last days that she began to wear a skirt, and that was by compulsion, not by her choice.

Close by Easter Carter's house was a small hut in which Molly Stevens lived. With regard to Molly, Mann stated: "No one keeps her memory green. She must have made life unhappy for the gentle Easter, unless history is at fault."[16]

Just beyond where the so-called Commons bars stood on the Dogtown Road, not far from Easter Carter's house, was the Isaac Dade house. As an English boy living in or near London, Isaac had been impressed for service on a new man-of-war. During the Revolutionary War, while the warship was anchored at Gloucester, he was sent to row an officer ashore. Instead of returning to his ship, however, Isaac boarded a Gloucester vessel just ready to sail for Virginia with a cargo of fish. In Virginia he joined the Continental Army. After the war, he married a southern lady, Fanny Brundle, whose father's plantation adjoined that of the mother of George Washington. Several years later, being in poor health, Isaac returned to Gloucester, with the hope that a change in climate would benefit him, and settled in Dogtown.

On the southern side of Dogtown Road, opposite the Dade cellar, is an old pasture where a tragic bullfight occurred, on September 10, 1892. A few years earlier, James Merry, a Gloucester young man, had shipped as a seaman on a vessel

---

16 Mann, *op. cit.*, p. 46.

which brought salt from the Mediterranean. He visited Spain where he witnessed several bullfights and met some of the toreadors. After his return, he talked so much about bull-fighting that some of his friends finally suggested that he show them how it was done. Not to be outdared, he began to wrestle with a young bull-calf pastured at Dogtown. Since Merry was six feet seven inches tall and weighed two hundred and fifty pounds, he had no difficulty in throwing the bull, and presently he staged several exhibitions of bullfighting for his friends. The next year, the three-year-old bull was much heavier and stronger, but Merry continued wrestling it. In his first exhibition that summer, after a long struggle with the bull, Merry went limp from exhaustion and had to be rescued by the spectators. Several weeks later he went to the pasture alone one morning for a private match with the bull. Late that afternoon, when he had not returned, neighbors went on a search for him and found his lifeless body in the pasture. The bull was feeding calmly nearby. The blood on the rocks and the trampled grass showed that Merry's body had been thrown against the boulders many times by the bull. Three boulders in the field mark the scene of the fight.

Several hundred yards beyond the site of Isaac Dade's house we come to what was known in Dogtown as a parting path. To the left is Wharf Road, the path which connects Dogtown Road with the Commons Road. To the right is a path which soon divides into two paths, one leading to the vicinity of the old sawmill on Wine Brook, and the other to Gloucester. The area where Dogtown Road, Wharf Road, and the parting path meet is now called Dogtown Square, and in this neighborhood there are several points of interest.

On the point between Wharf Road and the parting path Granny Day's house stood. She was the school mistress, and the village schoolhouse was situated just across Wharf Road from her home. Back of the schoolhouse was Granny Day's Swamp, where village cattle sometimes became mired.

Southeast of Dogtown Square, near the junction of the path to the old sawmill and the path to Gloucester, the house of Col. William Pearce was situated. Col. Pearce was one of the wealthiest merchants in Gloucester. During the War of 1812, he became apprehensive over the raids by British ships at Annisquam Harbor, and in 1814 he moved from his home on Washington Street, near the millpond, to the house in Dogtown, where he resided for about two years. The British raiders sought him out even in Dogtown, however, and in June 1814 seamen from a British barge made their way from Lobster Cove or Mill River to Dogtown. They did not find Col. Pearce, but they did carry off some of his sheep. After the war was over and the raids ceased, Col. Pearce returned to his former residence.

In the vicinity of Dogtown Square and along the path to Gloucester are some of the most picturesque boulders in Dogtown. On the faces of several of them mottoes were carved, some thirty years ago, at the instance of Roger W. Babson, the well-known native of Gloucester. The letters in the mottoes are ten inches tall and they were carved with expert workmanship. The following are examples of them:

Get A Job	*Prosperity Follows Service*
Help Mother	*Be On Time*
Save	*If Work Stops, Values Decline*
Never Try, Never Win	*Keep Out Of Debt*

The boulders on which the mottoes were carved are located on a tract of eleven hundred acres which Mr. Babson gave to the City of Gloucester in the watershed of the Babson Reservoir. By the terms of the gift the tract is always to be kept as a public park for the use of all the inhabitants of Cape Ann.

On the right-hand side of Wharf Road, as we proceed from Dogtown Square toward the Commons Road, was the residence of Abram Wharf, one of the sturdy villagers, and near the site of his house are the remains of an old well. The Wharf Road is especially notable now, however, for its borders of blueberry and huckleberry bushes, whose deep purple foliage in the autum is set off, here and there, by bright yellow witch-hazel leaves. Along this road, too, are some of the most picturesque cedars in Dogtown.

When we reach the Commons Road we first will turn right. As we proceed northward on that road, we pass Peter's Pulpit, a big boulder which stands close to the road. Several hundred yards beyond Peter's Pulpit a path leads off to the left to the Whale's Jaw, one of the most notable landmarks in Dogtown. The Whale's Jaw is a large boulder that was split long ago by some natural force to resemble the jaws of a whale pointing toward the sky. At the Whale's Jaw, paths lead off from Dogtown to Annisquam and Pigeon Cove.

The Commons Road, to the east of the path to the Whale's Jaw, winds on for half a mile or so to end at Brier Swamp, also known as Great Swamp and Wine Swamp, the source of Wine Brook, already described on page 20. In addition to its iron ore, Brier Swamp is notable for certain rare plants, including buckbean, pitcher plant, sundew, and white fringed orchid.

Let us now retrace our steps on the Commons Road to its junction with Wharf Roard. Near the junction the village blacksmith shop stood, and farther along the road toward Riverdale was a grocery store. Thus, at the height of its prosperity, Dogtown had a schoolhouse, a blacksmith shop, and a grocery store. There also was a cobbler shop, to which we shall come shortly.

On a hill to the west of the Commons Road, also near the junction with Wharf Road, was the so-called Beech Pasture. It affords a particularly fine view of Ipswich Bay, with Coffin's Beach and the sand dunes in the background. On that hill, back some distance from the road, stood one of the most famous houses in Dogtown. It was the home of Peter Lurvey, who was killed in a battle between the townspeople and the British Warship *Falcon* at Gloucester Harbor, August 8, 1775. His widow continued to live in the house until she died, at the age of 104. Subsequently her daughter and son-in-law, John Morgan Stanwood, lived there for a few years. Then, as the building was becoming more and more dilapidated, Molly Jakups (Jacobs) and her friend Sarah Phipps, better known as Sally Jakups, another friend, Mrs. Stanley, and Mrs. Stanley's grandson "Sammy Stanley" moved in.

Molly and Sally apparently whiled away their time, when the weather permitted them to get out of bed, by playing cards. Mann reports that Molly was smarter than Sally: "Sarah would get mad at Molly and say 'I shan't tell you where I hid the keerds. I hid them behind the old chest, but I shan't tell you.' "[17] In the winter they spent much of their time in bed, under a coverlet which sometimes became white with snow that drifted in through the cracks when it stormed.

Sammy Stanley, whose real name was Sam Maskey, took care of the old women until they were removed to the poorhouse to live. Although Sammy wore men's trousers, he had been brought up by his grandmother as though he were a girl, and wherever he went he wore a handkerchief tied over his head. Until she went to the almshouse, Sammy's grandmother had kept him busy at housework. When he was left to shift for himself, he moved to Sandy Bay and earned a livelihood there by going out to work for his neighbors as a "washerwoman." Despite his attire and his domestic occupation, however, Sammy had sufficient innate shrewdness to lead him to save enough money from his earnings at Sandy Bay to enable him to become a stockholder in the cotton mill that was established there.

After Molly Jakups and her friends left the Lurvey house, the oak frame was sold to two Day brothers, who took it down

---

17 Mann *op. cit.*, p. 60.

and removed it to a site on Washington Street, near the corner of Reynard Street, across from where the old mill stood. With the use of that frame a sturdy house was built on the new site, and it is still there. One wonders if the River- dale tenants ever knew what had gone on within that old frame in its Dogtown days.

Farther along the Commons Road toward Riverdale, just before the point where a brook flows over the road, was the house where Judy Rhines lived. Judy was a tall, rawboned woman who had been born in Sandy Bay in 1771. She made a precarious living, as several other Dogtown dames did, by going out occasionally for housework, picking blueberries, and telling fortunes, and by other unrecorded means. She is re- puted to have had great courage, which was so respected that no intruder dared approach nearer to her house after she bade him to stop.

Judy Rhines, like some of the other penurious Dogtown women, is said to have had many friends. We judge that those friends were attracted to her not by pity, but by her heartiness, her broad compassion, and perhaps by a freedom from conventional restraints.

One of the last kindhearted acts of Judy Rhines was to persuade "Black Neil" to move to her house. Black Neil was a big, powerful Negro, with prominent protruding teeth. He worked at various jobs, including that of itinerant hog butcher. Shortly before Molly Jakups and her friends left the Lurvey house to go to the poorhouse, Black Neil had moved into the cellar of that building. He patched the floor to keep out some of the rain and snow, but the cellar soon became unlivable, and it was then that Judy Rhines took him in. After she died and the walls of the house fell in, Black Neil lived in the cellar there. Finally, on a bitter cold day in the winter of 1830, at the instigation of residents of Riverdale, a constable took Black Neil to the poorhouse. The cellar in which he was living was full of ice and some of his toes were frozen. The

41

comforts of the poorhouse were too much for him, however, and he passed away within a week after he arrived there.

Black Neil had been convinced that Molly Jakups had buried treasure in the cellar of the Lurvey house, and he never ceased searching for it, but without success. He was the last inhabitant of Dogtown.

Near the southern end of the Commons Road, as it approaches Gee Avenue, was the home of John Morgan Stanwood, otherwise known as Johnny Morgan, Morgan Stanwood, and Granther Stannard. Those various names were not aliases but rather the terms used by friendly neighbors when referring to a thoroughly estimable member of the community. In his later years, Granther Stannard became the village cobbler. At first he did his cobbling in a little shed attached to the house, but he had a large number of children, and as they grew up, they and their callers caused so much confusion around the house that the old gentleman built a hut near a big rock by the side of the road, where he could cobble in peace. The hut was made of slabs and covered with turf, and the hole in the bank where it stood is still clearly visible.

Before he became too lame to travel about, Granther Stannard also practiced itinerant dentistry. On one occasion Tammy Younger sent for him to extract from her upper jaw two rather large teeth which had become painful. Granther pulled each tooth part way out and then left the two of them dangling there for a time, telling Tammy that her teeth were so obstinate that he could do nothing more with them. He had his joke but he also received more than an earful of Tammy's choicest language.

There is a legend, oft repeated, that Dogtown was settled by people who went up there to escape the pirates and other marauders along the shore and that when those dangers had passed, the settlers moved back to the Harbor and other villages on the coast. Although that legend has a certain romantic appeal, it does not jibe with the facts, for Col. Pearce

42

was the only person who moved there for that reason, and it was almost a hundred years after Dogtown was first settled that he went there to live. The period when Dogtown was settled coincided with the period when the fishing industry was first beginning to thrive at Gloucester. That was when the population at the harbor was starting to show a marked increase and the center of the community was beginning to shift from The Green to the harbor. Furthermore, in the next generation, as industry and trade continued to prosper at the harbor, and also at Annisquam and Sandy Bay, the younger people at Dogtown were attracted away from that village, and it finally became deserted. Pirates had nothing to do with the founding or the desertion of Dogtown.

The settlement at Dogtown was merely something of an eddy in the course of the history of Cape Ann. When Dogtown was settled, the conditions already were becoming unfavorable for the success of such a settlement. The settlers were the victims of circumstances which they did not foresee and were powerless to combat. The tragedies of the deserted village, however, do add a personal poignancy to the somber grandeur of the Dogtown boulders.

The Harbor Village

Soon after 1700, a commercial fishing industry began to develop at Gloucester; foreign trade started to grow; and the shipbuilding industry became more and more active. The wood-coasting trade also continued to thrive. As a result of these commercial and industrial activities, the area around the harbor gradually became the business center of the Cape and presently it was the most populous district. The change, however, took place slowly. As late as the time of the Revolutionary War, only three streets were formally laid out in the harbor village, Front Street, Middle Street, and Back Street. Front Street (now Main Street) had been laid out in 1698. Then Cornhill, which became Middle Street, was laid out in 1737. Back Street (now Prospect Street) was laid out a few months later. Until after the Revolution, Pleasant Street was only a path with a few homes on it. North of Back Street, in what is now the Maplewood Avenue and Cleveland Street area of the city, lay the Harbor Swamp. That large swamp, which then had not been drained for farming, extended back to the foot of the ridge along the top of which ran the road between the sawmill on Wine Brook and The Green.

As the shipowners and traders prospered, some of them built mansions on Front Street. On that street too, were several stores, and at the foot of Front Street, near the head of Harbor Cove, stood Lowe's Tavern from which Mr. Lowe's stagecoaches departed for Salem and Boston. From Front Street several paths and rough roads led to the wharves and

44

beaches along the water front. At that time there was no
street directly along the water front; Rogers Street was not
opened until 1864.

The new meetinghouse for what then became the First
Parish was built on Middle Street in 1738, and since that
date Middle Street has been a primary location for churches.
Also on this street, where the Y. M. C. A. building now
stands, was the whipping post where public offenders were
chastised until about 1780. Two lots to the east of the whipping post, on the site now designated as 79 Middle Street,
the Broome Tavern was located. It is said to have been a
popular gathering place as early as 1725. And farther east,
at the corner of Middle Street and the Pleasant Street path,
a barber shop was operated for many years in the eighteenth
century by Rebecca Broome, who had a reputation of being
an expert barber. Apparently she also was a genial hostess,
for John J. Babson reports that "her shop was long a place
of resort for all the wits and genteel idlers of the town."

Thus the commercial and industrial prosperity of the village not only provided jobs with the fishing fleet and the overseas traders, but it also produced a new meetinghouse, a
couple of taverns, a barber shop, new stores, and "genteel
idlers." It was while this new sort of life was appearing at
the harbor, moreover, that the settlement at Dogtown was
struggling to become established. With such attractions at the
harbor, it is hardly surprising that the younger generations of
Dogtowners were lured away from the moors, and that the
settlement ultimately was deserted.

The prosperity of the merchants and fleet owners also
led to the building of several fine homes in the harbor village.
At 58 Middle Street, for example, stands a house which was
built about 1750 by Daniel Rogers, the father of twenty-one
children, and the great-great grandfather of Elliott C. Rogers.
At the time of his death, Daniel Rogers owned the largest
fleet sailing out of Gloucester.

Daniel Rogers apparently preached what he practiced. He is reputed to have given a house to each of his twenty-one children when they married, and to have presented a silver porringer to each new grandchild. He was rather temperamental, however, and in one instance he was feeling so displeased with one of his daughters that he did not send her a porringer when a new baby arrived. The daughter was not lacking in resourcefulness: when her father presently had occasion to call at her home, she saw him coming and quickly instructed the nurse to be heating the baby's food in a tin cup over the coals as grandfather entered the house. Soon thereafter the baby received his silver porringer.

At 81 Middle Street stood the house of Captain Jack Davis. Captain Davis was renowned for having recaptured his schooner, the *Pickering*, after she had been taken by the British. He and his father put the prize crew in irons and safely worked their vessel back to Gloucester. The Davis house was a fine mansion and like many of the other houses on Middle Street in the eighteenth century had a lovely garden which extended through to Front Street.

Nathaniel Ellery also lived on Middle Street, in a house later occupied by Addison Gilbert and known as the Gilbert house. Mr. Ellery was a well-known merchant and an avid gunner, especially for pigeons and water fowl. He owned fifteen slaves, who frequently grumbled, it was reported, at having to pick the feathers from all the birds shot by Mr. Ellery— a further indication of how life changed at the harbor village from what it had been at The Green.

Still another historic house on Middle Street is the Sargent-Murray-Gilman house, which is now greatly admired for its fine wood carvings and balustrades. Although the house itself has been well known ever since it was built in 1786, there is a lot of local history connected with it, directly and indirectly, which heretofore has been largely neglected or ignored in the literature of Cape Ann. We think that that history is worth recording in some detail.

The Sargent-Murray-Gilman house was built by Winthrop Sargent, whose own home was on Front Street at the eastern corner of the lane that led to Duncan's Point. Winthrop was a successful merchant and shipowner. He had three children, Winthrop Jr., Fitzwilliam, and Judith.

After graduating from Harvard, Winthrop Sargent, Jr., went to sea as captain of one of his father's vessels. Then, during the Revolutionary War, he became an officer in the Continental Army. After the war ended, he participated in the formation of the Ohio Company, which was organized to develop the Northwest Territory, a position which he held for twelve years. In 1798 he was appointed by President Adams to be the first governor of the newly acquired Mississippi Territory. He was austere and tactless, however, and antagonized many of the people in Natchez. Consequently, when Thomas Jefferson became President, he replaced Mr. Sargent as governor, but Mr. Sargent remained in Natchez as a cotton planter, and to the mansion in which he and his southern wife lived, he gave the name "Gloucester."

Fitzwilliam Sargent became a merchant in Gloucester. He was the lineal ancestor of John Singer Sargent, the famous American portrait painter, and of Charles Sprague Sargent, who for many years was the distinguished director of the Arnold Arboretum in Boston.

It was for his daughter Judith that Winthrop Sargent built the house on Middle Street. Judith's first husband was John Stevens, who became an unsuccessful merchant and trader. To avoid being jailed for debt, he fled in one of his father-in-law's vessels to the West Indies, where he died. Judith's second husband was the Reverend John Murray, founder of Universalism in America, and one of the most controversial characters in Gloucester and all along the northern Atlantic seaboard during the latter half of the eighteenth century.

John Murray was born in England in 1741, the son of an Episcopalian father and a Presbyterian mother. When he was eleven years old, his family moved to Ireland, where John and his father became disciples of John Wesley, the Methodist evangelist. After his father's death, John was adopted by a well-to-do family who had come to take an interest in him. That happy arrangement came to a sudden end, however, when his foster father happened to see John kissing his daughter's hand to console her for some minor emotional upset. John then returned to England, where he drifted about, became a "melancholy man of business," married, was thrown into debtors' prison, and became a convert of James Relly, the founder of the Universalist faith, who was already beginning to preach the doctrine of universal salvation.

When his first wife died in 1770 John Murray was so depressed that he decided to emigrate to America. The ship in which he took passage ran aground about sixty miles from Philadelphia, and there he was pressed into service as a preacher in a church which had been built by a local farmer who had long been waiting for the Lord to send him an acceptable minister. Within a short time Mr. Murray was being invited to preach in numerous cities and towns in eastern Pennsylvania, New Jersey, Maryland, New York, and New England. Thus he became a Universalist evangelist, and he continued his itinerant preaching for over thirty years. He was involved continually in controversy with orthodox clergymen, and he was often condemned and sometimes persecuted for preaching the doctrine of universal salvation.[18]

---

18 This summary of John Murray's life is based primarily on his autobiography, *The Life of Rev. John Murray, Preacher of Universal Salvation*, Written by Himself, with a continuation by Mrs. Judith Sargent Murray, new ed. (Boston, Universalist Publishing House, 1870). Some additional facts have been gathered from Rev. Richard Eddy, D. D., *Universalism in Gloucester, Mass.* (Gloucester, Procter Brothers, 1892).

GLOUCESTER HARBOR

Schooner with dory and seine boat. Pinkie in the foreground.

GLOUCESTER WATER FRONT
Note nest of dories on deck of schooner.

About the time that Mr. Murray came to America, a copy of a book written by James Relly was read by Winthrop Sargent and some of his friends in Gloucester. They wished to learn more about the Universalist doctrine. The opportunity came in 1774 on the occasion of Mr. Murray's second visit to Boston. At that time he was denounced vigorously by a Boston clergyman as being a preacher of Relly's doctrine. The Gloucester group learned of the accusation and at once sent Winthrop Sargent to Boston to invite Mr. Murray to visit Gloucester. He accepted the invitation and in November 1774, spent nine days in Gloucester. He was permitted to preach from the pulpit in the Meeting House of the First Parish on Middle Street on several evenings. Daily services also were held in Mr. Sargent's parlor.

A month later Mr. Murray paid a second visit to Gloucester, and decided to make it his permanent home. He again was permitted for a few days to speak in the First Parish Meeting House, but then it was closed permanently to him. Sunday services were held in Mr. Sargent's parlor.

In May 1775, Mr. Murray became a chaplain of the Rhode Island Brigade in the Continental Army. When General Washington took command of the Army, the other chaplains petitioned him to remove Mr. Murray because of his unorthodox teachings. General Washington however supported Mr. Murray and made his appointment official. After eight months' service with the Army, he became ill and was sent back to Gloucester.

In June 1776, the religious controversy in Gloucester began to gather heat. Several of the friends of Mr. Murray ceased attending the regular services in the First Parish Meeting House. Their action aroused so much anger that a crowd gathered around Mr. Sargent's house, where Mr. Murray was staying, and threatened to ride Mr. Murray out of town, presumably on a rail, unless he left of his own accord. Under the sanction of an old provincial law, an attempt also was made to expel him as a vagrant. And widespread attempts were being made by orthodox clergy and laymen in Gloucester and elsewhere to discredit him because he did not accept their beliefs in hell-fire and brimstone. Feelings ran so high that sometimes as he walked the streets of Gloucester, curses, anathemas, and stones were hurled at him.

In February 1777, while he was ill, Mr. Murray was forced to appear before the local Committee of Public Safety, which is said to have subjected him to insulting questioning. The Committee then notified him that he must leave town within five days. He remained. In March the matter was brought up at town meeting, where the Committee's action was upheld by a vote of 54 to 8, but Mr. Murray did not leave.

The attacks on Mr. Murray and his followers continued. In September 1778, Winthrop Sargent, his daughter Mrs. Judith Stevens, his brother Epes Sargent, David Pearce, and eleven other persons were suspended from the First Parish Church, and four months later they and their friends organized the "Independent Church of Christ," with Mr. Murray as their minister. The following year they erected a new House of Worship on the western corner of what is now Main and Water Streets, near Winthrop Sargent's residence. The section of Main Street from Pleasant Street to Union Hill was then called Spring Street. Winthrop Sargent contributed over forty per cent of the cost of building the new church, the first Universalist Church in America.

Even after the new church was established, the assessors of the First Parish claimed that the Universalists were still obligated to contribute, by taxation, to the support of the First Parish. The Universalists denied that liability and based their denial on the Bill of Rights prefixed to the Constitution of the Commonwealth of Massachusetts. To enforce their demands the assessors, in 1782, seized property of three Universalists and sold it at auction. The property seized included silver plate from Epes Sargent, linen from another, perhaps Winthrop Sargent, and an anchor from a vessel about to sail, probably one owned by David Pearce. William Pearce, who had been a prominent member of the mob which had once threatened to ride Mr. Murray out of town, and who later had become a convert to Universalism, resisted the tax collector and was thrown into jail in Salem. William Pearce was the prominent merchant who owned the largest and best farm in Dogtown.

A suit was brought by the Universalists against the assessors and after four years of litigation, the Universalists obtained a verdict in their favor from the Supreme Court of the Commonwealth. That decision was of great significance, not only for the Universalists, but also for all the other independent sects in Massachusetts, and it constituted a precedent for the rest of the country. It established the right of freedom of worship and of voluntary support of the church of the worshiper's choice. No longer did a person have to contribute to the support of a church which he did not attend.

The victory of the Universalists in obtaining legal recognition of their right to set up their own church free from local parish jurisdiction broke the control by the Commonwealth over religious organization. Theretofore under the Puritan system each town was divided into parishes, and to facilitate the collection of church taxes the boundaries of each parish were fixed specifically by the Commonwealth legislature, as had been done when new parishes were set up in Gloucester in 1716, 1728, 1742, and 1754. The decision in the Universalist case destroyed the significance of any parish boundaries and made legislative action on such matters meaningless. From a broad standpoint, that decision was in keeping with the spirit of freedom for which the Revolutionary War, then in progress, was being fought.

While the tax case was in the courts, Mr. Murray also was prosecuted for performing a marriage ceremony, on the ground that he was not an ordained minister. In 1777 he was found guilty and fined fifty pounds. Inasmuch as he had performed numerous other marriage ceremonies, this prosecution opened the way for many more fines. Consequently, in January 1778, Mr. Murray went to England to avoid further litigation. Shortly thereafter the state legislature passed an act which decreed that he was an ordained minister. Thereby the marriages which he had performed were legalized. The Reverend Murray then returned to Gloucester and at once announced his intentions of marrying Mrs. Judith Sargent Stevens, who had become a widow. They were married in October 1778, and for the next five years they resided in the Sargent-Murray-Gilman house on Middle Street.

In October 1793, the Reverend and Mrs. Murray moved to Boston, where he became pastor of the Universalist Church in that city. On their departure, they sold their house on Middle Street to Major Frederick Gilman.

Major Gilman, who came to Gloucester from Exeter, N. H., married Abigail Somes, the daughter of a Front Street tavern keeper. Their son Samuel, born in the house on Middle Street, went to Harvard and became famous as the author of the college song "Fair Harvard." The Reverend Samuel Gilman was for many years pastor of a Unitarian church in Charleston, S. C.

The turbulent religious controversy was only one aspect of the life in the village at Gloucester Harbor during the eighteenth century. But before recounting some of the other episodes of that period, reference should be made to a few more old houses.

The Somes-Webber house at what is now 20 Middle Street, near the Joan of Arc Statue, was built by Captain John Somes, who was president of the first bank founded in Gloucester, in 1796. When the first Universalist Church was built, Captain Somes presented to it an organ which he had captured as captain of a privateer, from an English merchant ship during the Revolutionary War. His lovely old house has been occupied for many years by the Webber family.

There were, of course, many other new homes of both the finer and the ordinary types built on Middle Street, Front Street, Back Street, and adjacent paths during the prosperous days of the harbor village in the eighteenth century.

At the Garrison house on Back Street, where a parochial residence now stands, one of the most famous characters in the history of Gloucester lived in the middle of the eighteenth century. She was Peg Wesson, a witch who could ride a broomstick. In 1745 a group of Gloucester soldiers who were about to embark for Cape Breton to take part in the siege of Louisburg in the French-American war decided to pay a visit to Peg Wesson. During their visit some of the young men made Peg so angry that she vowed she would wreak vengeance on them. On a cold, raw day in the following spring, while they were still in camp before Louisburg, a large crow kept hovering over the camp. The crow's raucous calls annoyed the uncomfortable, homesick soldiers and they tried, without success, to shoot it down. Then it occurred to one of them that the taunting crow might be a witch in disguise, and a witch, of course, could not be brought down with bullets made of a base metal. Silver bullets were needed for that game. Consequently, he rammed a silver cuff button into his gun and fired it at the bird, breaking its leg. When the soldiers returned to Gloucester a few weeks later, they inquired about Peg Wesson and learned that on the same day that the crow had been shot at Louisburg, Peg had fallen at Garrison house and suffered a broken leg. Furthermore, when a doctor examined her leg, he found in the wound a silver cuff button like that which had been fired at the crow in Louisburg.

Another old landmark near the harbor, of which nothing now remains, was the windmill which once stood near Pavilion Beach, at the northeastern end of the shore boulevard where the Gloucester Tavern now is located. In 1814 a grist-

mill situated on the brook which ran from the Harbor Swamp, near Prospect Street, to Pavilion Beach was being dismantled. Captain Ignatius Webber, who had retired from the sea, bought the equipment in the old mill and installed it in his new windmill on the shore of the harbor. The cost of erecting and equipping the windmill was about $5,000, and it incurred a loss of $2,000 in the first six months of its operation. Captain Webber then tried to sell the mill, but no buyer could be found, either at private sale or at public auction. He continued to operate the mill, apparently without too heavy losses, until 1824. In that year the vanes were damaged by a storm and the mill never was put into operation again. It remained, however, as an exotic, idle landmark on the shore of the harbor until 1876, when damage by fire led to its being completely dismantled.

The village which grew up at the harbor after 1700 was tributary, of course, to the water front. It was from the harbor that the fishing craft and the foreign traders sailed. It was at the harbor that they landed their catches and their return cargoes. At several points on the water front were yards for building ships. On the wharves tributary industries became established. And along the water front colorful episodes occurred from time to time.

The harbor spans the history of the Cape. On its western side lies Stage Fort Park where the Dorchester men located their fishing stage and the cabin in which some of their number spent the winters of 1623 and 1624. It was there, too, that Captain Myles Standish and Messrs. Oldham, Lyford, and Conant almost came to blows in 1625. As a protection against invasion, a fort was built in that area at the time of the Revolutionary War, and rebuilt in 1812. The early name of the Park was Fisherman's Field.

Between Stage Fort Park and the bronze statue of the old fishing captain on the esplanade, is the bridge over the "Cut" which provides an entrance to the Annisquam River from Gloucester Harbor. For three hundred years, until the bridge on Route 128 was completed in 1953, the Cut Bridge was the only road over which the island section of the Cape east of the river could be reached.

Gloucester Harbor actually consists of two harbors, the outer harbor, a large anchorage basin formerly called the "Southwest Harbor," which since 1904 has been protected by the Dog Bar Breakwater at Eastern Point, and the inner harbor, which is afforded additional protection from heavy seas by Ten Pound Island and Rocky Neck.

Ten Pound Island, according to tradition, got its name from the sum which the early settlers paid the Indians for title to it. The deal with the Indians also included the smaller Five Pound Island, located at the head of the inner harbor where the Commonwealth Fish Pier now stands.

We have run across absolutely no information as to when that deal with the Indians was made or what prompted the settlers to make any such payment. In an interesting little book[19] by John S. Webber, Jr., there is a copy of a document by which Samuel English, an Indian, transferred to the Town of Gloucester all his rights and title to the Cape Ann Territory in 1700. He received seven pounds in payment therefor. Samuel English entered into that transaction as the grandson and rightful heir of Masshanomett, the "Sacamore of Agawam," who apparently was recognized as having been the legal owner of the Cape. That transfer purported to include all the islands belonging to the Cape.

Why did the white men make a payment in 1700, nearly sixty years after their fathers had settled on the Cape? Was there actually another deal for the purchase of Ten Pound and Five Pound Islands? If so, with what Indians was that made, and was it made earlier or later than the trade with Samuel English? And why should fifteen pounds have been

---

19 *In and Around Cape Ann* (Gloucester, Cape Ann Advertiser Office, 1885), pp. 6-8.

paid for two small islands in the harbor and only seven pounds for the whole cape, including its islands? Those are intriguing questions to which we have no answers. The fact remains, however, that the island marking one side of the entrance to the inner harbor and the commercial water front at Gloucester long has been known as Ten Pound Island.

The point opposite Ten Pound Island, now known as The Fort, originally was called Watch House Point. In 1743 the Massachusetts legislature made a grant for the erection of a breastwork and the installation of eight twelve-pound cannon on the point. Hence it came to be called The Fort. The purpose of building a fort at Watch House Point was to provide protection for the ships in the inner harbor from enemy warships and pirates. The date of the building of the fort is significant. By 1743 the fishing and trading fleets at Gloucester had become large enough to merit protection.

The major battle at The Fort, however, occurred on August 8, 1775, when the British sloop-of-war *Falcon* attempted to land men there to burn the town. The *Falcon*, which just previously had been foiled in attempted raids at Annisquam, chased a Gloucester West Indiaman into the harbor. The Gloucester vessel was grounded by its crew at the head of the harbor, and when the captain of the *Falcon* undertook to send a landing crew to board her, it was fired on from The Fort and from other spots on the shore. The resistance so infuriated the captain of the *Falcon* that he not only fired a cannon ball through the steeple of a church on Middle Street whose bell had constantly been ringing an alarm, but he also sent another boat ashore at The Fort to set fire to the town. The landing crew, however, were made prisoners by the Gloucester defenders, and the *Falcon* had to depart without its prize West Indiaman and without some of its crew. That was the battle in which Peter Lurvey of Dogtown was killed.

In the middle of the nineteenth century a part of Watch House Point became a residential area, with a large Irish

57

population. When the Irish residents moved out, Italians moved in, and for several decades now The Fort has been the scene of the colorful annual fiesta of the Italian residents of Gloucester. Along the shore front at The Fort, of course, are wharves and fish processing plants.

Next to The Fort lies Harbor Cove, at the head of which is the town landing. There was once a beach of fine white sand at Harbor Cove and along the inner shore of Watch House Point, which then was a popular bathing place for Gloucester residents.

It was on a wharf next to the town landing that a fire originated in 1830 which destroyed many of the buildings on Front Street and some of those on the water front.

At Central Wharf, which was located roughly halfway between the foot of what is now Hancock Street and Duncan Street, David Pearce had his place of business in the latter half of the eighteenth century. He was a vessel owner and a merchant. His vessels were employed in the whale fishery and in trade with Europe, India, and the West Indies. On Central Wharf he had a distillery where cargoes of Surinam molasses were landed and converted into rum. He also had an oil works, for refining whale and fish oil, and warehouses for storing hogsheads of sugar, molasses, cocoa, coffee, and other merchandise, large quantities of which were trans-shipped from Gloucester by freighter to Boston. At one time David Pearce was reputed to be worth $300,000, a very large estate for Gloucester.

David Pearce, it will be recalled, was one of the followers of the Reverend John Murray, and for several years after Winthrop Sargent's fortune had greatly shrunk, Mr. Pearce was the largest contributor to the Universalist Church. Eventually, however, through loss of ships and other adversities, he too became impoverished.

David's brother William had a wharf farther along the

water front, at Vincent's Cove. Left an orphan at an early age, he went to sea and when about twenty-one years old became master of a vessel in the India trade. In a few years he had accumulated enough capital to set himself up in business as a shipowner and trader. He also acquired a sizable fortune. When a new Universalist church was built on Middle Street in 1806 to replace the original outgrown meetinghouse, William Pearce was the largest subscriber. Like his brother, however, he finally ended up in financial embarrassment.

Still farther along the water front toward the head of the inner harbor, was Dr. Coffin's wharf, where there were goings-on which have a certain current political suggestiveness. In referring to Dr. Coffin's wharf, the writer of an article published in the *Gloucester Daily Times*, July 10, 1889, said: "It was a small wharf and a noted resort (about 1830) where Town Meeting orators, waxing warm with each other in the discussion of local affairs, would adjourn and fight it out. It was the scene of many a hotly contested rough-and-tumble fight over questions which agitated the minds of those who were interested in town affairs—and perhaps had imbibed too much of the famous New England rum of that period. There was not much business at this wharf as it served more for a landing for small boats." From the foregoing statement it appears that even a century and a quarter ago, politics in Gloucester were turbulent, and there was an arena for combat then which might have been useful for certain members of the City Council in 1955-56.

The Gloucester traders of the eighteenth and early nineteenth centuries did not hesitate to outwit the customs authorities when opportunity offered. Shortly before the Revolution, for example, a schooner owned by Col. Joseph Foster arrived in Gloucester at night with a foreign cargo, and the landing of the cargo was immediately begun. Nevertheless, at sunrise over half the cargo was still aboard the ship and Col. Foster knew that a royal customs officer from Salem would soon be arriving. Consequently, the aid of a watchman at the Cut was enlisted. There had been an alarm about a smallpox epidemic and a stout Irishman, John McKean, had been stationed in a watch house at the Cut to stop all strangers entering the town and subject them to fumigation. When His Majesty's customs officer arrived at the Cut that morning, John McKean insisted that he must be fumigated, a process which in that instance took all day. By the time the customs officer was released, Col. Foster's cargo was neatly stored away on shore.

Another case which involved a United States Customs officer occurred in 1813. In that instance, the schooner *Adolph*, nominally of Swedish registry, arrived in Gloucester Harbor from Halifax with a cargo of sugar, and also a considerable quantity of contraband goods of British manufacture. The ship's papers had been forged to indicate that she came from St. Bartholomew. The sugar was unloaded and the contraband smuggled ashore. The *Adolph* took a cargo of flour and sailed supposedly for St. Bartholomew, but actually for Halifax. In fourteen days the *Adolph* was back in Gloucester Harbor with another cargo of sugar and contraband. Inasmuch as fourteen days obviously was too short a time for a trip to the West Indies and return, the customs collector seized the vessel, stripped off her sails and took them ashore, and placed an inspector on board. Some of the contraband already had been landed, however, and some of it had been sunk under the vessel for later recovery.

While the *Adolph* was still at anchor in the harbor, a heavy snowstorm came up at night, and under cover of the storm the sails were retrieved from the collector's storage place and returned to the schooner, which then prepared to put to sea. As the vessel left its anchorage, the customs inspector, who had been kept locked in the cabin, was placed in his revenue boat, with a bottle of wine and some food, and left to return to shore as best he might.

During Prohibition days in the 1920's, Gloucester also had a reputation for rum-running activity, and a squadron of "rum chasers," as the Coast Guard boats were called, had its headquarters at the head of the inner harbor.

The harbor, of course, also has been the center of the Gloucester fishing industry, with its forests of masts when the fleet was in, its nets drying on the wharves, its odors of fish gurry, tar, bilge water, and pogy oil, and its ships' crews coming and going with their gear or indulging in the shore divertisements of a seaport town.

East Gloucester and the Back Shore

WHILE NUMEROUS OLD landmarks are still to be found around The Green, Dogtown, and the harbor, similar reminders of the early days are scarce in the East Gloucester and back shore area. That area extends along the eastern shore of the harbor and the southern side of the Cape, from the head of the harbor to the Rockport line. It includes East Gloucester, Rocky Neck, Eastern Point, Bass Rocks, Little Good Harbor Beach, Brier Neck and Joppa. With the exception of a small district along the East Gloucester water front where fishermen lived, most of the area was farm land until the latter part of the nineteenth century. During the first couple of hundred years after the white settlers arrived, life in the farming community in East Gloucester and on the back shore seems to have been relatively uneventful. There were occasional neighborhood rows, to be sure, over such matters as rights of way to the shore, but there were no public buildings or taverns located there. No records of scandals or witches have been found. And there seem to have been only a few notorious characters among the residents of the area. It was just a peaceful farming community.

Then, toward the middle of the nineteenth century, almost exactly two hundred years after the first settlers had begun to establish homes around The Green, summer vacationers appeared and their coming opened a new chapter in the saga of the Cape. Although almost contemporaneously the back shore, Pigeon Cove, and Annisquam also began to attract summer visitors, East Gloucester was one of the first vacation spots on the Cape. The summer folks started to come by stagecoach. Then when the railroad was built, their numbers increased. And when the automobile came into general use, summer visitors arrived in larger flocks.

The first summer visitors stayed mostly at farmhouses and other private homes. Then summer boardinghouses and hotels were opened. Presently private cottages and fine summer mansions were built; bathing and sailing facilities were provided; and a golf course was constructed. If some of the old farmers who settled in Joppa could now see the bathing suits at Little Good Harbor Beach and the pajama costumes of Rocky Neck, or witness grown men and women chasing little white balls around their old cow pasture in the hot summer day after day, they might suspect that all witchcraft had not vanished!

A memorandum which has come into our hands indicates that the summer boarder business in East Gloucester got its start in 1843. In that year Joseph Kidder, a Boston druggist, and his wife made a recreational visit to Gloucester, staying in a hotel which then stood at the corner of Main and Washington Streets. Before returning to Boston, Mr. and Mrs. Kidder decided to make arrangements, if possible, for some of their children and the children's cousins to come to Gloucester for a vacation on a farm. They finally prevailed upon Mrs. Judith Wonson of East Gloucester to take in the children as boarders, Mrs. Kidder assuring Mrs. Wonson that the children would be no more trouble than kittens.

Mrs. Wonson, who then was twenty-three, neglected to ask the ages of the children who were to be her guests, with the result that she presently experienced a big surprise. When they arrived—a whole stagecoach full—she was somewhat dismayed to find that the "children" were quite grown up. One of the boys had just graduated from college and two of the girls were older than Mrs. Wonson herself.

To feed the boarders, vegetables, eggs, milk, chickens, and other produce were provided, of course, from the farm.

Supplementary groceries were purchased at the general store which then was located in the Square at East Gloucester. Meat was bought occasionally from an itinerant butcher's cart. And fish and lobsters were obtained from the nearby ocean. The food was cooked over an open fire on the hearth and in the brick ovens in the old farmhouse.

The Kidder "children" enjoyed themselves so thoroughly at the Wonson farm that they came back year after year and brought more and more of their friends with them. Mrs. Wonson acquired a neighboring property to house her growing clientele, and from that start a large summer boarding business developed in East Gloucester. Other farmhouses began to take in summer boarders and in the 1870's the building of summer hotels in that neighborhood was started.

The Wonson farm was located on the shore of the harbor where the Hawthorne Inn later was built, a short distance beyond the sand bar which then connected Rocky Neck with the mainland. The farm was only a couple of stones' throws from where the Indiaman had been beached in 1775 to escape the British *Falcon*. It likewise was only a short distance from the beach where Champlain had landed when he visited "Beau Port," as he called the place, in 1605 and 1606. From the farm the boarders had an excellent view, of course, of all the traffic in the harbor, which then was active with bankers and mackerel seiners and Surinam traders, many of them sleek schooners whose prototype had been launched in a nearby shipyard in 1713.

One of the most distinguished early summer residents of East Gloucester was Elizabeth Stuart Phelps. Miss Phelps made her first visit to East Gloucester about 1868, when she was twenty-four years old. She then was just starting on her literary career. She had engaged rooms in a village outside Cape Ann in the region of Ipswich Bay, but not on the shore. After a week's sojourn there, she tired of the spot and started out on an exploring expedition which took her to Cape Ann.

Miss Phelps described finding Eastern Point:

We drove on for seven miles, crossing the noisiest and dirtiest and fishiest of little cities, without enthusiasm. Gloucester, as to her business sections, did not prove alluring, but we pushed on eastward down her harbor shore.

Suddenly, at the end of our journey, hot, dusty and discouraged, toiling up what is known as Patch's Hill, we brought our tired pony to a halt, and drew the breath of unexpected and undreamed of delight. We had discovered Eastern Point.

Out of the salt dust, out of the narrow scorching streets, by the fishflakes and the fish teams, past the rude roads whose boulders seemed to have been "spatted" down by the whimsical street-commissioner Time, we came upon the fairest face of all the New England coast —the Eastern side of Gloucester Harbor.

She then added, "It would not be easy to find a lovelier bit of coast survey anywhere in the world."[20]

Miss Phelps took up her summer abode in a cottage on the Wonson farm where the Kidders had stayed. That cottage can still be identified from her description of it, "with the beautiful lava gorge in front where the tide rises almost to the piazza." After a few summers at Wonson's, Miss Phelps built her own chalet on the neighboring upland off Grapevine Road, which she called "Old Maids' Paradise," a title which she also bestowed upon one of her books. She continued to be a summer resident of East Gloucester from May to November, until she became an invalid in 1888.

While driving through the fishermen's district of East Gloucester one summer evening in the early years of her residence on the Cape, Miss Phelps found a large crowd gathered on the street. On inquiring she learned that a man had just

---

20 *Chapters From a Life* (Boston, Houghton, Mifflin and Company, 1896), p. 193.

been shot to death in a grog shop across the way. Although they were total strangers to her, she went immediately to visit the slain man's widow and twelve children. That experience so aroused her sympathies for wives and children of men who patronized the grog shops that she became a local temperance crusader and helped to support a Reform Club. On one occasion her friend Dr. Phillips Brooks came to talk to the fishermen of East Gloucester on the evils of drunkenness.

Among the many distinguished visitors entertained at Old Maids' Paradise by Miss Phelps were Henry Wadsworth Longfellow and Dr. Oliver Wendell Holmes. Miss Phelps stated that it was from her chalet that Longfellow had his first view of Norman's Woe across the harbor on the Magnolia shore. Longfellow in his poem already had wrecked the Hesperus upon that reef, but Miss Phelps stated that she understood he never had seen it until he viewed it from her home in East Gloucester.[21]

Rudyard Kipling also was a temporary resident of East Gloucester. He was living in Vermont, his wife's native state, in 1896, when he decided to write a sea story and he naturally came to Cape Ann to obtain a setting. While he was gathering his material for *Captains Courageous*, he and his family stayed at the "Fairview," a small inn in East Gloucester not far from the former summer home of Elizabeth Stuart Phelps. During his sojourn on Cape Ann, he also lived for a time in Annisquam.

Among the many other famous visitors to East Gloucester were Louisa May Alcott, who spent at least four summers at the Fairview Inn, and Lotta Crabtree, the actress, who usually stayed at the Pilgrim House.

Rocky Neck also shared in the growth of the summer boarder business. Rocky Neck formerly was an island at high tide, but sometime before the summer boarder influx began,

21 *Ibid.*, p. 157.

a broad stone wall had been built between the Neck and the mainland, presumably to protect the anchorages in Smith Cove and the inner harbor from the heavy seas which rolled in from the ocean when it was stormy. People could walk across to the Neck on the sand bar at low tide and on the stone wall when the tide was high. When the Cape was first settled, Rocky Neck was known as "Peter Mud's Neck," but we have not been able to find out much about Peter Mud or why he deserved to have a neck named for him. What a pity, nevertheless, that the original name of the Neck was not perpetuated!

When the first summer visitors came to East Gloucester, there were only a few houses and a paint factory on Rocky Neck. Nowadays in the summer time Rocky Neck bristles with activity. Smith's Cove just north of the causeway which has superseded the sea wall, is a popular mooring basin for sail boats and other pleasure craft in great variety. On the Neck are summer boardinghouses, an artists' colony, and several eating places specializing in sea food. On the Neck also is a marine railway, where commercial vessels and pleasure craft are hauled out for cleaning and repairs. One of the vessels periodically overhauled there in recent years has been the *Yankee*, in which Captain and Mrs. Irving Johnson made their well-known South Sea cruises, and it was from Rocky Neck that the *Yankee* made its departure on each of these cruises.

The paint factory located on Rocky Neck was the first in America in which copper paint was produced. Copper paint had been invented earlier in France, but in 1863 a Gloucester firm greatly improved the product and began its manufacture at Rocky Neck. Copper paint was used to give the bottoms of sailing vessels a coating which protected them against the accumulation of barnacles and other marine growths. The noxious ingredient in the paint which checked those foul growths was yellow ochre, the bog iron ore pig-

67

ment obtained from the swamps of Cape Ann. Incidentally, Elliott Rogers' maternal grandfather, Mr. Friend, sold fifteen hundred dollars' worth of bog iron ore to the copper paint factory at Rocky Neck in the middle of the nineteenth century. The ore was dug on Mr. Friend's farm on the old Harbor Swamp, near what is now Myrtle Square on Maplewood Avenue, and it was hauled to the factory by oxcart. The Kidder "children" may even have seen that oxcart crossing the sand bar to Rocky Neck while they were vacationing in East Gloucester.

The promotion of a section of the back shore as a summer resort followed closely upon the heels of the East Gloucester development. The land where that promotion took place had been known for many years as the Harbor Pasture. It was common land in which farmers living in that section of the Cape owned "cow rights." About 1846 George H. Rogers, a prominent Gloucester merchant, began to purchase those cow rights and eventually he obtained title to all the pasture land. He then laid out streets and roads and broke up the pasture into building lots. He spent a large sum of money in that development but he died before he could reap a profit. After Mr. Rogers' death, the property was sold to Henry Souther, of South Boston, who in turn sold it to the Gloucester Land Company. The company built a small hotel and sold a few building lots, but the property presently reverted to Mr. Souther, who then carried the development through to success. A large addition was built to the hotel; more cottages were erected; the roads were improved; a golf course was constructed; and Bass Rocks, as the new settlement was named because of the striped bass which lurked there in season, became a fashionable summer resort.

The shore at Bass Rocks, with its jagged ledges and big boulders, is one of the most rugged stretches of the Cape, and when a heavy storm rages, the surf there is especially spectacular.

Although the farms on Eastern Point adjoined both East Gloucester and Bass Rocks, they were not converted into summer estates until a considerably later date. The Niles farm—four hundred acres—was the largest holding on Eastern Point. It extended from Niles Beach, on the shore of Gloucester Harbor, to Brace Cove on the outside of the Cape. One of the early owners of the farm stipulated in his will that the land should not be divided until his younger grandson had reached the age of twenty-one. Consequently until about 1885 the only nonagricultural developments on the Niles farm were a lighthouse, a quarry, and a fort.

For the seafarers of Cape Ann, Eastern Point always has been an outstanding landmark. Located at a sharp angle on a rocky shore, it indicates dangerous rocks and reefs to be shunned and marks the entrance to Gloucester Harbor from the east, a point to be rounded to reach a haven of safety in foul weather. Despite the significance of Eastern Point to the seafarers, however, it was not until 1812 that steps were taken to provide a beacon light there. In that year the United States Government purchased an acre of land from Mr. Niles and erected a stone beacon at the tip of Eastern Point. On the top of the beacon a lantern was placed. In 1831 the beacon was superseded by a modern lighthouse.

Nearly a century after the first light was put up on Eastern Point, another step was taken for the protection of mariners. In 1904 a breakwater was built westward from Eastern Point. It is nearly half a mile long and extends out over the dangerous Dog Bar Reef. On the outer end of the breakwater is another small lighthouse, to supplement the Eastern Point Light. In addition to providing protection against the reef for inbound ships, the breakwater also is especially useful in making the outer harbor a safe anchorage for vessels in stormy weather. The violence of the storms which that breakwater sometimes has to withstand is attested by the fact that in one storm in recent years a couple of slabs of granite, each weighing twelve or thirteen tons, were picked up from the top of the breakwater by the waves and tossed over into the harbor.

As an additional aid to navigation, a whistling buoy was placed, about 1880, in the ocean off Eastern Point. It stirred up a controversy between the summer residents in nearby East Gloucester and the fishermen which was typical of several other controversies during the last seventy-five years. In one letter which was published in the *Cape Ann Advertiser* in answer to previous letters of remonstrance, the writer said, among other things: "I would ask . . . whether the visitors who spend a few weeks here during the summer months are of more financial importance to Gloucester than its fisheries; whether the possible slight annoyance of a few should be allowed to outweigh the fact of the great benefit which must arise from the establishment of this signal."

One of the summer residents who was especially annoyed by the groans of the whistling buoy was Elizabeth Stuart Phelps, who then was suffering from a nervous ailment. As a consequence of her complaint, the United States Secretary of the Navy, it was reported, instructed a local government official to have the buoy taken up in May and put out again in October. Shortly thereafter, however, Miss Phelps married the Reverend Herbert Ward, a young man sixteen years her junior, who had just graduated from a theological seminary. While Mr. Ward was spending a summer in Gloucester, where a new sloop was being built for him in a local boat yard, he boarded in a cottage owned by Miss Phelps and before the summer was over they were married. After the marriage the following item appeared in the *Boston Record*: "Since her marriage Mrs. Ward is much better, and the officer who had to remove the buoy has put it back with the assurance that next summer he will have no orders to disturb it."

On the seaward shore of Eastern Point, not far from the lighthouse, is a ledge which so resembles the head and body of a woman that it is known as "Mother Ann." The fishermen used to call it "Woman in the Rocks."

Just inside the breakwater, on the harbor shore, a project was started in 1836 of which no trace now remains. In that year a Boston contractor acquired land there from the Niles family and opened a quarry. That was one of the early quarries on Cape Ann, but it was operated for only seven years.

During the Civil War the federal government leased a piece of land from the Niles family, several hundred yards inland from the Eastern Point lighthouse, and built a fort on it. Ten large guns were mounted on the fort but no invaders appeared and there never was occasion to use the guns. The earthworks of that old fort, roughly an acre in extent, are still standing.

About 1885 the Niles farm was purchased by the Eastern Point Associates, a group of men who planned to develop it for summer residences. The whole farm was laid out in one-acre lots. A road was built along the shore of the harbor to the lighthouse. Another was built to the old fort, and numerous other streets and roads were planned. In order to maintain it as a private colony, the roads were built and kept in repair by the Associates, not by the city. Also to ensure privacy, a gate was erected at the entrance to the estate, near the northern end of Niles Beach, where a watchman could be stationed to turn away any picnickers and undesirable intruders.

After they had spent considerable sums in developing the property but before their plans were consummated, the Eastern Point Associates went into bankruptcy and two of their members bought the property at a foreclosure sale. The new owners continued to build roads and they even attempted to lay out a golf course, but they made little headway in attracting summer settlers. Then about 1915, John W. Prentiss, of New York, purchased a large tract of this land near Brace

Cove. Mr. Prentiss built a beautiful summer home, called "Blighty," landscaped the grounds, and constructed a road around Niles Pond. Between 1920 and 1930 several other estates were developed on the old Niles farm, and about 1930 a syndicate of the residents established the Eastern Point Yacht Club.

About ten years after Mr. Prentiss built "Blighty," a small cottage was built on the harbor side of Eastern Point which presently became one of the most notable modern landmarks on Cape Ann, the Sleeper house—"Beauport," a title deriving from Champlain's designation of Gloucester Harbor. The owner of the cottage was Henry Davis Sleeper. After graduating from college, Mr. Sleeper had gone to Paris to study architecture, but on his return to America, instead of entering that profession, he accepted employment with a publishing firm. He enjoyed good living and friendly entertainment. Consequently he bought a smallish lot of land near the tip of Eastern Point, on which he built a modest little cottage for recreation and hospitality.

One day when he was traveling through Essex, Mr. Sleeper learned that an old eighteenth-century house which had been built by William Cogswell was to be torn down because of its decrepitude. He bought the pine paneling and flooring of that old house and utilized them in the construction of a new front hall in his cottage at Eastern Point. That step led to others, and more and more rooms were added. His aim, he said, was "to have a house in which each room could recapture some of the specific mood or phase or 'period' of our American life from the time of the Plymouth Colony down through the Revolution and the early Republic."[22] In 1909 there were twenty-six rooms at Beauport.

22 Samuel Chamberlain and Paul Hollister, *Beauport* (New York, Hastings House, 1951). This volume has 71 pages of excellent photographs by Mr. Chamberlain and a brief but pungent text by Mr. Hollister.

In 1914 Mr. Sleeper joined with his Eastern Point neighbor, A. Piatt Andrew, later a long-term Congressman from eastern Massachusetts, and William Hereford of New York, to organize, staff, and supply the American Field Service for operating ambulances between the battle lines and the Allied hospitals in France. For the next four years, Mr. Sleeper devoted all his time and most of his financial resources to that undertaking.

To obtain funds for adding to his collections at Beauport Mr. Sleeper became active in architecture and interior decoration after his return from France. And when he died in 1934 there were over forty rooms at Beauport, each designed and furnished in accordance with Mr. Sleeper's original objective. Beauport thus became an establishment of great historic and artistic significance.

The rooms are small, the Octagon Room, for example, one of the largest, being only twenty feet across. Among the other rooms are the pine kitchen, furnished in true Plymouth style; the Mariner's Room, Paul Revere Room, Franklin Room, and Golden Step Room—a summer dining room with a large model of a square-rigged vessel and a 180-degree view of Gloucester Harbor; the Jacobean Room, with a narrow panel at one end which hides a spiral staircase by way of which fugitive witches might escape; and the Chinese Hall, the walls of which are covered with hand-painted scenic paper depicting the arts and crafts of China. That paper had been imported by some New England skipper sailing to the Far East, and had been reposing in its original boxes in an attic in Marblehead for a century or longer before it was discovered by Mr. Sleeper.

Mr. Sleeper was a gracious entertainer and the list of his guests at Beauport was long and illustrious—sculptors, architects, painters, writers (Glasgow, Benet, Wister, Henry James, Amy Lowell, Booth Tarkington and so on), gentlemen of music, theatre people (Hayes, Coward, Eames, Rob-

73

son, Janis, Tree, Manners, and others), statesmen, generals, men of capital, and other distinguished persons such as Alice Longworth, Eleanor Roosevelt, and the Crown Prince and Princess of Sweden.

Thus through Miss Phelps, Mr. Sleeper, and other residents of the area, many prominent people have visited East Gloucester and Eastern Point during the last hundred years.

One natural feature of the Eastern Point area which deserves special mention in passing is Niles Pond, a good-sized fresh-water pond that lies so close to the ocean at Brace Cove that the surf breaks over into it during heavy storms, but the water in the pond remains fresh. It must be fed by springs which flow in sufficient volume, even in dry weather, to cause the fresh water to seep out at a rate which prevents the salt water from seeping in.

On the back shore to the east of Bass Rocks, another summer colony was built up some time after the Bass Rocks development took place. It was located on Brier Neck, a rocky promontory facing Salt Island. And between Bass Rocks and Brier Neck lies Little Good Harbor Beach, a natural feature of the shore which has provided one of the major attractions for summer vacationists.

One of the traditions of Cape Ann is that Little Good Harbor Beach was so named by an Indian whose English vocabulary was so limited that to him "little good" meant "not good." The Indian was referring, of course, to the harbor outside the beach, not the beach itself. That is an intriguing tradition, but there is evidence that it originated in the mind of one of the imaginative citizens of Gloucester rather than in the mouth of an Indian.

At the southwestern end of the beach, a creek, after winding through the marsh behind the beach, flows into the cove. When the Cape was first settled, that creek apparently was considerably wider and deeper than it is today. And on an old map we have found a basin in the creek, near the

74

mainland, designated as "Little Good Harbor." The boats of the early residents of the Cape were small craft, and that basin in the creek, though little, would have been large enough to accommodate them. Inasmuch as it was fairly well protected from the sea by the marsh, it also was "good"; hence "Little Good Harbor."

One of the old roads on the Cape, now called Witham Street, led down through Joppa to that harbor. And from Joppa, as stated earlier, another road apparently ran to the first sawmill on Wine Brook. Hence, Little Good Harbor was one of the points from which lumber sawn at the mill could be shipped by water, and it presumably also was a point from which cordwood was shipped when that trade developed. Little Good Harbor was the most sheltered spot for vessels to anchor between the inner harbor at Gloucester and Sandy Bay.

Joppa, on the mainland back of Little Good Harbor and Brier Neck, was one of the early farming districts on the Cape. John Rowe settled there in 1651 and presently other farmers arrived. After the forests had been cleared away, the district to which the biblical name of "Joppa" became attached, for reasons now unknown, was fairly level and tillable and it was only about three miles from The Green. When the village at Gloucester Harbor grew up, Joppa was only a couple of miles from its center, and it was on one of the roads from the harbor to Sandy Bay. That Joppa became quite a prosperous little community is indicated by several sturdy old houses which are still standing there.

In 1651, however, the corner of Witham Street and Eastern Avenue, where John Rowe built his house, was a lonely place, deep in a trackless wilderness, and life in the Rowe home was hardly a peaceful one. In 1656, on two occasions, Mr. Rowe declared publicly that if he "had his wife off his mind" he would burn down the house and leave before the next break of day, in order to get away from

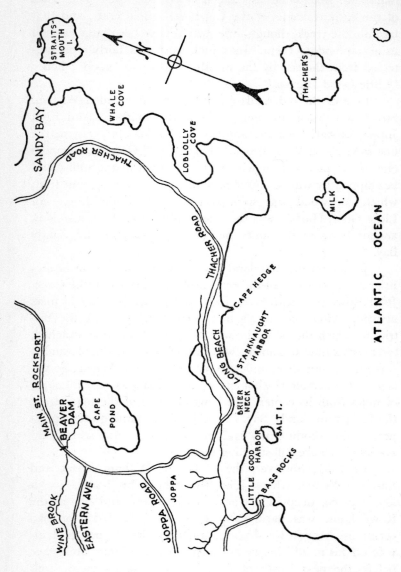

ATLANTIC OCEAN

BASS ROCKS TO SANDY BAY

"such a company of hell-hounds." His two sons apparently were causing him great discomfiture. For making such a statement, he was fined twenty shillings by the Quarterly Court and ordered to make a public confession at the next town meeting in Gloucester.

Besides being a farming community, Joppa in later years also had a lobster business. Lobsters were plentiful in the ocean off the back shore, and when a market became available, lobstering was developed as a commercial enterprise. There is no record, so far as we are aware, of the origin of the lobster business on the Cape or of its growth. We do not even know when or by whom or where the lobster pot was invented. But the Parsons family at Joppa were among the pioneers in the Cape Ann lobster business. In a newspaper article published in 1889 it was stated that the Parsons family had been engaged in catching lobsters "for generations."

According to that article, Joseph Parsons, then living at Joppa, had begun helping his grandfather, Mr. Coos, set lobster traps over fifty years earlier. In the grandfather's time he and his grandson handled eighty traps a day in the waters along the back shore. The lobsters were landed at Salt Island, off Brier Neck, and then carried to the Coos's home to be boiled. Then Mr. Coos took them in a wheelbarrow to the harbor for sale, the largest commonly being sold for twenty-five cents apiece. Mr. Coos at that time was the only lobster vendor in Gloucester. By 1889 Mr. Parsons and his sons were setting over four hundred traps each season. Most of the lobsters then caught in the spring and fall were being sent to Boston alive in barrels. The remainder were boiled for the Gloucester market.

One other spot of minor historical significance in this general area should be mentioned for the record. We had run across several casual references to Starknaught Harbor, but it was not until we examined an old map of the shore that we found out where it was located. That map designated the shallow cove beyond the eastern end of Brier Neck, where Long Beach begins, as Starknaught Harbor. It was not well protected from the sea, and apparently was used commercially for only a short time. Cordwood may have been shipped from there, and perhaps lumber sawed at a mill located on Saw Mill Brook, about half a mile inland from that point, also may have been loaded there for shipment along the coast.

Along the northern boundary of the whole back shore area lies a prehistoric geological landmark, a long stretch of uncovered terminal moraine. In his classic report on the geology of Cape Ann,[23] Professor Shaler stated that the terminal moraine occupies about three-quarters of the area of Cape Ann east of the Annisquam River. It is evidenced by the boulders on Dogtown and elsewhere. But only on the ridge north of East Gloucester, Joppa, and Beaver Dam is there a long uncovered stretch.

The terminal moraine consists of rocks and boulders of many shapes and sizes which were shoved forward at the front of the second glacier that covered this region many centuries ago. The exposed moraine extends in length for about three miles. From Lamb's Ledge just above Webster Street, near the end of traffic Route 128, the frontal moraine stretches out in a somewhat irregular fashion to the Raccoon Ledges above Beaver Dam, and on to the vicinity of Great Hill in Rockport. In width, the open moraine varies from perhaps a hundred yards to a mile or thereabouts. Over much of the stretch exposed boulders rise almost perpendicularly for forty to over one hundred feet.

The moraine has remained exposed along this front because here it is composed of such a high percentage of large boulders. The crevices between them are often fifteen or

---

23 Nathaniel S. Shaler, *The Geology of Cape Ann, Massachusetts*, a report submitted to the United States Geological Survey, June 20, 1888, and published as part of a larger report on a study of the Atlantic coast line. The report contains many excellent photographs.

twenty feet deep, and their arrangement is such as generally to avoid the collection of sediment. Where a little soil has accumulated, trees have taken root. In several instances, furthermore, they are even growing out of small cracks in the boulders.

In and around the moraine are several swamps where pockets, which have little drainage, were gouged out of the bedrock by the ice sheet as it inched its way relentlessly onward. In the swamps trees, shrubs, flowers, and mosses grow luxuriantly and afford a striking contrast to the grim piles of boulders only a few yards away.

The terminal moraine marks the end of the southward movement of the second ice sheet to cover this region. Here the glacier stopped and began to melt away, leaving this ponderous evidence of its depth and force. In Dogtown gigantic boulders stand as isolated monuments of the ice age. The exposed terminal moraine, on the other hand, affords a manifestation of the titanic natural force which shoved along windrows of massive rocks irresistibly, either grinding opposition to gravelly powder or breaking it off in huge chunks to be added to the rolling mass.

Ships and Shipbuilders

ALONG WITH THE ERECTION of crude dwellings for shelter and the planting of a few crops, boatbuilding was one of the first concerns of the New England colonists, including those of Cape Ann. Boats were needed for catching fish for food. Boats also were essential for travel and transportation. Horses were not numerous and the early roads were only wild trails. Many of the early colonists were of a restless sort, and there was a good deal of traveling back and forth between settlements, but usually it was much easier and much simpler to travel by boat than to journey by land. These observations held fully as true for Cape Ann as for its neighboring settlements. In fact, the contour of Cape Ann and the Cut which connected the Annisquam River with Gloucester Harbor after 1643 especially favored travel and transportation by water in this region.

The forests of Cape Ann furnished readily available timber, and its brooks provided power for sawmills to convert the timber into materials for boatbuilding.

The first boats built here were shallops and pinnaces, small craft with shallow draft, which could be propelled with either oars or sails, and could be built wherever there was a cove or beach for launching. That sort of boatbuilding was so common and so obvious that no records were kept as to where or by whom the boats were built.

In 1642, however, a more ambitious shipbuilding project was undertaken when William Stevens, a shipwright, was induced to settle at Gloucester. That was the year, it will be recalled, in which the settlement really began to take form.

"Woman-in-the-Rocks" (Mother Ann), Eastern Point

LOBSTERMAN
With Pot in Dory.

In 1642 the town was incorporated, a minister was obtained for the new parish, a meetinghouse was built, and a sawmill was set up on Wine Brook. It was then that community life began on Cape Ann, and it is significant that shipbuilding was deemed to be so essential that substantial inducements were made to attract that new industry.

When William Stevens came to Gloucester he had been in New England for ten years. As an inducement for him to settle here, he was granted eight acres of land on the shore of Gloucester Harbor near the Cut, six acres of land on Meeting House Neck, and five hundred acres between the Chebacco and Annisquam Rivers. Forty-six years later the land west of the Annisquam River became the Coffin farm.

The first vessel that Stevens built was 68 feet long with 23 foot beam and a 9½ foot hold. This was a large vessel for those days. Besides building vessels and operating a farm, Stevens was a member of the first board of selectmen in Gloucester, and he also served as a member of the General Court of the Massachusetts Bay Colony. He was an ardent Puritan, however, and after the Restoration he was so vehement and so outspoken in his denunciations of King Charles II that the royal governor had him sentenced to a month in prison in 1667. He also was fined twenty pounds and lost his privileges as a freeman.

Presumably to raise funds with which to pay his fine and perhaps to meet other financial obligations, he mortgaged his land west of the river. He was not able to redeem the mortgage, and he therefore lost the property, including the buildings which he had erected on it. It was through that mortgage transaction that the property came into the hands of Mr. Willoughby of London, who sold it to Tristam Coffin in 1688.

Although William Stevens built a few vessels, no regular shipbuilding industry resulted from his coming. The raw material was here. The skill was here. And production sites were available. But at that time there was no adequate market for

Gloucester-built vessels. Boatbuilding, therefore, was confined mostly to small coastal craft.

It was not until more than fifty years after William Stevens was persuaded to settle on Cape Ann that large-scale shipbuilding got under way here. That development came largely as a result of the opening up of potential new markets for Cape Ann products and services, and it coincided roughly with the shift of the center of the town from The Green to Gloucester Harbor, the settlement of Dogtown, Pigeon Cove, and Sandy Bay, the spurt of shipping activity at Annisquam, the arrangements for the new road and ferries in the West Parish, and the opening of the first public school at The Green.

This new era of economic and social activity on the Cape was brought about by a variety of influences, some of which were of far distant origin. One of the immediate factors was the growth of nearby cities. During the period from 1628 to 1700, or thereabouts, the population of the Massachusetts Bay Colony, of which Gloucester was a part, had been increasing, and several cities, such as Salem and Boston, were beginning to manifest urban needs which had to be supplied, in part, from outside sources. Lumber for building, wood for fuel, and food for existence were some of the items which had to be brought in from the more primitive settlements, and many of these cargoes were carried by water.

During the latter part of the seventeenth century and the early eighteenth century, moreover, a development of overseas trade that helped to provide a market for Cape Ann ships was fostered by both colonial and more distant events. As the colonial wilderness was conquered, and agriculture, industry, and trade prospered, the standard of living in the New England colonies was rising, with the result that the demand for products manufactured in the mother country and for articles produced in the West Indies and the southern colonies was effectively enhanced.

By 1700, moreover, a large market was appearing in the southern colonies and the West Indies for New England dried fish as food for slaves. In South Carolina, for example, by 1708 two-thirds of the population were Negro slaves and in Virginia and the other southern colonies the number of slaves had been growing rapidly. The development of those markets for dried fish encouraged the building of ships on Cape Ann for use in catching fish and also for use in shipping the fish to the regions where it was sold.

The foregoing trends which stimulated the shipbuilding on Cape Ann were given further impetus by two events which occurred in 1713. The first of these was the signing of the Treaty of Utrecht by England and France which suspended colonial warfare and ushered in a thirty-year period of peace. For the preceding sixty years the English and French had been engaged in almost continuous struggles for possession of New-foundland and Nova Scotia, and that warfare, of course, had interfered with fishing and trade activities at Cape Ann. By the Treaty of Utrecht, however, France relinquished posses-sion of those territories to England. Thereby the surrounding waters became safely accessible to Cape Ann fishermen. The Treaty of Utrecht also made foreign trade safer. This cessa-tion of warfare thus removed obstacles to fishing and foreign trade at just a time when the market opportunities were favor-able for an expansion of these activities.

The second event of special significance which occurred in 1713 was the launching of the first schooner. Between 1702, when the building of larger vessels really got under way, and 1712, over 35 sloops and 10 brigantines were built on Cape Ann. A few of the sloops were of about 50 tons burden and the brigantines were of 80 to 100 tons displacement. Those vessels were all conventional in design. Then in 1713 Captain Andrew Robinson, of Gloucester, built a "schooner," a great American invention.

The distinctive feature of the schooner was not the design of the hull but the type of its rigging. Until the schooner rig was invented, sails on the vessels then in use generally were of the square-rigger type on large ships and of the lateen type on small craft. The lateen type was the one in which the upper edge of the sail was fastened to a long, heavy spar that reached on a slant from just above the deck to a point considerably higher than the top of the mast by which it was supported. In the schooner rig, which could be used on both large and small craft, there was a short gaff at the top of the sail and a longer boom at the bottom. The inner ends of the gaff and of the boom had a prong that fitted onto the mast. The luff of the sail, that is its inside edge, was fastened to hoops which slid up and down the mast as the sail was raised or lowered. By that means the luff was held close to the mast but the sail could be swung freely to either side to catch the wind, or hauled close to sail against a head wind. Sails could be raised and lowered with less labor, and the vessels could sail closer to the wind. The vessel's speed was increased and valuable time was saved in reaching the fishing grounds and in returning to port with the fare.

The schooners built in the eighteenth century each had two masts, with the mainmast stepped nearly amidships and a smaller foremast nearer the bow. Because of the design of the rigging the masts could be placed nearer together than those of earlier vessels, and the speed and maneuverability of the vessel were thereby further enhanced.

The yard where Captain Robinson built his new craft was located at the head of the inner harbor at Gloucester. As the vessel slid smoothly down the ways into the water when she was being launched, one of the spectators standing beside Captain Robinson exclaimed: "Oh, how she scoons!", and the Captain then and there decided to call her a "scooner."

While the introduction of the schooner was the most outstanding innovation in American shipbuilding in the eighteenth century, improvements in the design of the hull also were made from time to time, both on Cape Ann and elsewhere. And one of the notable types of vessel which emerged from the Cape Ann shipyards during that period was the "pinkie," built chiefly at Chebacco.

The forerunner of the pinkie was the "Chebacco boat." Unlike other boats of its period, it had a pointed stern. It typically was not over 30 feet long and had a displacement of 10 to 12 tons. It had a high freeboard and was decked over fore and aft, with a cuddy for the crew in the bow and a hold in the stern. In the center of the boat was an open space reaching from side to side, where the crew stood to fish. In bad weather the standing room could be covered by hatches. The boat had two masts, but no shrouds or stays and no bowsprit. Because of the type of its construction, the Chebacco boat was very buoyant and well-suited to the choppy waters along the Cape Ann coast. Many Chebacco boats were built during the last half of the seventeenth century.

Toward the end of that century larger vessels with the same type of hull as the Chebacco boats began to be built and were called pinkies; and they, too, were built largely at Chebacco. The pinkies ranged up to 35 tons in size and each had a bowsprit. After the schooner rig was invented, the pinkies were usually equipped with it. The early pinkies' sails were made of hemp, and when the wind was light or moderate, the sails were wetted to close the pores. For wetting the sails, a pinkie carried a "scout horn," a pole about fifteen feet long with a leather pocket at the end which held about a pint of water.

Since no stoves were carried on ships at that time, a brick fireplace was placed in the cuddy below the forward deck of the pinkie with a brick chimney or a chimney made of wood and heavily plastered on the inside. The chimney afforded a convenient place for occasionally smoking a halibut or a pollock.

85

The pinkie was an especially seaworthy vessel.[24] It had a deep draft aft, one vessel of only 26 tons displacement drawing 10 feet aft, though much less forward. Its full, "apple" bow prevented deep plunging in a heavy sea and it lifted quickly on the waves. The pinkie also was a durable craft, one built in Essex in 1780 remaining in service for 101 years, and another built in 1835, for over 95 years.

Although a pinkie occasionally took a long trip, vessels of that type were employed chiefly for fishing in nearby waters. While many pinkies were built after 1700, more and more square-sterned ships were turned out at the Cape Ann shipyards. These had greater carrying capacity and therefore were more economical for use in fishing on the Grand Bank and other distant grounds to which the Gloucester seafarers traveled when the fishing industry became so active after 1700.

Shipbuilding continued to be one of the major industries of Cape Ann from 1700 until the outbreak of the Revolutionary War. And the ships built in the local yards not only were employed in fishing and foreign trade, but occasionally were sold along with their cargoes. One of the results of this colonial shipbuilding at Cape Ann and elsewhere was to cause English ship carpenters to complain of the competition by the American shipbuilders, and the activities of the latter contributed to the growing friction with England.

During the Revolutionary War period many Cape Ann vessels were destroyed by the British and few new ones were built. For thirty years after the end of that war, moreover, the obstacles to foreign trade and the harassment of American shipping slowed down a revival of activity in the Cape Ann shipyards. Vessels were built then, of course, but not in such large numbers as in earlier years.

After the conclusion of the War of 1812, however, shipbuilding picked up again on Cape Ann. The growth of popu-

---

24 Judge Robert W. Hill, "Our Coastal Pioneers," reprinted from *The Essex Institute Historical Collections* (January, 1942), p. 8.

lation in the cities along the Atlantic seaboard provided markets for fish. The invention of the cotton gin in 1790 stimulated a great expansion of cotton growing in the southern states, with a resultant increase in the slave population, and that market for fish became correspondingly greater. Foreign trade also expanded.

In 1668 the town of Ipswich set aside an acre of land on the Chebacco River where the townspeople could build boats.[25] The shipyard was at the northern end of the causeway, where the famous A. D. Story yard was located in later years. During the next 160 years after the public yard was provided, however, many boats were built in the front yards of the builders and hauled to the river to be launched. When the hull was finished, it was loaded on two pairs of wheels, and oxen then were hitched to the forward wheels to start the trip to the river. For the larger vessels ten or twelve yoke of oxen were required to do the hauling. When the vessel arrived at the launching place, the wheels were eased into the water until the vessel floated. The largest vessel hauled to the river and launched in that way was a craft of 35 tons. Each "boat-hauling" was quite an event and was attended by most of the folk in the village.

The last boat-hauling in Essex (the name given Chebacco when the parish was set off from Ipswich as a separate town in 1819) took place in 1835. Thereafter the increased size of the vessels being built and other developments in the local shipbuilding industry resulted in the construction of vessels only at the yards on the shore of the river.

Shipbuilding got its start at Chebacco, as at other points on Cape Ann, because of its local timber supply and the facilities for sawing lumber. Between 1656 and 1682, five sawmills were put into operation in Chebacco. The local forests furnished an adequate supply of timber for the Chebacco

---

25 Reverend Robert Crowell, *History of the Town of Essex, from 1634-1868* (Essex, 1868), p. 60.

boatbuilding industry until after the War of 1812. Then, with the stepping-up of production and the increased size of the vessels being built, more and more shipbuilding materials were brought in from outside—masts and small spars, for example, from New Hampshire, and white oak planking from the southern states, in exchange for fish and other produce shipped from Cape Ann.

To facilitate the shipping of timber from New Hampshire to Essex for shipbuilding, an inland waterway was opened in 1820, presumably one of the first inland waterways in the United States. A canal was cut through the marsh back of Castle Hill, from Essex Bay to the Ipswich River, only a short distance from where Plum Island Sound, the Parker River, and the Ipswich River meet. After that canal was opened, timber was rafted down the Merrimack to Newburyport, then through Plum Island Sound to the Ipswich River, and then through the Canal to Essex Bay and the Essex River. The raft was propelled by oars and on each raft was a small house in which the crew lived. The facility for shipping timber from faraway sources by water without having to transport it across the open sea obviously was of substantial advantage to the Essex boatbuilders.

The canal from the Ipswich River to Essex Bay is no longer navigable. It has been narrowed by the encroachment of the marshes along its banks and closed at one point by the construction of the road to Crane's Beach in Ipswich, but its course is still clearly discernible.

During the period from 1820 to 1830, shipbuilding was an active industry at Annisquam, but after the latter date it tapered off there. At the Gloucester Harbor yards ships were built throughout the nineteenth century—down until World War I, as a matter of fact. In Essex shipbuilding continued to flourish, with occasional ups and downs, till an even later date.

Around the middle of the nineteenth century a new era in ship design began which lasted as long as fishing schooners were built. The opening of that era was marked by the construction of the *Romp,* designed and built by Andrew Story of Essex about 1850. The *Romp* had a narrow, sharp bow of the clipper type. Her design was such a radical change from the blunt-nosed schooners previously built that the fishermen generally were afraid to sail in her. She was more graceful and faster than the old type, however, and gradually the fishermen's apprehensions were allayed, with the result that by 1890 the clipper schooners began to come into general use.

When the new type began to gain popularity, vessels of that design were built both in Essex and in Gloucester and among the first of them was the *Nannie C. Bohlin,* which was built in the yard at Vincent Cove, Gloucester Harbor, in 1890. The *Bohlin* was 110 feet long, 131 gross tons, had a 23.5 foot beam, and was 11.2 feet deep. She had a clipper bow, a long bowsprit and tall masts. The *Bohlin* was immortalized by James B. Connolly as the *Nannie O* in his popular book *Out of Gloucester.* Her skipper, Captain Thomas Bohlin, was the "Tommie Ohlson" in Connolly's story.

The *Bohlin* was a fast vessel and her skipper delighted in driving her to the utmost. Their most publicized feat was the trip home from Norway, in September 1893, when the *Bohlin* covered the distance of about forty-seven hundred miles in twenty-two days, despite bad weather. On that trip, "Captain Tommie" undertook to beat the *Valkyrie,* the British challenger for the American cup, which was sailing from England at the same time. And he succeeded. The *Valkyrie's* course was about eight hundred miles shorter, but she took nearly eight days longer to make the crossing. During the passage, the *Bohlin* lost two jibs and her mainsail, but new sails were hurriedly bent on, and Captain Tommie resumed his relentless drive. He was proud of his schooner and she responded enthusiastically, especially in heavy weather.

Because of the drive to which she was subjected the *Nannie C. Bohlin* probably carried away more spars and topmasts than any vessel from this port. It is said that she carried away five sets of spars.[26]

Another vessel of that era was the *Grayling* designed by Captain George M. McLain of Rockport, one of the pioneers in developing the clipper type of fishing schooner, and the most prolific designer of Gloucester vessels during the 1890's.[27] The *Grayling*, launched at Essex in 1891, was one of the fastest vessels in the Gloucester fishing fleet in that decade.

The *Grayling*, like many another Gloucester fisherman, had several harrowing experiences. On December 16, 1896, for example, she was running before a heavy gale, about twenty-five miles south of Cape Sable, when a gigantic wave rose astern and washed over the deck. The helmsman, who was lashed to the wheel, was thrown against the wheel so hard that he was killed. The other seaman on watch, who was clinging desperately to the boom, was washed overboard and then swept back again. The wave carried away the boom, the gaffs, the dories, and the mainsail and smashed the hatches, companionways, and taffrail.

The *Grayling* also encountered the notorious "Portland gale" on the night of November 26, 1898, while headed for Gloucester. About 12 miles off Thachers she passed close to a big white steamer, presumably the *Portland,* which shortly thereafter went down with a loss of 176 lives. The *Grayling*, however, did not fare so badly in that storm as in the earlier gale off Cape Sable.

On July 11, 1911, the *Grayling* was wrecked on a sunken reef in a Greenland cove, where she had anchored for safety in another heavy storm. The crew rowed ashore in their eight

---

26 Gordon W. Thomas, *Builders of Gloucester's Prosperity* (Gloucester, 1952), pp. 70-72. In this little volume Mr. Thomas gives an interesting and detailed description of the design and eventful lives of 38 Gloucester schooners.
27 *Ibid.,* p. 50.

dories in bitterly cold weather, spent the night on a deserted island, and then rowed forty miles down the coast to Holsteinborg, the nearest settlement. Such experiences have been an inherent part of the saga of Cape Ann.

The *Effie M. Morrissey* was still another of the vessels built with a clipper bow. She was constructed at Essex in the winter of 1893-94. After serving in the Gloucester fishing fleet for twenty years, the *Morrissey* was sold to a Nova Scotia buyer, who later sold her to Captain Bob Bartlett, who had commanded Admiral Peary's ship on Peary's successful trip to the North Pole. Captain Bartlett had a diesel engine installed in the *Morrissey* in 1926 and took her on numerous scientific trips to the Arctic. She was a very staunch vessel.

In 1891 another local experiment in ship design was tried, which was not successful but was a forerunner of a later development. In that year the yawl *Resolute* was built at Essex and equipped for beam trawling. A steam engine was installed for hoisting the sails and hauling the trawl, but not for propulsion. After a year's trial, however, with several mishaps, it was decided that the *Resolute* was too light for beam trawling and she was converted to a schooner rig. Ten years later power-trawlers began to revolutionize the fishing industry.

From 1623 until 1900 the fishing industry of Cape Ann was carried on in sailing vessels. Then in the latter year an auxiliary engine was installed in a schooner, and that was the beginning of the end for the picturesque sailing craft which had made Gloucester so famous.

The first large Gloucester fishing vessel to be equipped with an auxiliary engine was the *Helen Miller Gould*, built at Vincent Cove and launched in March 1900. She was designed by Captain McLain with a clipper bow and was equipped with a 150 horsepower gasoline engine to supplement her sail power. The *Gould* was very successful in mackerel fishing but she had only a short life. She was destroyed by fire after only eighteen months of service.

After the loss of the *Gould*, her owner arranged for the construction of a fishing steamer, the *Alice M. Jacobs*, launched at Essex in 1902. The *Jacobs* was a large vessel— 220 gross tons, 141 feet long, and 24 foot beam. She carried sails, but mainly to steady her in certain operations, not for power. The *Jacobs* was the first large steamer built for a Gloucester fishing firm,[28] but not the first steamer used in the industry. A Gloucester captain had chartered a steamer for use in fishing as early as 1885, and steamers also had been operated out of other fishing ports between 1885 and 1902.

Like the *Gould*, the *Jacobs* had a short life. During a heavy storm in December 1903, she ran on a reef near the Newfoundland shore. The rescue of the crew, another epic of the Cape Ann fishing industry, was described as follows by Gordon Thomas. He wrote:

> It was indeed fortunate that she was carrying two nests of dories. Two of these small craft were put over and both were pounded to pieces. By this time the vessel heeled over, forming a lee, and a third dory was launched successfully. Austin George [a member of the crew] succeeded in rowing to the shore, where he made a line fast to a rock. The remainder of the crew left in more dories and were pulled to safety by means of this rope. All were frost-bitten. Austin George had fingers and ears frozen. His courageous act had saved his shipmates. The island on which they landed was uninhabited. A dory was dragged over the island, which was 3½ miles wide, to the main channel separating it from the mainland. Without much difficulty they rowed to the mainland and safety.[29]

---

28 Gordon W. Thomas, *op. cit.*, p. 16.
29 *Ibid*, p. 18.

The use of steamers for certain types of fishing operations continued to increase, but they were not built on Cape Ann.

After the advantages of equipping a fishing vessel with an auxiliary engine had been demonstrated by the *Helen Miller Gould* and by vessels built elsewhere, auxiliary engines were installed in more and more Gloucester schooners. In fact, the *Thomas S. Gorton*, built at Essex in 1905, was the last Gloucester schooner to be constructed without an engine. By the time that World War I broke out, most of the vessels in the Gloucester fishing fleet had auxiliary engines, installed either at time of building or at some later date.

With World War I shipbuilding, except for small craft and pleasure boats, came to an end in Gloucester, but not in Essex. Among the vessels built at Essex between 1922 and 1930 were the *Puritan*, the *Columbia* and the *Gertrude L. Thebaud*.

The *Puritan*, built at Essex in 1922, was designed by the famous yacht designer, W. S. Burgess. She was 124 feet in length and had 149 gross tonnage, and the object of her owners was to produce a vessel fast enough to win back the International Fisherman's Cup from the Nova Scotians. The *Puritan* was exceptionally fast, but with her tall mainmast and large spread of canvas she was tricky and hard to handle. Unfortunately she was wrecked before she had an opportunity to enter a race. Three months after she was launched she ran across a bar at Sable Island into shallow water and became a total loss.

After the *Puritan* was lost, several members of the syndicate which had owned her proceeded to arrange for the construction of a new schooner, the *Columbia*, to take her place. The *Columbia*, also designed by W. S. Burgess, was built at Essex in 1923. She was somewhat smaller than the *Puritan* and not quite so fast, but more manageable. She participated in one International Fisherman's Race before she was lost with her crew of twenty-two men, in a gale off Sable

Island in October 1927. In June of that year the *Columbia* had brought in the last fare of salt codfish caught by a Gloucester dory hand-trawler.

The *Gertrude L. Thebaud*, built in Essex in the winter of 1929-30, was the last schooner to be built for the Gloucester fishing industry. She cost sixty thousand dollars. Of that sum, forty-five thousand was contributed by Louis Thebaud, a summer resident of Gloucester, and members of his family, and the remainder by a group of men interested in obtaining a vessel which could win the International Fisherman's Cup. The *Thebaud* engaged in fishing and racing, and in 1933 she sailed from Gloucester to Chicago, by way of the St. Lawrence River and the Great Lakes, to serve as the Massachusetts exhibition at the World's Fair. In 1937 she was chartered by Commander Donald B. MacMillan, the noted explorer, for a trip to the Arctic, which covered some eight thousand miles. During World War II she served in the Coast Guard patrol. She ended her career as a freighter in the Caribbean, being wrecked off Venezuela in February 1948. With the *Thebaud*, the three-hundred-year-old shipbuilding industry of Cape Ann virtually came to an end.

On Cape Ann, as well as elsewhere, shipbuilding shared with ship-sailing the romance of the sea. A new ship always was launched with high hopes—hopes that she would be seaworthy and responsive, that she would be lucky in escaping disaster, and that she would bring a fortune to her owner. The sea captains were a hard-bitten lot, inured to peril, hard work, and the vagaries of the sometimes elusive fish. The captains, however, had a tender feeling for the craft which they commanded. To them a vessel had individuality and character and was almost a living creature, and when a new vessel was launched there always was animated suspense while her owners and crew were waiting to learn what traits she would manifest in the ocean habitat for which she was designed. Hence a launching was always something of a gala occasion.

In Essex, as has been stated, most of the village turned out for the boat-haulings in the eighteenth and early nineteenth century. In later years, when larger vessels were launched, the launchings, both in Essex and Gloucester, became more festive occasions. When the *Grayling* was launched in 1891, for instance, a party of twenty-five persons made the trip on her when she was towed from Essex to Gloucester, where her masts were to be stepped and she was to be fitted out. When the *Helen Miller Gould* was launched at Vincent Cove in 1900 a crowd of about three thousand people were on hand to watch the skipper's daughter break the traditional bottle of wine on her bow as she started to slide down the ways. At the launching of the *Oriole* in Essex in 1908 the party included guests of the owner from New York, New Jersey, Missouri, and Virginia.

Usually the launching went off smoothly, but once in a while a mishap occurred. When the *Onato* was being launched at Essex in 1904, she fell over on her side and as the guests aboard were thrown to the deck they became daubed with fresh paint.

After the masts had been stepped in a new vessel and rigging and sails had been fitted, came the eagerly awaited trial run, to find out how she would behave under sail and how fast she could go. The trial trip was the second gala event for a new craft. On the trial trip of the *Mesquita* in 1905, for example, 250 guests enjoyed a sail from Gloucester to Salem and return, with an orchestra on board to provide entertainment for them. In another instance, the *Atalanta*, on her trial trip in 1894, engaged in an impromptu race with another schooner from the outer harbor to Minot's Light and return. One hundred thrilled guests were aboard.

The last schooners to be built on Cape Ann, in the 1920's, were designed, as has been stated, for racing as well as for fishing. Impromptu racing between the skippers of Gloucester fishing vessels began at an early date. Whenever two or more vessels left port for the fishing grounds or headed home with their fares at the same time, the skippers frequently undertook to best each other on the run. Pride in their ships and the zest of competition, with perhaps a monetary reward in the form of higher prices for an early landing of the fares, all stimulated those old sea dogs to drive their ships and their crews and to guide their courses craftily to win such races. Many are the tales of high adventure in those races with gales and heavy seas, as well as with calms and fair weather, and also with ruses and wiles to outtrick the other fellow. There probably was hardly a vessel out of Gloucester which did not engage in many such brushes.

The first formal fisherman's race was held off Gloucester in August 1892, as a feature of the 250th anniversary of the founding of the town. The First Class race was for schooners measuring 85 to 100 feet at the water line. Seven vessels were entered in that race, including the *Nannie C. Bohlin, Ethel B. Jacobs, Grayling, Joseph Rowe,* and *Harry L. Belden.* The race was run during a raging northeast storm; the fishermen never would think of postponing the race merely because the wind was blowing a gale and the sea running high. Since much of their ballast had been removed to lighten them for the race, all the participants, except the *Harry L. Belden* which won, had a tough experience in the storm.

The first International Fisherman's Race was held in the autumn of 1920, off Halifax. That race resulted from a challenge sent to Gloucester by the *Halifax Herald,* proposing to match the Canadian *Delawana* against the fastest Gloucester fishing schooner for a cash prize of five thousand dollars and a trophy for the winner. The conditions of the challenge stipulated that the entrants must be regular fishing schooners carrying their ordinary sails with the usual weight of duck, and manned by a crew not to exceed twenty-five in number. Each captain must have had at least one year's experience fishing on the banks. The vessels could carry only their usual

MENDING A NET

FISHERMAN'S LUCK

ballast of iron or stone and no racing equipment was to be added. It also was stipulated that the vessels must not be over 150 feet in length. These conditions, it is to be noted, were devised to make it strictly a fisherman's race, not a yacht contest.

The *Esperanto* was selected to uphold the honor of the Gloucester fishermen. The *Esperanto* had been built in 1907. She was 107 feet in length, had 140 gross tonnage, and was one of the few schooners in Gloucester which by 1920 had not been equipped with an auxiliary engine. For the race she was manned by a picked crew and her skipper was Captain Marty Welch.

In the first race, sailed over a forty-mile triangular course, the *Esperanto* finished 18 minutes and 28 seconds ahead of the *Delawana*. Before the second race the crew of the *Delawana* altered her ballast, removing part of it and shifting the position of the remainder. This time she led for the first thirty miles, but on the last leg along the rocky, kelp-laden shore of Devil's Island, Captain Marty boldly cut in close to the dangerous shore and the *Esperanto* went on to win again, by 7 minutes and 25 seconds.

In 1921 the Gloucester schooner *Elsie* was defeated by the Canadian *Bluenose* in another race off Halifax. It was after that race that arrangements were made for the construction of the ill-fated *Puritan*. Then came the *Columbia*. Under Captain Ben Pine of Gloucester, the *Columbia* raced the *Bluenose* off Halifax in October 1923. The first race was won by the *Bluenose,* which crossed the finish line 1 minute and 20 seconds ahead of the *Columbia*. The second race, six days later, also was won by the *Bluenose,* by a margin of 2 minutes. The first race had been protested by Captain Pine, however, on the ground that the *Columbia* had been fouled by the *Bluenose* during the race, and the protest was upheld by the race committee. That left the race tied, with one win for each schooner, but Captain Angus Walters of the

Bluenose refused to accept the verdict of the committee and no third race was held to determine a winner.

In October 1930, the new Gloucester schooner *Gertrude L. Thebaud* engaged in two races against the *Bluenose* off Gloucester. The International Cup was not put at stake for those races. The *Thebaud* won both of them by substantial margins. The following year a cup contest was held between the same two vessels off Halifax, and the *Bluenose* won two straight races.

The final races for the International Cup were held off Gloucester in 1938 between the *Bluenose,* under Captain Angus Walters, and the *Thebaud,* under Captain Ben Pine. The *Thebaud* won the first race by 2 minutes, 50 seconds, the *Bluenose* the second by 12 minutes, 10 seconds, and the third by 6 minutes, 37 seconds. The fourth race was won by the *Thebaud* by 2 minutes, 44 seconds. But the *Bluenose* took the fifth and deciding race by 2 minutes, 50 seconds. Captain Pine was forced by illness to retire from command of the *Thebaud* after the second race. Those races in 1938 marked the end of an intense rivalry between Captain Pine and Captain Walters. They also marked the end of international fisherman's racing. Thereafter there were no schooners in the Gloucester fishing fleet. Technological changes in the fishing industry had brought to a conclusion a series of picturesque events, in which ingenious ship designing, canny seamanship, and local loyalties had roused great emotional excitement.

As the bronze old captain gazes out across Gloucester Harbor from his base near the Cut, he must be filled, nowadays, with feelings of nostalgia. No longer does he see a fleet of sleek schooners swinging at their moorings, sailing vibrantly out around Eastern Point with their white sails gleaming in the sun, or racing back to port, low in the water with their fares of fish. The modern, power-driven vessels which ply the harbor may be more efficient but they are far less picturesque than the schooners which he watched for so many years.

The Seafarers

THE SACRED COD hangs in the State House on Beacon Hill in Boston, but it is to Cape Ann that the cod really belongs. It was the cod which brought the first upsurge of prosperity to Cape Ann, and it was from Gloucester that salt codfish was distributed far and wide in the western world. If modern ballyhoo had been in vogue a century or two ago, Gloucester might have been hailed as the "Codfish Capital of the World," and perhaps it might have toasted a "Codfish Queen." Numerous other species of fish have been included in Cape Ann fares, of course, but for many years the attention of the fishermen was focussed principally on the cod.

Cape Ann was destined by nature to be the home of a seafaring people. Living on a rocky promontory thrust out into the Atlantic Ocean, with a large natural harbor at Gloucester and smaller harbors at Annisquam and Sandy Bay, the inhabitants of Cape Ann turned naturally to the sea when a market for cod became available. The land on the Cape suitable for farming was not great enough in acreage to support a large population, but from the ocean abundant crops of fish could be gathered. Sometimes fish were elusive, to be sure, but they always were available somewhere in the ocean, if they could be found.

During the first sixty or seventy years after the Cape was settled, a Gloucester vessel occasionally made a trip to distant fishing grounds, but fishing then was a secondary employment for the local inhabitants and was confined mostly to nearby waters. About 1700, however, as was explained in the preceding chapter, conditions became favorable for the development of a large commercial fishing industry, and then the Gloucester fishermen began to journey regularly to the grounds off Nova Scotia and Newfoundland where they usually could count on finding cod.

The largest of those fishing grounds was the Grand Bank with an area of about thirty-six thousand square miles, located ninety miles southeast of Newfoundland. Several smaller banks lay to the west of the Grand Bank, forty to sixty miles south of Newfoundland and Nova Scotia. Those banks were part of the continental shelf, with water twenty to one hundred and fifty fathoms in depth and an abundant supply of food for the fish. Cod thrived there.

The Newfoundland banks were discovered by French navigators early in the sixteenth century and presently they became fishing grounds not only for the French but also for the British and other Europeans. To secure domination of those fishing grounds was one of the objectives of both the French and the English in their struggle for control of Newfoundland and Nova Scotia during the seventeenth and eighteenth centuries. When the Treaty of Utrecht was signed in 1713, the opportunity was opened to the Gloucester fishermen to operate on those banks without molestation, and they immediately took advantage of it.

Soon after 1713 Gloucester vessels were making regular trips to the banks. On such a trip a vessel usually did not return to port until it had caught a full fare of fish, or until it had exhausted its supply of salt or bait. Hence a trip commonly lasted two or three months and for that period of time the members of the crew were working and living together continuously, day and night, within the somewhat cramped confines of their craft.

Until the middle of the nineteenth century the traditional method of fishing for cod was by hand line, over the rail of the schooner as it rode at anchor on the fishing grounds. All the crew took part in the fishing, of course, and each man shared in the proceeds of the trip in accordance with the number of fish that he caught. He cut out the tongue of each cod that he landed and threw the tongue into a bucket which he delivered to the captain at the end of the day. Thereby the captain kept a record of the number of fish caught by each of the men. Thus each went "on his own hook," an expression which spread from the fishing industry to become common usage in New England for indicating individual action and responsibility.

Every fisherman, salt or fresh-water, knows that some men are "luckier" than others in catching fish, even when they sit or stand side by side in the same boat. That "luck" comes from skill in baiting the hook, in judging the depth at which to deploy the bait, in sensing the bites, in handling the line, and in other phases of the art of fishing. It was differences in individual skill and luck which led to the arrangement whereby each member of the crew of a fishing schooner went "on his own hook." That those differences were real is indicated by the record of the schooner *Abigail,* for example, which made three trips to the Grand Bank in 1757. The number of cod caught by the skipper and each member of the crew was as follows: Paul Hughes, (skipper) 6,643; B. Foster, 5,000; Job Galloway, 4,274; Nathaniel Day, 3,929; Rufus Stacy, 3,784; and William Smith, 3,435.[30]

When trawls came into use in cod fishing after 1861, the crew fished in pairs. Then the record was kept for each pair of men to determine the share of the proceeds of the catch which they would receive.

For trawl fishing a schooner carried six to ten dories, about sixteen feet long, each equipped with two pairs of stout oars. On arriving at the fishing bank the schooner anchored, the trawls were placed in each dory, and the dories took off

30 *The Fisheries of Gloucester, from 1623 to 1876* (Gloucester, Procter Brothers, 1876), p. 24.

in different directions—two men to a boat. Each dory usually was equipped with six tubs in which were six trawl lines about three hundred feet long. From each line gangings three to six feet in length were suspended at intervals of about six feet, and on the lower end of each ganging was a baited hook. Thus there usually were about 50 hooks to a line, 300 to a tub, 1800 to a dory, and when a schooner carried ten dories, 18,000 hooks to a schooner. That was the cod fisherman's device for obtaining mass production.

At the start of the trip the dory crews drew lots for trawl positions, and as soon as the schooner had been anchored at its fishing berth, each dory proceeded to set its trawls in its assigned position. A trawl anchor with buoy attached was first heaved overboard. The first end of the top trawl line in one of the tubs had been tied to the trawl anchor line, and as soon as the anchor line was out, one of the men in the dory began to pay out the trawl, with its hooks already baited, as the other member of the dory crew rowed away from the neighborhood of the schooner. The trawl was arranged so that the hooks dropped nearly to the bottom of the sea. When the end of the first trawl line was reached, it was fastened to the top end of the next line, and so on until all the lines in the six tubs had been paid out. When the end of the last line was reached, another anchor to which a buoy was attached was heaved overboard, and the trawl, over a mile and a half in length, was all set.

In the earlier days, when hand lines had been used in cod fishing, clams ordinarily had been used for bait—clams which had been dug on the flats along the Annisquam and Essex Rivers. When trawls came to be used extensively, however, the supply of clams was not adequate to provide bait for all the thousands of trawl hooks. That was when the fishermen began to use more herring for bait. The torchers operating out of Annisquam furnished part of the supply needed, but the Gloucester schooners also used large quan-

102

tities of herring which had been shipped to Gloucester from Newfoundland during the winter or were purchased at Newfoundland ports during the trip. Squid also were used as bait when they could be obtained.

The herring was cut into small chunks for bait, and it presumably was with the Gloucester fishing fleet that the admonishing phrase originated that one must either "fish or cut bait."

The trawl remained set for several hours, sometimes overnight, before it was hauled. To aid the fishermen in hauling the trawl, the line was run over a pulley, called a "gurdy," placed on the gunwale of the dory near its bow. Even with that mechanical assistance, however, hauling in a trawl loaded with struggling fish was heavy work.

Setting and hauling the trawl, nevertheless, did not constitute a full day's work for the fishermen. After the last line had been hauled aboard the dory and either rebaited and heaved back or coiled in its tub for a new set the next day, the men rowed their dory back to the schooner, unloaded the day's catch, and then "dressed off" the fish. The process of dressing off included cutting off the heads, splitting the fish open, removing the livers, which were carefully saved for sale to producers of cod-liver oil, removing the entrails, and finally salting the fish either in the hold of the schooner or in barrels. In the early years of bank fishing, the roe of the fish also was saved and salted for sale in the European market, but roe salvage had ceased before trawls came into use.

The labor of baiting, setting, and hauling the trawls was arduous enough on calm, clear days. But the work also had to be done, of course, on many days when the sea was rough, with the dory bobbing around like a wooden eggshell. Fog, however, brought the greatest peril to the men in the dories. It was common on the banks, and it often shut in so suddenly and so thickly that the men in a dory could not see the schooner even when it was only a short distance away. Then they had to rely on the schooner's foghorn, if they could hear it, to guide them back to the ship. If they could not find the schooner in the fog, they could only hope that they might be picked up by some other vessel or that they might be able to reach a distant shore.

Sometimes the fishermen lost in the fog were fortunate enough to be rescued. On October 7, 1874, for example, soon after two members of the crew of the *Marathon* left the schooner at 4.30 P.M. to visit their trawls, a fog shut in and they could not find their way back. The weather remained foggy, with only occasional brief liftings, and they rowed around for seven days in the hope of finding their own schooner or some other vessel. They had no food but they did catch fresh rain water in one of the trawl tubs. On the eighth day they were picked up by a steamer en route to New York.

Two of the crew of the *Edward A. Horton* were caught in a fog on July 1, 1880. After rowing for five days, they reached the Newfoundland coast.

On July 6, 1882, two men from the *Solomon Poole* became lost in a fog. After spending eight days and seven nights in their dory without food, they were picked up by a vessel bound for Pernambuco. They reached their homes in Gloucester nine weeks later. In August of that same year two fishermen from the schooner *Restless* also became lost in the fog. They were picked up by a steamer bound for Liverpool, England, and they returned to Gloucester seven and one-half weeks later.

Such experiences were common among the crews of the fishing fleet, and many men lost in the fog never were heard from again. In 1874, for instance, eleven men were lost in dories on the Grand Bank and ten on the Western Bank. In 1875, twenty-two men were similarly lost. The number of such losses varied from year to year, but every year the fog mercilessly baffled its victims.

When a schooner returned to Gloucester with word that some of the members of her crew had been lost in the fog, the families of the lost men went through weeks of agonizing suspense, always hoping that their husbands, fathers, or sons had been picked up by some other ship and that eventually they would come home. Many of those hopes were not fulfilled.

Nowadays we take rapid communication by telegraph, telephone, and radio so completely for granted that we are prone to forget how long it took word to travel even less than a hundred years ago.

The steamers crossing the banks picked up some of the lost dory men, but the steamers also were a menace to the fishing schooners. Occasionally a schooner was run down in a fog by a passenger or freight steamer. On May 31, 1865, the Gloucester schooner *Northern Chief* was sunk by an English steamer off Cape Sable. The *Northern Chief* had a crew of eleven men, five of whom succeeded in reaching the deck of the steamer by scrambling up the rigging of the schooner. The other six members of the crew were drowned.

At a later date, in 1916, the Gloucester schooner *Oriole* was rammed by a Norwegian steamer forty miles off Nova Scotia. The steamer's whistle was heard by the watch on the *Oriole* and all hands were called on deck just before the bow of the steamer crashed into the schooner amidships, cutting her almost in two. Five members of the crew climbed the rigging of the schooner and thus reached the deck of the steamer. Several others escaped by launching dories or by grasping trawl buoys which kept them afloat until they could be rescued. But four men were lost. The *Oriole* sank four minutes after she was hit. Thus the time for escape was terribly short. The *Northern Chief* and the *Oriole* were only two of several Gloucester schooners run down and sunk in a fog.

It should be added, perhaps, that fog and collisions were not the only hazards encountered by the Gloucester fishermen. One of the members of the crew of the schooner *Christie Campbell,* for instance, died while on a fishing trip in 1859 from the effects of swallowing a match.

For many years the banks in the vicinity of Nova Scotia and Newfoundland were the chief offshore grounds for Gloucester fishermen, but eventually they fished on other banks, among them the Georges.

The Georges bank, which incidentally was the scene of Kipling's *Captains Courageous,* did not become an active fishing ground for Gloucester schooners until 1831. The Georges had an area of approximately 8,500 square miles and was located 190 miles east of Cape Cod, about a twenty-hour run for a schooner from Gloucester in fair weather. The sea on Georges varied from two fathoms to fifty fathoms in depth, and the tide ran very swiftly there. It was the strong tide and the rips on the shallows in the bank which long deterred the Gloucester captains from venturing there for fish. They were apprehensive that their vessels would drag their anchors or perhaps be sucked under by the tide.

In 1831, however, a shortage in the supply of cod for the Boston market led to new efforts to catch fish on the Georges and thereafter a winter and spring fishing industry developed there. It was on the Georges, furthermore, that halibut fishing gained its first momentum.

For over a hundred years after commercial fishing got under way at Cape Ann, halibut were looked upon as trash fish, a nuisance to be thrown away when caught; and if they became too numerous around a fishing boat, the crew pulled anchor and shifted to what was hoped would be a less infested berth. A halibut is a flat fish, shaped like a flounder, and commonly weighs up to two hundred pounds. In September 1819, a small Gloucester boat, the *Madison,* while fishing for cod on the Middle Bank, about twenty miles southeast of

106

Cape Ann, ran into a school of halibut. The Captain and his crew of two men caught 140 of the fish, which were sold in Boston for one dollar each, that is, for less than one cent a pound. That seems to have been the start of commercial halibut fishing, but it was a dozen years before any substantial number of fish were caught.

In 1827 Captain John Fletcher Wonson of Gloucester caught two halibut on the Georges while his vessel was hove to there on the return from a longer voyage. He put over a line just "to try his luck" and unexpectedly landed the halibut. Three years later, on March 5, 1830, Captain Wonson sailed for the Georges in the *Nautilus* on a halibut fishing trip, the first trip made intentionally for that purpose. Only twenty fish were caught, and one of the crew who had gone fishing alone in a dory was nearly lost. He had anchored the dory to fish while the *Nautilus* drifted away on the tide. Toward evening the crew of the *Nautilus* sighted the dory at a distance and wondered why the man in it was not rowing back toward the ship. The *Nautilus* reached the boat just before dark, with a storm coming on, and then found that the fisherman had forgotten to take his oars with him when he launched the dory.

A few days after the *Nautilus* sailed for the Georges, another Gloucester schooner, the *Romeo,* also started on a similar trip. She caught three thousand pounds of halibut, but the demand was still undeveloped, and the fare was sold for three cents a pound. About five or six years later, however, the fish had gained sufficient popularity in the market to lead numerous other vessels to engage in halibut fishing, not only on the Georges but also on other banks. In 1847 the Gloucester fleet landed over three million pounds of halibut.

As the demand for halibut continued strong, Gloucester schooners made trips to even more distant grounds—to Greenland, starting in 1869, and to Iceland, starting in 1873. In 1870 Captain John McQuinn, for example, in the schooner

Caleb Eaton, brought in a fare of 177,300 pounds of fletched halibut from Greenland, and in 1888 Captain John Marshall, in the schooner *Landseer,* landed a fare of 200,630 pounds caught in Iceland waters. Those were exceptionally large fares, but they indicate the magnitude to which the halibut fishing industry had expanded. Captain Marshall's fare, incidentally, was sold for $13,519, or at a little more than six cents a pound.

A halibut fishing trip to Greenland usually lasted for four or five months, and the fish were preserved by "fletching," a process by which the fish were boned, sliced, and salted. After the fare was landed, the fletched halibut were smoked, chips from the Essex shipyards providing part of the fuel for smoking halibut, as well as other fish, in Gloucester.

Because of the depletion of the supply of halibut on the banks, the catch tapered off after 1879, with considerable variations from year to year. The last fare of fletched halibut—forty thousand pounds—was landed by the schooner *Atalanta* in Gloucester in September 1916. Thereafter for about twenty years fresh halibut trips were landed here.

Halibut were caught for the most part with hand lines over the rail of the schooner. Hence there was not the danger that men would be lost in dories during a fog. Halibut fishing on the Georges nevertheless involved plenty of hardships. It was carried on there largely in the late winter and early spring, when ice, sleet, and snow, as well as fog and tide rips, made life uncomfortable for the fishermen.

One of the worst disasters on the Georges occurred on February 24, 1862. On that date there were about seventy schooners fishing there, and on one of them was a fisherman who was making his first and last trip to the Georges. His account of his experience was forcefully reported in *The Fishermen's Memorial Record Book.*

When the schooner arrived, the vessels in the fleet were anchored one-half mile to one mile distant from each other, and the crews were pulling in cod as rapidly as they could move their hands and arms. Occasionally a halibut was caught. The crew of the newcomer started fishing at once and when the man who was making his first trip caught a halibut, it was given due recognition. He stated: "Our steward, a Portuguese, was a clever fellow, and, in honor of my first halibut, brought me a mugful of hot coffee and a pancake with plums in it, called by the fishermen a 'Joe-flogger'."

He then went on to say: "The crew were a jolly set, and for several days the weather was fine, the fish abundant, and the fun immense. We had changed our berth twice, each time drawing nearer to the body of the fleet, and each time finding the fish more plentiful."

On the evening of February 24, there was a sudden change in the weather. The wind shifted to the northeast and soon was blowing with gale force. The sky turned inky black and snow began to fall. The skipper ordered the crew to pay out some ten fathoms more of cable, so that the anchor would be less likely to drag. The storm grew worse.

"It was now about eleven o'clock. The wind had risen fearfully, the snow came down spitefully, and the sea rose higher than I had ever supposed it possible for it to rise, and was covered with snow caps of foam. The sensation of being tossed up and down so violently, together with the darkness and the storm, were not pleasing, and it seemed to me that every plunge of the vessel would be her last."

The schooner rode the storm through the night. Then about nine o'clock the next morning the skipper suddenly called out to a crewman stationed in the bow: "There's a vessel adrift right ahead of us! Stand by with your hatchet, but don't cut till you hear the word." If necessary, the anchor cable was to be cut to avert a collision.

"The drifting vessel was coming directly for us; a moment more, and the signal to cut must be given! With the swiftness of a gull she passed by, so near that I could have leaped aboard, just clearing us, and we were saved from that danger, thank God! The hopeless, terror-stricken faces of the crew we saw but a moment, as they went on to certain death. We watched the doomed craft, as she sped her course. She struck one of the fleet, a short distance astern, and we saw the waters close over both vessels, almost instantly, and as we gazed, both disappeared." [31]

Fifteen Gloucester vessels, with their crews of 125 men, were lost in that gale on the Georges. At home, to mourn their loss, were 70 widows and 140 fatherless children.

In 1852 five Gloucester schooners and forty men were lost on the Georges; in 1860, five vessels and forty-eight men; in 1864, eight vessels and seventy-five men; in 1871, ten vessels and eighty-one men; and thus it went from year to year.

Halibut fishing on the Grand Bank also had its perils. In March 1875, for instance, while a fleet of Gloucester schooners was fishing on the northern section of the Grand Bank, ice floes began to drift in from the Arctic regions, and the water became so cold that the frozen herring which the fishermen were using for bait scarcely would thaw in fifty fathoms of water. As the ice floe spread farther and farther over the bank, the schooners were forced to shift their berths into deeper water. That shifting of berths, incidentally, led to a discovery that halibut could be caught at greater depths —83 to 135 fathoms—than had been thought possible.

At that time the men were trawl-fishing, and a number of dories became caught in the ice before they could return to their schooners. The ice closed in on two dories from the schooner *Howard* while they were still about two hundred yards from the schooner's stern. One of the crew on the vessel, however, threw a buoy, with a line attached, out on the ice and the men in one of the dories were able to pick up the

---

31 George H. Procter, *The Fishermen's Memorial and Record Book* (Gloucester, Procter Brothers, 1873), pp. 54-59.

buoy as it drifted by. The line was made fast to the bow of one dory and the other dory tied astern.

After they got the line aboard from the schooner, the men in the dories were in no danger of being carried away by the tide, but they still were two hundred yards distant from the schooner. They covered about half that distance by jumping out on the ice and pulling the dories over the large cakes through which there was no passage. At last they reached clear water and were hauled aboard the schooner. No lives were lost on that occasion, but several fishermen had to take refuge on vessels other than the ones to which they belonged.

Shortly before halibut fishing was taken up commercially on Cape Ann, mackerel had begun to receive attention from the fishermen, and eventually Gloucester became as well known for salt mackerel as for salt cod.

In the case of mackerel, as well as in the case of halibut, the market for the fish seems to have opened up without any developmental efforts by the fishermen. A considerable quantity of mackerel had been caught in Massachusetts Bay as early as 1630, and in 1653 salt mackerel were shipped from Boston to England. But for about 150 years thereafter mackerel fishing remained a small, desultory occupation. Undoubtedly mackerel were present in the waters around Cape Ann during that whole period, in greater or less abundance, but the potential market was not activated.

About 1800, fish peddlers in Charlestown and Boston found that they could sell fresh mackerel to their customers in large enough quantities to warrant more effort by the fishermen to provide a supply, and presently new methods of catching and preserving mackerel were devised. Mackerel, unlike cod and halibut, are migratory, surface fish which travel the ocean in schools, and they cannot be caught in any considerable quantity merely by anchoring a boat and throwing over a baited hook. Mackerel can best be taken by moving lures or by use of a net.

111

When the Boston market for fresh mackerel began to be appreciated by the Gloucester fishermen, small boats went out in the summer to the Inner Bank, about a dozen miles southeast of Cape Ann, to catch them. Only the largest fish were saved, the smaller ones being thrown away. The fish were preserved in fresh condition by placing them in tubs of salt water after they had been dressed, the water in the tubs being changed about once an hour. The fish generally were landed at Boston and Charlestown just before daybreak, so that the peddlers could sell them while they were still fresh. A boat at that time typically had a crew of three men and two boys, and if it stocked fifty dollars a week, that was considered a satisfactory return.

Within a short time after that type of mackerel fishing got under way, new methods of catching the fish were introduced, and markets for salt mackerel began to be discovered. About 1812 larger vessels took up mackerel fishing and the "trailing" method of catching fish came into use. For trailing, long poles, like outriggers, were fastened to each side of the vessel. The forward poles were about seventeen feet long and they tapered toward the stern in shorter lengths, the aft pole being five feet long. To the end of each pole a line about twenty fathoms long was fastened with a lead sinker and, of course, a hook at the end. Some of the fishermen tied a little piece of white cloth to the hook as a lure—primitive but effective. A fisherman stood by each pole to land whatever fish were hooked. The vessel sailed back and forth through the school of mackerel when it was sighted, and eight or ten barrels of mackerel might be caught in a day by this method.

In 1816 Abraham Lurvey of Pigeon Cove invented the mackerel jig,[32] a small gadget but a major invention. The mackerel jig was a small hook on the shank of which was an elongated, tear-shaped casting of lead. The lead served both

---

32 George H. Procter, *op. cit.*, p. 61.

as a sinker and as a lure when the line was jigged up and down by swift jerks from the fisherman. Mr. Lurvey kept his invention secret for many months, but when it was discovered by the other fishermen, jigging rapidly superseded trailing, and for thirty years or so, jigging was the prevalent method of mackerel fishing, both for the pinkies which fished in waters fairly near Cape Ann and for the schooners which went much farther asea.

When they took up jigging, the mackerel fishermen soon discovered that they could multiply their catch by using chum to toll the fish to the vicinity of the jigs. Chum was prepared by grinding clams, herring, small mackerel, or trash fish into small bits which were then cast overboard to spread out on the tide and settle gradually downward in the water. As the clams lay in barrels on deck before being ground, they often became "ripe," but the riper the chum, the better the mackerel liked it. As the mackerel swam in to pick up the chum, they were attracted by the jigs. The jigs themselves were not baited, but the chum served as bait.

The chum at first was cut by hand, and the men on watch often worked far into the night cutting up chum for the next day's fishing. Then about 1820 Gorham Burnham of Gloucester invented a "bait mill," which ground the bait finer and much faster, and presently every mackerel fishing vessel was equipped with a bait mill. Thomas Pulsifer, the Annisquam blacksmith, was one of the manufacturers of bait mills. With the use of a bait mill, as much as fifteen barrels of bait a day sometimes were thrown over by one schooner. While jigging, the vessel lay to, of course, and merely drifted with the tide.

Since mackerel were caught near the surface, the lines were short and each member of the crew fished with two lines over the rail of the vessel. When the fish were biting freely, it was quite an art for a fisherman to jerk in one of his lines, swing the fish so that it dropped into the barrel where his catch was kept, flip the fish off the hook, and cast the line back into the ocean, all in one motion, and then immediately repeat the operation with the other hand—all without getting his lines tangled.

Inasmuch as mackerel were surface fish, they often came in close to shore and small boats and pinkies participated extensively in mackerel fishing. In fact, pinkies often were called "jiggers." To exploit the potential demand that was becoming manifest, however, mackerel fishing was taken up on a larger scale by schooners.

The Cape Ann fishermen were not adept at market development, but once some one discovered a promising market for them, they showed ingenuity in procuring the fish to be sold there. We have referred to the introduction of trailing in 1812, the invention of the jig in 1816, and the invention of the bait mill in 1820. In 1817 and 1818, furthermore, a method of preserving mackerel by salting them down in barrels was introduced, and schooners began to make trips farther offshore, and at the start of the season, as far south as the Virginia capes in search of the fish. In 1830 Gloucester schooners began to follow the mackerel as far north as the Gulf of St. Lawrence.

From about 1820 until 1855 mackerel were caught by jigging. Then in the latter year the use of the purse seine was introduced and within a decade it had almost completely superseded the jig. This revolution in mackerel fishing, it is to be noted, came at just about the same time that trawls were taking the place of hand lines in cod fishing, and both were primarily means of increasing the productivity of the men engaged in fishing. Purse seining, furthermore, not only was a much more productive method of catching mackerel, but a more exciting one as well.

A purse seine used in mackerel fishing was about 225 fathoms in length and 18 fathoms in depth. It was made of light, tarred twine, equipped on the top with cork floats to keep that part of the net on the surface, and on the bottom with lead weights to make it sink quickly while being set. On the bottom of the net also were iron rings through which was passed the purse line, a rope by means of which the bottom of the net could be pulled together to form the purse as soon as the net had been set.

While the schooner was cruising in search of mackerel, the seine was carried in the seine boat, towed astern. When the watch aloft, a man standing on the crosstrees high up on the mainmast, sighted a school, the vessel was headed toward it and the entire crew sprang into action. The crew usually included seventeen men, and as the vessel approached the school, the captain and members of the crew entered the seine boat and rowed rapidly toward the school, the captain steering the seine boat with a long oar in the stern. At what he deemed to be the proper moment, the captain ordered the two men in the bow to "let go the twine!" One end of the net was left in a dory and then the seine boat was rowed as rapidly as possible around the school of fish, back to the dory, where the two ends of the purse line were quickly pulled in, to close the bottom of the net. Then the net gradually was hauled into the seine boat, until only a small section, which held the fish, was left in the water. At that point, the schooner, which had been left in the cook's charge, was brought alongside, and the catch was dipped out on to the deck of the schooner.

As soon as all the mackerel had been bailed out of the net, the crew began dressing them. Each fish was slit open by cutting through the back from head to tail and then it was gibbed by removing the head and entrails. The fish were placed in barrels and salted as they were dressed.

The dressing had to be done promptly to prevent the fish from becoming soft. Hence, when a large catch was landed late in the day, the crew worked far into the night, by the light of torches hung in the rigging. Occasionally they had barely turned into their bunks before there was a fresh call of "School O," and they had to turn out hurriedly to man the seine boat and take off to set the seine again. No matter how tired the crew might be, no opportunity to make a set was passed up.

There is a gamble in all fishing, but that was especially true in mackerel fishing. The fish would be abundant one year and scarce the next. They would be found in one locality at one time, and somewhere else the next. A school of mackerel, moreover, appeared only as a dark spot in a wide expanse of ocean and it might be missed by the watch in the crosstrees, especially when the water was roughened by a breeze. If other vessels were in the vicinity, furthermore, one of their seine boats might reach the school first and thus foreclose to others the opportunity to make a set. Frequently there were hot races between the seine boats of rival schooners to reach a school first, and the law of the sea was that the boat which let go its twine first had the right to the school.

When a seine had been set around a school of mackerel it did not always follow that the fish would be caught. Sometimes they became quickly alarmed and dove for the bottom before the purse line could be pulled tight. That was known among the fishermen as a "water haul." When fish were caught, each set might yield anywhere from 25 to 150 barrels, and when the fish were plentiful, several sets were made each day. Purse seining thus enabled a schooner to catch a substantially larger quantity of mackerel than it could have caught by jigging during the same period of time.

On a Gloucester fishing schooner, whether it was engaged in cod, halibut, or mackerel fishing, the captain held a position of great responsibility, and it was essential that he be a man of hardy physique, great physical and moral courage, and sound judgment. He had to be an expert mariner, a competent judge of where to find the fish, an able manager, and a forceful leader of men.

116

Before sailing, it was the captain's responsibility to make sure that the vessel was fit and to arrange to have her supplied with extra sails, ropes, and other gear with which to make repairs at sea, should an emergency arise. The large butts in the forehold had to be filled with fresh water for drinking and cooking, and coal and wood had to be provided for the stove. He also hired his crew. A skipper who had a high reputation as a competent mariner, a canny fisherman, and a forceful leader of men often had a crew who sailed with him trip after trip. Other skippers had more or less frequent changes.

When mackerel fishing was at its height in the latter half of the nineteenth century, the crews were recruited largely from out of town men, some of whom indulged themselves freely, when ashore, in the saloons and brothels around the water front. It occasionally happened that a man who had been hired for a trip had not shown up when the schooner was ready to sail. Her departure, however, was not delayed thereby. The captain merely ordered that the missing man's dunnage, including mattress, quilts, blankets, and oil skins, be placed on the wharf, and the captain went out and picked up some other sailor to fill the berth.

At sea, the captain decided on the course to be steered, chose the spots where to fish, assigned tasks to the members of the crew, supervised the dressing and storing of the fish, kept the records of the catch, decided where to look for any members of the crew who became lost, directed repairs to rigging and gear, and took charge in whatever emergencies arose. He was in command and he could not "pass the buck" to anyone else.

The captain also had the task of maintaining an *esprit de corps*, if possible, among a group of fifteen to twenty-five men who were living a hard life in cramped quarters, with no means of escaping from one anothers' company for several weeks or months. The captain had to keep an eye on the antagonisms and horseplay among the members of the crew, in order to avoid having emotions get out of control. When the ship returned to port, he sold the fare and paid off the crew in accordance with the standard practice.

Those were the men typified by the bronze old captain standing on the shore of Gloucester Harbor, gazing eastward to the sea. Some skippers, furthermore, first took command of fishing schooners when they were only 19, 20, or 21 years old.

For nearly the first 150 years after commercial fishing got under way at Gloucester, most of the schooner captains were Cape Ann Yankees. By the middle of the nineteenth century, however, skippers from Maine, Nova Scotia, and Newfoundland were taking over command of the Gloucester fishing fleet and before long Irish, Scandinavian, Portuguese, and Italian names became common in the list of captains.

Next to the skipper, the most important person aboard a fishing schooner was the cook. And the skipper himself could not keep a hard-working crew contented unless they had plenty of good grub. To the cook was delegated the job of procuring the food supplies before the schooner sailed—meat, salt pork, vegetables, seasonings; flour and other ingredients with which to make bread, cookies, puddings, cakes and pies; coffee, tea, sugar, and all the other items that would be needed to provide three meals a day for a hungry crew for perhaps two or three months. The only food item which was not bought before sailing was fish.

There is a tradition, incidentally, that it was some unsung cook on a Gloucester schooner fishing for cod who discovered the art of smoking halibut to make a tasty dish. When one of the crew caught a halibut, the cook sliced it in strips and hung it over the fire in the cook stove until it became well cured by the smoke. It then was cooked, seasoned, and served with butter. The fishermen enjoyed smoked halibut long before it gained acceptance in the marketplace.

At sea, the cook was complete boss of the forecastle. When the weather was too inclement for fishing, the members

118

of the crew who were not on watch could use the forecastle as a place for loafing, spinning sea yarns, or playing cards, but while there they had to take orders from the cook.

For nearly a century and a half after commercial fishing got under way at Gloucester, the crews of the fishing fleet, as has been stated, were largely natives of Cape Ann, bound together by many local and family ties. Thereafter more and more of them came from the Canadian Maritime Provinces, European countries, and the Azores. But whatever their origin and however rough, individualistic, or taciturn they might be, the members of a crew of a fishing schooner always were ready, on the instant, to spring to the assistance of a crewmate who was in danger or of a ship in distress. When a life was at stake, they practiced the Golden Rule without the slightest hesitation.

The saga of the Gloucester fishing fleet includes innumerable accounts of daring rescues and brave sacrifices by members of the crews. Despite all the attempts at rescue, however, ships and men were lost every year. We have not undertaken to compile a complete necrology for the Gloucester fishermen, but in March 1766, for instance, nineteen fishing vessels sailed from Gloucester for the Grand Bank, and of the nineteen, nine were lost in a heavy storm. In a later and much longer period, from 1830 to 1883 inclusive, 450 vessels and about 2,550 men from Gloucester were lost in marine disasters. The fishing industry, despite all its thrills and glamor, did take a heavy toll from Cape Ann. No wonder the bronze old sea captain on the water front has an anxious look in his eyes! He knows that the sea can be grim as well as alluring.

II

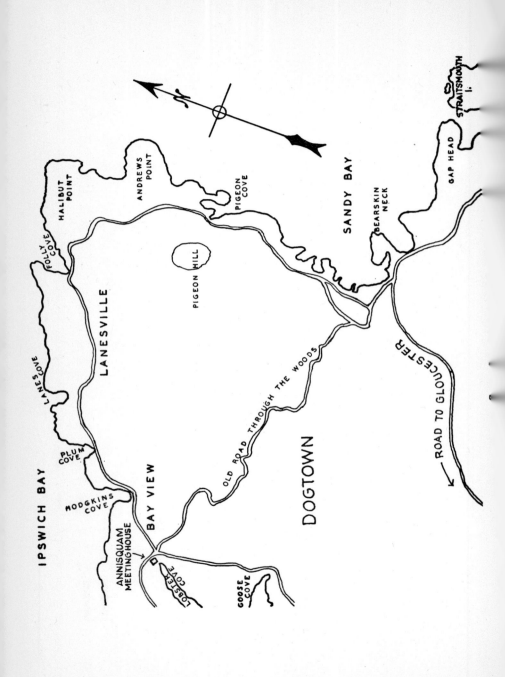

IPSWICH BAY

FOLLY COVE
HALIBUT POINT
ANDREWS POINT

LANES COVE

LANESVILLE

PLUM COVE

HODGKINS COVE

BAY VIEW

ANNISQUAM MEETINGHOUSE

LOBSTER COVE

GOOSE COVE

OLD ROAD THROUGH THE WOODS

PIGEON HILL

PIGEON COVE

SANDY BAY

BEARSKIN NECK

GAP HEAD

STRAITSMOUTH I.

DOGTOWN

ROAD TO GLOUCESTER

Rockport

THE FIRST WHITE MEN's homes in what is now the town of
Rockport were built at Pigeon Cove, Halibut Point, and
Sandy Bay, near the end of the seventeenth century, about
fifty years after the settlement was started around The Green
in Gloucester. Previously men had come to Gap Head from
Ipswich and Chebacco for summer fishing and had put up
wooden shanties there for temporary shelter, but it was not
until 1692 that the first house was built on the outer end of
Cape Ann. That house, according to tradition, was erected
in the woods at Pigeon Cove by two young men from Salem
for their mother, who had been convicted as a witch. She
was one of three women condemned at one of the notorious
witch trials in Salem in 1692. Her two fellow witches were
executed, but she was pregnant, and since it would have been
unlawful to kill an unborn child, even though its mother was
a witch, she was allowed to depart with her two sons, to live
in exile in the wilderness on Cape Ann. Here she was not
molested. However intolerant the residents of Cape Ann may
have been toward some of the other persons who came into
their villages, they apparently were always indulgent toward
witches. The house built for the Salem refugee eventually
became known as the "Old House." In later years it was re-
modeled and enlarged by other owners and it is still standing.[1]

Within a few years after the Salem refugee came to Cape
Ann, half a dozen other families settled around Pigeon Cove,

---

1 Henry C. Leonard, *Pigeon Cove and Vicinity* (Boston, F. A. Searle,
1873), p. 20.

Andrews Point, and Halibut Point, one of the first settlers at Halibut Point being Samuel Gott, whose house still stands there.

At Sandy Bay, now the center of the town of Rockport, land was granted to John Babson in 1695 for a fishing station at Gap Head, on the mainland opposite Straitsmouth Island, and he built a cabin there. Two years later Richard Tarr sailed into Sandy Bay from Marblehead and decided to remain there. He built a house on what is now Main Street. In 1700 John Poole came to Sandy Bay from Beverly and put up a house on what is now King Street, at the corner of Smith Street. He established the first sawmill at Sandy Bay, on the town brook, and in 1710 he shipped several boatloads of hemlock timber to Boston for wharf building. He also was the first shipbuilder at Sandy Bay.

From those beginnings the settlements at Sandy Bay and Pigeon Cove gradually grew, and in 1707 the selectmen of the Town of Gloucester laid out a road through the woods from Annisquam to Pigeon Cove and Sandy Bay. From 1728 until Sandy Bay was set off as the Fifth Parish in 1754 with its own meetinghouse, the residents of Pigeon Cove and Sandy Bay walked or rode over the road through the woods to the meetinghouse at the head of Lobster Cove in Annisquam for services each Sunday.

For perspective, it should be noted that the settlements at Pigeon Cove and Sandy Bay were getting under way at approximately the same time that Dogtown was being settled and the movement from The Green to Gloucester Harbor was beginning to take place.

From 1700 till after 1820 the settlements at Sandy Bay and Pigeon Cove increased only slowly in population. Farming, wood-coasting, and the shore fisheries were the chief occupations of the inhabitants of that period. The harbors on that section of the Cape were too small and too exposed to the sea to facilitate an extensive development of the sort of offshore

124

fishing and foreign trading which took place at Gloucester Harbor and Annisquam in the eighteenth century.

In 1823, however, a new industry—granite quarrying— began to develop on a large scale at Pigeon Cove and in neighboring areas, and that led to such a growth of trade and such an increase of population that a movement eventually was started among the residents of Sandy Bay, Pigeon Cove, and adjoining neighborhoods to have that part of the Cape separated from Gloucester and set off as an independent town. As a result, in 1840, by action of the State Legislature, the Town of Rockport came into being. The name "Rockport" never had been applied previously to that district; it was coined for the purpose and chosen by the residents to be the designation of the new town.

Efforts were made from time to time to develop other industries besides fishing and quarrying at Rockport in order to furnish more industrial employment. One of these ventures was the establishment of a cotton mill in 1848. The mill, which manufactured cotton duck, stood on Broadway and was of massive granite construction. It had 18,000 spindles and 262 looms, and employed 225 people. It continued in operation for thirty-five years, until gutted by fire, but after the fire no serious attempt was made to revive the enterprise. Rockport, in fact, was not a favorable location for a textile manufacturing plant. It had no water-power resources or other local advantages, such as were found in the mill towns along the Merrimack and at various other points in New England. With hindsight, moreover, it now may appear fortunate for Rockport that it was not successful in becoming a mill town. As a mill town the village would have lost much of the attractiveness that led to the growth of quite a different sort of business—that of catering to summer visitors.

Summer visitors began to arrive in Rockport about 1840 and that business continued to thrive long after most of the quarries had become mere swimming pools or gaping chasms in the landscape, and also long after many of the New England mill towns had turned into distressed communities.

Among the first of many well-known summer visitors to Rockport was Richard H. Dana, the poet and essayist, who started spending his summers at Pigeon Cove in 1840. Two years later, William Cullen Bryant also spent the summer at Pigeon Cove, and with him was a Mr. Brackett, a sculptor who was working on a bust of Mr. Bryant. Mr. Dana and Mr. Brackett had rooms that summer in a tavern at Pigeon Cove. Mr. Bryant boarded at the "Old House."

Improvements in travel facilities helped the summer resort business to grow. A post office had been opened at Sandy Bay in 1825, with deliveries three times a week by two-wheeled chaise from Gloucester Harbor. The post chaise carried passengers, to the extent of its capacity, between Sandy Bay and Gloucester, where connections could be made with the stagecoach to Salem and Boston. That was the first public transportation service for Rockport. By 1840, however, Boston stagecoaches were running through to Pigeon Cove and the availability of that means of travel contributed substantially to the growth of the summer resort business in Rockport. The opening of the railroad from Gloucester to Boston in 1847 gave further impetus to the expansion.

In 1861 a branch railroad was opened from Rockport to Gloucester. Since the Eastern Railroad Company, which then operated the Gloucester-Boston line, was not willing to extend it to Rockport, the Town of Rockport, on authorization by the State Legislature, subscribed $75,000 for building the branch; individual stockholders invested $13,000, and $2,607 was borrowed. The branch was so prosperous that the debt was paid off from earnings; the stockholders received good dividends; and in 1868 the branch was sold to the Eastern Railroad Company at cost.

Although several summer hotels were built at Pigeon Cove and elsewhere in Rockport, many of the summer visitors took rooms in private homes which expanded their accommodations for that purpose. In later years, especially after the automobile came into general use, numerous private summer residences were built in Rockport. Thus the summer business in Rockport was not dependent upon the patronage of a few large hotels and at least partially for that reason, it acquired a high degree of permanency and stability.

For summer visitors the lure of Rockport, as well as of other parts of Cape Ann, has been a blend of many attractions —the ever-changing sea, sometimes serene and peaceful, at other times seemingly implacable in its rage and fury; the fishing craft and the picturesque wharves and fishermen's shanties; the fishing nets spread out to dry in the sun; the lobster pots and the lobsters caught in them; the smells and odors to be found only in a fishing village; sailing and pleasure boating, in all their varied forms; beaches for bathing; strolls under stately old trees, and walks through the woods or over the moors for those still inclined to indulge in such old-fashioned pleasures; blueberries and huckleberries to be had for the picking; grey ledges and somber boulders of many shapes and sizes; colorful quarries, with intriguing shadows and delicate shadings reflected in the waters with which most of them eventually became filled; weather-stained old houses as well as attractive modern homes; and over all the tangy air, compounded from sea and forest and rocky shores. Mingled with those physical attractions have been the legends and traditions which have long been an integral part of Cape Ann.

The first Englishman's association with Cape Ann had a romantic tinge which for three and a half centuries probably has not been equalled. In 1614 Captain John Smith, of Pocahontas fame, was sent out by a group of London merchants to catch whales and to seek sources of gold and copper in the New World. The trip ended up as a fishing enterprise off the coast of Maine. While the crews of his two ships were engaged in catching codfish in the waters around Monhegan

Island, Captain Smith set out with a few men in a small boat and sailed along the coast to the southward as far as Cape Cod. He made a map of that stretch of coast, and to the headland later to be known as Cape Ann, he gave the name "Tragabigzanda" to commemorate a fair Turkish lady, he said, who had befriended him while he was a prisoner of war in her homeland. The three islands off the southeastern point of the Cape he called the "Three Turks' Heads," in memory of three Turks whom he gallantly had slain while he was crusading as a volunteer in the forces of the Emperor of Austria.

Captain Smith's romantic place names did not stick. Tragabigzanda became Cape Ann, and the Three Turks' Heads presently were christened, prosaically, Thachers, Milk, and Straitsmouth Islands.

The largest and most prominent of those islands is Thachers. It got its permanent name from a tragic shipwreck which occurred near its shore.

In August 1635, a pinnace with twenty-three persons on board sailed from Ipswich for Marblehead, where the Reverend John Avery, one of the passengers, was to become minister of a parish. When off Cape Ann, the pinnace was caught in a hurricane. The description of the storm, written at the time by Governor Bradford of Plymouth,[2] shows that it was very similar to the hurricanes which hit New England in 1938 and three subsequent years. The storm struck with great suddenness, just before daybreak, with a wave twenty-five feet high. Houses were blown down and thousands of trees were uprooted in the vicinity of Plymouth, and the storm must have hit Cape Ann with similar fury. It continued, without abating, for five or six hours.

When the hurricane struck, the pinnace from Ipswich was anchored off Sandy Bay, about a mile from a large island.

---

2 William Bradford, *Of Plymouth Plantation, 1620-1647*, Samuel Eliot Morrison, ed. (New York, Alfred Knopf, 1952), p. 279.

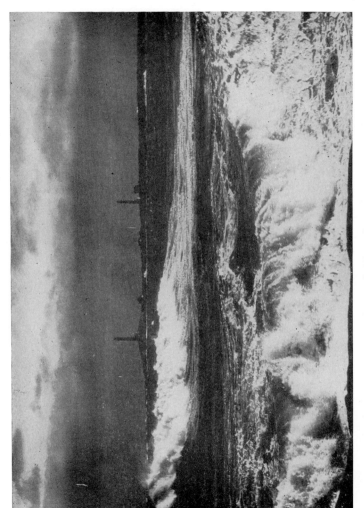

THACHER'S TWIN LIGHTS

THE WALL OF A QUARRY PIT

At bottom foreground lies half an engine boiler, used as a bucket for
hoisting out grout.

The ship dragged its anchor, of course, and was driven on a ledge submerged in about four feet of water. Mr. Anthony Thacher and his wife, who were two of the passengers, were carried away by the tide and rather miraculously they were washed ashore on the island. All the other passengers, including four Thacher children and six Avery children, were lost. After two days on the island, Mr. and Mrs. Thacher were rescued by a passing boat. Thachers Island was named for them. Avery's Ledge, just outside the Rockport breakwater, commemorates the Avery name.

This tragedy may well have given rise to the efforts which were started within the next three years to have a cut made through the marsh from the Annisquam River to Gloucester Harbor, so that the perils of sailing around the Cape in small boats could be avoided.

The colonial government purchased Thachers Island in 1771 and immediately built two lighthouses on it, together with a dwelling for a caretaker. The island is about eighty acres in size and it provided pasturage for the caretaker's cattle. In 1861 the federal government erected two new lighthouses on the island, in a north-south line, and although only one of the lighthouses has been kept in operation in recent years, the twin lights of Thachers are still a famous landmark for mariners.

For a period of about three years recently Thachers was a prolific breeding place for terns—common terns, Arctic terns, and a few roseate terns. Hundreds of those birds laid their eggs and raised their young there each summer. The terns built no nests; they simply laid their eggs on the ledges, wherever there was a slight depression which served to keep the eggs from rolling off. In 1957, on one of our trips to Thachers, it was estimated by John Kieran and Lawrence Jodrey that there were about two thousand terns on the island, but in the following year there were none. They had been driven off, presumably, by the larger, rapacious herring gulls which ate the terns' eggs and chicks.

Milk Island, to the southwest of Thachers, is a small, low-lying island which had enough fertile land within its pebbly beaches to provide summer pasturage, a century or so ago, for a few sheep. The animals were ferried over from the mainland in the spring and taken back in the fall. On the island at one time there was a structure of some sort, as indicated by the remains of a foundation which were visible about fifty years ago. The structure presumably was a shelter for the animals, and well they must have needed it when a northeaster was drenching the island with rain and clouds of spray. As to when the use of the island as a pasture began, there is no record. The use continued until about the end of the nineteenth century. There also is no record as to whence the island got its name.

Milk Island now is a bird sanctuary, inhabited by herring gulls, great black-backed gulls, night herons, and cormorants which breed there. Each of the four species of birds has its own residential precinct, which seems to be respected by members of the other species. The great black-backed gulls, or parson gulls as they sometimes are called, occupy a relatively small area on the western end of the island. The night herons build their nests in scrubby bushes in the south center of the island. Along the northeastern point are the nests of the cormorants, which are built of small sticks artfully woven together to form structures often about a foot in height. The cormorants' nests are along the crest of the beach, just beyond the reach of the big waves which roll in during a heavy storm. They stand out in the open, devoid of any protection whatsoever from the elements.

The herring gulls, which are by far the most numerous species, occupy all the rest of the island and fill the air with an ear-splitting din whenever a visitor lands on the beach. There are so many herring gulls on the island, in fact, that a person has to walk carefully to avoid stepping on the camouflaged eggs or the little chicks and partly grown birds which blend into the rocks and debris and low vegetation so thoroughly that often they are not seen until they move. Here and there in the herring-gull domain lies the corpse of a gull slain by his mates, presumably because he had transgressed one of the rules of the colony. The nest of a herring gull is a very crude affair, usually a hollow spot in the ground with perhaps a few twigs around the edges.

On the shore of the mainland across from Milk Island, and across the tidal inlet known as Saratoga, lies Cape Hedge, at the westerly end of Pebbly Beach. A short distance easterly along the shore is where the laying of an Atlantic cable from Dover, England, to the United States was completed in 1884.

Westward from Cape Hedge, Long Beach extends to the Gloucester line near Brier Neck. Long Beach became especially popular during the trolley-car era, when it was an attraction for excursion trips from Gloucester. It is now one of the most populous summer colonies on the Cape. The land on which the cottages stand at Long Beach is still owned by the Town of Rockport, but the houses were privately constructed on long-term land leases.

To the east of Cape Hedge lies Pebbly Beach which rises quite abruptly for ten or fifteen feet, and is composed of pebbles, many of which are about the size of a man's fist, all nicely smoothed and rounded. At one period in the development of the fishing industry at Gloucester, many tons of pebbles were hauled in tip-carts from Pebbly Beach to Gloucester wharves to be loaded on the fishing schooners for ballast. Out on the fishing grounds, as a vessel filled its holds with fish the ballast was no longer needed, and the pebbles were thrown overboard. Thus Cape Ann pebbles, as well as the remains of Gloucester wrecks, came to be scattered over the Grand Bank and other offshore fishing grounds.

On the outer shore of the Cape, between Thachers and Straitsmouth, lie two small coves, Loblolly Cove and Whale Cove. There is no record as to how Loblolly Cove got its name, but the designation is an old one. Whale Cove was given that name when a seventy-six foot whale was driven ashore there in March 1798. The area between Thachers and Straitsmouth is especially noteworthy, however, for the marine mishaps and disasters which have occurred there, from the Thacher wreck in 1635 down to the present time. During a storm the seas run heavy around Thachers, and a navigator who fails to clear it is headed for trouble. At times the fog also rolls in thick around Thachers.

One of the most famous mishaps in that area occurred during the Revolutionary War. A brig which was carrying a load of coal, iron, and livestock from Nova Scotia to the British troops in Boston, was feeling her way along in a dense fog and unintentionally nosed in between Thachers and Straitsmouth. When the skipper heard the roar of the surf on the rocky shore which he could not see, he anchored. Shortly thereafter the fog lifted momentarily, as it often does, and then shut in again. The interval of light was not long enough for the brig to get under way again, but it was sufficient to enable it to be seen from the shore. Word that a prize was just offshore spread rapidly in the little village and despite the fog, a fishing boat with a good-sized crew put out from the harbor and captured the brig. The cattle were unloaded at Sandy Bay, and when the weather had cleared the brig was sailed around to Annisquam Harbor. The coal and iron were unloaded at Captain Gee's wharf on Wheeler's Point, but the brig was lost; she slid off into the channel of the river and sank.

The hazards of navigation in the neighborhood of Thachers and Straitsmouth are rendered substantially more serious by the Salvages—the "savage rocks"—which lie outside Straitsmouth. The Little Salvages are about a mile offshore and the Big Salvages, a half-mile farther out. On a clear day the Big Salvages glisten in the sun, whitened by the droppings of myriads of gulls, but in stormy weather those ledges have brought disaster to many a ship.

During the last century still another hazard to navigation off Sandy Bay has developed from what was intended to be a protection to shipping. In 1882 a movement was started to secure for Rockport the construction of a large harbor to foster a greater maritime business. In that year a committee of Rockport men was appointed to draft a petition to Congress for a survey of Sandy Bay, with a view to the construction of a breakwater and a harbor of refuge there. The survey was made and construction was authorized by Congress, at an estimated total cost of $4,000,000. Work on the breakwater began in 1885, with the dumping of granite from the Pigeon Cove quarries to start forming the base. The breakwater was about a mile offshore and the original plan provided that it should be nine thousand feet long. Actually only about six thousand feet of the foundation were laid and on only a part of that foundation was the superstructure completed. In 1912 Congress decided to discontinue appropriations for the project and work was stopped. Up to that date approximately $1,750,000 of government funds had been spent on the breakwater.

The local campaign to have the breakwater completed continued without success until 1942, when World War II diverted attention to other matters. The work on the breakwater was stopped so abruptly in 1912 that no provision was made to prevent the partially constructed superstructure from being tumbled down by heavy seas. As a consequence, the superstructure now is considerably shorter than it was when the work on it was suspended, and the huge blocks of granite barely submerged under the surface of the sea constitute a serious hazard to ignorant or unwary skippers, even in clear weather.

On the mainland, the most colorful spot at Sandy Bay is Bearskin Neck. Shortly after John Babson built his cabin at Gap Head in 1695, he encountered a bear nearby, which, tradition says, he killed with his knife. After skinning the bear, Mr. Babson spread out the skin to dry on a rock at the end of a neck jutting out into Sandy Bay Harbor. Fishermen from Chebacco or Ipswich who happened to be sailing by saw the skin on the rock and thenceforth called that place "Bearskin Neck."

During the War of 1812 a fort was erected on Bearskin Neck and a company of militia was stationed there. In 1814, on a foggy night, the British frigate *Nymphe* sailed quietly into Sandy Bay Harbor and sent barges ashore to capture the town. One barge landed at Bearskin Neck and found the guards asleep. They were taken prisoners; the cannon in the fort were spiked; and the guardhouse was set on fire. Another barge, meanwhile, was landing at the town beach, but the crew of that barge was captured by the townspeople, who were more alert than the guard at the fort. On the next day a truce was called; prisoners were exchanged; and the frigate sailed away. The only thing which the Britishers left behind on that raid was a cannon ball which they had shot into the meetinghouse steeple.

Bearskin Neck also was the site of one of the unique industrial enterprises of Sandy Bay. In 1822 William Hall began the manufacture of isinglass in a small fishhouse on Bearskin Neck, and for about fifty years, it is said,[3] he was the only producer of isinglass in the United States. His raw material was hake sounds (air bladders), which previously had been thrown away as waste. He paid three to five cents a pound for them and converted them into isinglass by the use of hand rollers. His business prospered for years, but in 1876 financial embarrassment caused it to be closed down.

---

3 *History of the Town of Rockport* (compiled by a local committee, published 1888), p. 8.

The vicinity of Bearskin Neck also was once the scene of a temperance crusade. On July 8, 1856, a band of Rockport women decided to make a demonstration against the shops and stores in Sandy Bay which were unlawfully selling spirituous liquors. They raided thirteen grog shops, some of them on Bearskin Neck, and seized casks, demijohns, and other containers and emptied their contents into the street. The odors which then rose from the gutters tantalized the parching throats of the poor menfolk who looked on but dared not stoop to take a drink. There is no record as to how long a drought followed the raid.

In the eighteenth century, Bearskin Neck was the site of fishermen's shanties, boatbuilding shops, stores which sold boat gear, bait and clams, an old tavern, and the "lean-to" where William Haskell, who wore earrings and did up his hair on curl papers, sold homemade ginger pop and molasses candy. In the twentieth century most of the fishermen's shanties and other buildings on Bearskin Neck were taken over by artists for camps and studios, and the Neck became the center of a large artists' colony. One of the fishermen's shanties on the Neck has been the subject of so many paintings that it has become famed locally as "Motif No. 1."

While Sandy Bay and Pigeon Cove have been the two chief villages in the Town of Rockport, each has had its own personality, so to speak. Pigeon Cove was the center of the quarry industry on the outer Cape and in recent years it has had a metal working plant, but it has remained largely a summer resort area, with less bustle and commotion than are to be encountered around Bearskin Neck and Sandy Bay.

Pigeon Cove got its name, according to tradition, from a disaster which overtook flocks of wild pigeons migrating from Maine and New Hampshire to Cape Ann on their annual pilgrimage to the south. The pigeons were caught offshore in a storm which was so severe that many of them became exhausted and could not reach land. They fell into the sea and the little cove where their bodies were washed ashore in great numbers henceforth was called "Pigeon Cove." That slaughter must have occurred soon after the first settlers came to Cape Ann, because Pigeon Cove is one of the oldest place names on the Cape.

A short distance back from the shore at Pigeon Cove stands Pigeon Hill, which is especially noteworthy from a geological standpoint. Pigeon Hill is a drumlin. Whereas all the other hills around Cape Ann, with one exception, are composed of ledge or boulders, Pigeon Hill is a compact mass of clay. The other exception is the hill on Hog Island which rises out of the Essex marshes. Hog Island also is a drumlin.

Pigeon Hill is about two hundred feet high and mostly symmetrical in form. The clay of which it was formed presumably was part of a large mass of that material left on the surface of the earth hereabouts when the ice sheet of the first glacial period melted away. During the interval of thousands of years between the first and second glacial periods, the clay deposit was eroded by rivers and the sea, and when the second ice sheet came to cover the area, it wore away still more of the clay deposit. But here and there it left a rounded hill of that material, known as a drumlin. Shaler states[4] that Pigeon Hill is a remarkably good example of this type of geological formation.

Halibut Point, at the northeastern end of the Cape, is another landmark familiar to all local mariners. On its outer edge is a huge grout pile, formed of waste granite dumped there from the quarries, and adding to the prominence of the Point when seen from the ocean. For those who go to Halibut Point by land, there is a lovely view on a clear day across the bay, extending from the sandy beaches and dunes in West

---

4 Nathaniel S. Shaler, *The Geology of Cape Ann, Massachusetts*, p. 550. Report submitted to the United States Geological Survey (June 20, 1888) and published as part of a larger report on a study of the Atlantic coast line. The report contains many excellent photographs.

Gloucester, Essex, and Ipswich to Plum Island, the New Hampshire shore, and sometimes even to the Isles of Shoals and Mount Agamenticus in Maine.

The origin of the name Halibut Point is not wholly clear, but the most commonly accepted explanation is that early settlers in sailing around the Cape to or from Ipswich Bay had to "haul about" their boats and reset their sails when they rounded that point. Presently the words, as in so many other place names, became corrupted into "Halibut Point."

To the west of Halibut Point lies Folly Cove, the last spot in Rockport when touring the Cape counterclockwise. On the old maps Folly Cove was designated as "Gallups Folly." The story is that a man named Gallup or Gallop carelessly took the little cove for the entrance to some larger harbor, and lost his vessel when she ran ashore there. Since his neighbors went so far in perpetuating the memory of his mistake as to give the cove his name, one wonders whether Mr. Gallup may not have been a somewhat arrogant or boastful person. Or perhaps the christening may have been merely a bit of seventeenth-century humor.

Upstream a few hundred yards on the brook which flows into Folly Cove, is the site of an old milldam. Here, as elsewhere on the Cape, every little brook was utilized to provide water power for sawing lumber or grinding grain. The abundance of large trees in the forests on the Cape, and the facility with which the sawn timber could be shipped by water, made these little sawmills major industrial enterprises for the early settlers on Cape Ann. The mill at Folly Cove was known at one time as "Jumper's Mill," later as "Woodbury's."

When the quarry pits were opened on the hills back of Folly Cove, a stone dock was built on the shore of the cove and it thus became one of the granite shipping ports on the Cape. Thus Folly Cove shared with Pigeon Cove, Lanesville, and Bay View in the development of the quarry industry.

Lanesville, Bay View, and the Quarries

FOR NEARLY TWO HUNDRED years after the settlement of Cape Ann began, the area along its northern coast, like that along the back shore, had a rather uneventful history. In fact, it was not until the quarry industry spread into this section from Pigeon Cove that the villages at Lanesville and Bay View were anything more than small fishing and farming communities. At both places, as well as at Folly Cove, there were small coves with sandy beaches where boats could be hauled up, but they were not sufficiently protected for use by sailing vessels. It was only when the quarries began operations that sheltered harbors were constructed.

The rest of that section of the shore of Ipswich Bay was rocky, with several reefs not far offshore. They provided good fishing grounds, as evidenced by the fish traps and the large number of lobster pots which are still set there, but the rocks and reefs made inshore navigation somewhat hazardous.

Lanesville was first called Flatstone Cove, an obviously descriptive title. Sometime after John Lane settled there in 1700, the cove became known as Lane's Cove and the village as Lanesville. James Lane, who was the father of John Lane, had come to America from England in 1656, when John was four years old. The family had lived in Malden for two years and then moved to Casco Bay in Maine.[5] James Lane acquired a large area of land in Maine, but he was killed during an Indian raid in 1676, and in 1690 John Lane and his brother Samuel and their families narrowly escaped being

---

5 This information comes from an article by Margaret T. Doelger, published in the *Gloucester Daily Times*, January 14, 1958.

slain in another French and Indian attack. As a result of the continual trouble with the Indians, John and Samuel Lane finally decided to leave Maine, and they came to Cape Ann to settle.

In this connection it is worth noting that throughout the colonial period Cape Ann was unusually free from disturbance by Indians. Champlain reported that he found several camps of Indians on the Cape when he landed at "Beau Port" in 1606, and Indians later frequently came to Cape Ann in the summer, but there is no record of any friction between the white settlers and the Indians or of any Indian raids on Cape Ann. That experience is quite in contrast with what occurred not only on the Maine coast but also at Plymouth, Cape Cod, Weymouth, and numerous other places in New England. There is no obvious reason, so far as we are aware, why Cape Ann should have been spared from Indian molestation, but the fact is that it was spared.

When John Lane arrived at Flatstone Cove in 1700, there were five families living nearby. He bought land for farming and soon became a leading man in the community. He was a successful farmer and fisherman, and when he died in 1738, at the age of 86, his estate was valued at £978, a large sum in those days, and in his will the following items were listed:—"A dwelling house and barns with 30 acres of homestead, besides orchards, pasture, herbage, swamp and wood lands, flake yards, cattle, bills of credit, copper and silver money, iron, brass, glassware, cutlass and sword, and one-fourth part of an acre to be a burying place forever, and ye brook as a common priviledge of a watering place for cattle to all ye heirs of ye sd John Lane."

The old burying ground is still intact and a stone marks the grave where John Lane was buried.

He obviously was an enterprising man and he shared in the prosperity which Cape Ann began to enjoy soon after 1700. The list of items in his will, furthermore, gives some indication of the standard of living of a provincial colonist in the early eighteenth century.

Lanesville continued to be a small, placid farming and fishing community until 1828. Then quarries began to be opened on the hills back of the village and a new era opened. Before going further into the Lanesville quarries, however, let us first take a look at some of the broader background of that industry.

Granite not only has contributed to the picturesqueness of Cape Ann; it also has been put to utilitarian use. And some of the utilitarian uses, of course, long antedate the quarries. Stone was used from the early days for building the foundations of houses and other structures. Stones cleared from the fields were used to form the walls which marked property lines and public rights of way. Some of those old stone walls, incidentally, indicate that there once were farms and pastures where the land now is grown over with trees and brush.

Another primitive use of granite was for mooring stones. Early in the eighteenth century, for example, shipowners at Sandy Bay and other coves on the outer shore of the Cape employed Joshua Norwood to fashion mooring stones for their vessels. The mooring stone was a block of granite about six feet square and ten to fifteen inches thick. In the center of the block a hole about fifteen inches in diameter was drilled out. The trunk of an oak tree, with the top cut off about twenty feet from the base, then was shoved through the hole in the block. The roots were left on the oak trunk and kept it from pulling through the hole in the stone. A mooring rope then was fastened to the top of the oak trunk, and the mooring was deposited in the cove or harbor at the spot where it was desired to moor the boat. Since the stone weighed a couple of tons, there was slight danger that the boat would drag the mooring. In the water the oak retained its strength for years.

For the gristmills that were built to grind grain millstones were needed, and they, too, were fashioned from granite, with

140

surfaces ribbed to crush the grain as one stone rotated on top of another. A millstone was three or four feet in diameter and in thickness about five inches or more. Several of those old millstones are still to be found around the Cape, some in use as door stones and stone tables, and others just lying near where they were scrapped. Millstones occasionally were shipped from Cape Ann for use in mills in other towns along the coast.

Thus the colonists found essential, though primitive, uses for small quantities of the granite which was so abundant on the Cape. When the quarry industry was developed at Pigeon Cove and Lanesville, however, the excavation and processing of the stone became a large-scale operation.

The quarry industry got its start on Cape Ann[6] when Nehemiah Knowlton, in 1823, excavated some five hundred tons of stone at Pigeon Cove and advertised it for sale in a Boston newspaper. A Mr. Bates of Quincy, where quarries already were in operation, saw the advertisement and came to Pigeon Cove to investigate its resources. He deemed the prospects favorable and began operations there on a ledge which he leased. His venture was not successful, but a couple of years later William Torrey, who had been associated with Mr. Bates, opened a pit at another location in Pigeon Cove which became a large quarry. During the next fifteen years he supplied much of the granite used by the federal government in its construction work at Boston and Portsmouth, N. H.

About 1825 another firm opened a pit at Pigeon Cove, and to provide facilities for shipping stone, they built the wharf and breakwater at Gull Cove. In 1827 still another quarry was opened at Pigeon Cove by a firm which sold stone to buyers in Boston, Salem, Portsmouth, and other cities. While some of the granite from that quarry was used for construction purposes, including the foundations for the chain bridge over the Merrimack River above Newburyport, much of the

---

6 *History of the Town of Rockport*, pp. 237-39.

output was marketed for the production of cemetery monuments and gravestones.

The Lanesville Granite Company was incorporated in 1828, and it constructed a loading pier at Lane's Cove in Lanesville. A breakwater was built across the mouth of the cove, with an entrance just wide enough to permit a vessel to enter. Thus a small but well-protected harbor was created where the original Flatstone Cove had been.

From those beginnings the industry expanded, both in Pigeon Cove and in Lanesville. In 1860, John J. Babson reported that about 350 men were employed in quarrying the stone, in cutting it into the shapes and sizes called for in the market, in hauling the stone to the cutters and the shipping piers, and in manning the blacksmith shops which were always busy sharpening tools and repairing gear. Another 150 men then were employed on the sloops on which the stone was shipped.

With all this bustle of activity, Lanesville as well as Pigeon Cove became a small industrial community.

In 1848 the quarry industry spread to Bay View, which earlier had been known as Hogskin Cove, then Hodgkins Cove. Until a quarry was opened there, the only industry at Hodgkins Cove beside farming and fishing was a colonial sawmill located on the brook which flows down to the cove through the deep ravine on Mt. Misery. The mill was owned by John Harraden, and the remains of the milldam are still discernible through the thick brush in the ravine. As to the source of that lugubrious name "Mt. Misery," our curiosity remains unsatisfied. The hill is no higher, no steeper, and no bleaker than many neighboring hills, and there now are no signs of misery on the hill. We suspect that the name commemorates some otherwise unrecorded poignant episode of two or three hundred years ago.

The first quarry was opened at Bay View to provide stone for building a bridge across the brook at the head of the cove. While that quarry continued in operation from 1848 until 1865, under frequently changing ownership, it was only a small-scale venture. Then in 1869 the Cape Ann Granite Company was organized by Colonel Jonas H. French and his associates. They purchased the old pit and acquired additional ledges.

It was General Ben Butler who interested Colonel French in organizing that enterprise, and there we have another instance of a summer visitor's coming to take a keen interest in the affairs of Cape Ann, and in this case the summer visitor was an especially colorful character.

General Butler first came to Bay View in 1863. At that time he acquired land between Diamond Cove and Hodgkins Cove for a prospective summer home. In the summer of that year, after he had been relieved from his command of the Union troops at New Orleans, he lived in a tent on the shore of Diamond Cove, with his two sons and their tutor. Again, in the summer of 1865, after he had been relieved from another command, he and his boys returned to their tent at Diamond Cove, and in 1866 they spent a third summer there, sailing, fishing, and enjoying all the other pleasures of Ipswich Bay, which he described as a "beautiful and picturesque piece of water, where the sunsets are equal to those of the Bay of Naples."[7] It was General Butler who gave the name "Bay View" to the Hodgkins Cove area.

General Butler presently erected a summer residence near Diamond Cove, and on the large area of higher land above Davis Neck which he had purchased, his daughter and her husband, Major General Adelbert Ames, built a summer place which came to be known as the "Ames Estate," a title which it still carries. General Ames was a native of Maine and a graduate of West Point. He had had a distinguished career in the Civil War and in 1862, while still a colonel, he had served

---

7 Benj. F. Butler, *Butler's Book* (Boston, A. M. Thayer & Co., 1892), p. 920.

as the first commander of the famed Twentieth Maine Regiment.[8] Between 1868 and 1874 he served successively as Provisional Governor of Mississippi, United States Senator from Mississippi, and Governor of that state. After the political tide turned against him in Mississippi in 1874, he came to live in Lowell, Masachusetts, his wife's home town, and for about sixty years thereafter he regularly spent his summers at Bay View.

While General Butler was at Diamond Cove in the summer of 1866, John B. Alley, the local representative in Congress, informed the General that he had decided not to run again for Congress and suggested to General Butler that he become a candidate. General Butler's legal residence was in Lowell, in another congressional district, but although he was a "carpet-bagger," as he put it, and a very controversial figure in state politics and in military activities, he decided to seek election. He was elected in that year and was re-elected in 1868. As he stated: "I was elected to Congress while I lived in the tent on the beach." He obviously enjoyed his brash political venture.

It was while General Butler was in Congress that he made the proposal to Colonel French which led to the organization of the Cape Ann Granite Company. General Butler was so busy with his political activities and his law practice, however, that he apparently did not participate actively in the management of the quarry company. His name, nevertheless, is always associated locally with it.

To carry on its shipping operations, the quarry company constructed a big loading pier which jutted out into Hodgkins Cove, a long stone's throw from General Butler's summer home. The pier provided a protected deep-water berth for barges and added another harbor to the north shore of the Cape. After the quarry went out of business, the pier event-

---

8 John J. Pullen, *The Twentieth Maine* (Philadelphia, J. B. Lippincott Company, 1957), p. 1.

LANE'S COVE

Vessels being loaded with paving stones. Small ship in foreground, *I Am Here*, suggested name *We're Here* to Kipling.

VIEW FROM ADAMS HILL ACROSS LOBSTER COVE
Note Dogtown moors in the distance (picture taken around 1890).

ually came to be used as a storage and shipping depot for the Consolidated Lobster Company which now handles over four million live lobsters a year and ships its products not only to restaurants throughout the United States but also to Europe. Most of the lobsters which it handles are shipped by boat from Maine and the Canadian Maritime Provinces to Bay View, where they are stored in tanks of running salt water until shipped to market. Live lobsters thus have taken the place of granite building blocks and paving stones on the pier at Hodgkins Cove.

One of the pits of the Cape Ann Granite Company was known as Blood Ledge Quarry. That title derived not from any blood spilt by the quarry workers toiling in the pit but from the family name of the original owner of the pasture where the pit was excavated—James Blood. The Blood Ledge Quarry now is filled with water and beside it stands an attractive residence, with smooth lawns running down to the edge of the pit. That is only one of a number of picturesque homes which have been built around old quarry pits in the Lanesville-Bay View area. The pits have provided deep swimming pools for those who prefer fresh water to salt and who have no apprehension at diving into a hole twenty-five or thirty feet deep with no shelving shore on which to get a foothold.

Another large pit, with especially colorful stone in its perpendicular walls, which also was owned by the Cape Ann Granite Company, was called the Klondike Quarry. In 1956 it was converted into a reservoir for the Gloucester water supply system. One of the old pits in Rockport recently has become a reservoir for that town's water supply.

The Cape Ann Granite Company, like several of its neighbors, eventually experienced financial difficulties, and ownership passed into the hands of one of the Rockport companies. In his autobiography, General Butler said nothing about his promotion of the Cape Ann Granite Company, a silence which may have been occasioned by its impending financial problems.

Among the many buildings, in addition to those already mentioned, in the construction of which Cape Ann granite was used were the Post Office Building in Boston, the Danvers Insane Asylum, the Longfellow Bridge over the Charles River, the Myles Standish Monument at Duxbury, the Philadelphia Public Library, the West Point Military Academy, the fountain in the Union Station Plaza, Washington, D. C., and government buildings in San Francisco.

The production of stone for construction of buildings and monuments, furthermore, was supplemented, especially after the middle of the nineteenth century, by the output of paving stones which were sold not only to cities along the North Atlantic seaboard but also to New Orleans, Cuba, and South America. To prepare the paving blocks large slabs of granite, each weighing six or seven tons, were blasted out of the quarries. These rough slabs then were hauled over the quarry tracks to the cutters' sheds, where they were cut by hand drills to specified sizes. In some cities much larger paving stones were used than in others. A paving block for New Orleans, for example, was fifteen times as large as one for New York, twenty times as large as one for Philadelphia, and thirty times the size of a Boston block.

Paving stones also were produced, during the boom period, by numerous small operators who blasted out slabs of granite from the ledges and boulders on their own property or on leased land. Those were surface operations, called "motions," and their activities can be traced by the holes and chips which they left at many scattered points on the hills of Pigeon Cove, Lanesville, Bay View, and Annisquam. These small producers sold the blocks which they cut to the quarry companies at Lanesville, Bay View, and Pigeon Cove.

In the large quarries the direction of operations was a job for an expert. The supervisor or foreman had to select the ledges to be worked and to determine where the holes should be drilled for blasting. That required an understanding of the grain of the ledge and of its seam structure, in order that the rock might be split off to best advantage.

When the first quarries were opened, all the work was done by hand-power or ox-power. The holes in which blasting powder was to be exploded were drilled by pounding a square drill with a hammer. Round drills with V-shaped points presently superseded the square drills, but it was not until 1883 that the first steam drill came into use. In the early years, furthermore, the rough slabs of granite were hoisted out of the pits either by manpower or by oxen, and the pumping of the water which flowed into the pits from the surface of the ledge or from springs underneath was done by hand. It was in 1853 that a steam engine was first used for hoisting and pumping. Later in the nineteenth century numerous mechanical devices were introduced for drilling, cutting, and polishing the granite.

For transporting stone from the quarries to the finishing sheds and the piers, several quarry companies built inclined railroad tracks down which the loaded cars traveled by gravity. When empty, they were towed back by oxen. As the ownership of the quarries became largely concentrated in the hands of a few companies, the railroad tracks were extended over a larger area and steam locomotives came into use. The Rockport Granite Company, for example, with quarries both in Pigeon Cove and in Lanesville, operated seven miles of railroad track and three locomotives, one of which had the resounding name "Polyphemus."

Before the days of mechanization, quarrying was a seasonal business, with a curtailment of production during the winter months, and for about twenty-five years after the first quarries were opened, much of the labor was supplied by young men who came to Cape Ann from Maine and New Hampshire for the working season. In the middle of the nineteenth century the quarry industry, like many other New England industries, began to employ immigrant laborers. The first of those were Irish who had left the old country at the time of the potato famine in 1848. They formed a settlement near the quarries, on the outskirts of Lanesville, which was known locally as "Dublin."

When the first arrangements for employing Irish immigrants were broached in Pigeon Cove, strong opposition sprang up. "The house which was being prepared for them to occupy was two or three times blown up with powder; and other means were employed to keep out the unwelcome immigrants."[9] That opposition undoubtedly was kindled by apprehension that the newcomers would accept employment at wages lower than the rates then being paid.

Immigrants of other nationalities followed the Irish, and in 1875, for example, French Canadian as well as Irish laborers were employed for unskilled work in the quarries at Bay View, and presumably also in Lanesville and Pigeon Cove. English, Scotch, and Irish workmen, as well as Americans, were employed in the more skilled tasks of cutting, finishing, and polishing the stone; and a small group of skilled Italian workers was brought in from Genoa for sculpturing the stone to be used for the Boston Post Office, the Myles Standish Monument, and other structures.

About 1880 the quarry companies' continued search for strong-bodied laborers who would work for relatively low wages led to the bringing in of Finnish immigrants. At first the Finns were housed in a couple of old barns which had been converted into dormitories, but they soon established their families in permanent residences. Thus the population of Lanesville came to include a large Finnish colony.

Probably the most unique institution brought into the community by the Finns was their bathhouse or *sauna*. Until quite recent years, many of the Finnish homes in Lanes-

9 *History of Rockport*, p. 242.

ville had *saunas* for their own use and for use by their friends and neighbors. There also were larger *saunas* open to the general public. The fee for use of a *sauna* generally was fifteen cents; two for a quarter when two people took the bath together. There were at least twenty of these *saunas* in Lanesville.

The sauna usually was a small, two-room cabin. One room, unheated, was used as a dressing room; the other was the bath—a hot-air chamber in which smooth, round pebbles gathered from Cape Ann beaches were heated to a very high temperature by means of a firebox placed beneath the stones. The principle was the same as that traditionally used in a New England clambake. When the stones had been fully heated, all the coals from the fire were removed, so that there would be no smoke in the room.

Against one wall of the bathroom was a tier of three or four rows of pine-board benches, arranged bleacher fashion, upon which the bathers sat. The top row was used by the bathers for steaming, the lower rows for washing. Hot and cold water was stored in large wooden barrels on one side of the room, and wooden buckets were provided for dipping out the water. Water was thrown on the hot rocks and the air thus was heated to a temperature far higher than that of the ordinary steam bath. The bathers sat in that heat on the top benches until perspiration was flowing freely from their bodies.

When they were streaming with perspiration, they switched their bodies with aromatic switches made from the leafy, tender branches of birch trees, which were gathered in the spring so that the young leaves would not fall off even when used for innumerable switchings. The switching stimulated the bathers' circulation, then when their bodies were tingling all over from the combined effects of the heat and the switching, they came down from the top benches to start a rigorous soap and water scrubbing. This was followed by a brisk rinsing with cold water. In the old country in the winter young Finns followed their baths by a quick roll in the snow outside the bathhouse before dressing, but that was not a common practice in Lanesville. The cold water rinse or the roll in the snow hastened the drying of the perspiring bodies of the bathers by closing their skin pores, and thus provided protection when they emerged into the outside temperature after dressing.

Saturday was the traditional time for bathing in the *saunas* in Lanesville, and then there was great stir and activity in the Finnish community. The wood fires to heat the stones in the bathhouses had to be started at daybreak. Soon smoke was curling from the chimneys of the *saunas* and filled the air of the neighborhood with its exhilarating odor. By early afternoon the baths were ready for use and then one would see whole families walking to them, carrying bags of clean clothes into which to change after the bath. Neighbors chatted jovially with each other while waiting their turns at the *saunas,* and then after the bath they walked home in high spirits, with rosy, shining faces, ready for another week of hard work.

Cleanliness is an outstanding Finnish characteristic, and over one of the *saunas* the following inscription, printed in both English and Finnish, was placed: "The Church and the Sauna are holy places—cleanliness is next to Godliness."[10]

Although the *saunas* now have been largely supplanted in Lanesville by conventional bathing facilities, some of the people of Finnish descent who were brought up in the *saunas* still feel that it is impossible to get really clean anywhere else.

World War I practically marked the end of the quarry industry on Cape Ann. For some years now only one quarry has been in operation on the Cape. The industry fell victim to technological changes. New and improved methods for the manufacture of cement were introduced just before the start

---

[10] For this description of the *sauna*, we are indebted to Mrs. Evelyn E. Parsons of Lanesville.

of World War I, and the labor cost of putting up a building with reinforced concrete was so much less than the cost of erecting a building with granite blocks that granite construction, except for occasional trim, was largely discontinued. The rapid increase in the number of automobiles in use, which occurred at about the same time, called for smooth streets, and the market for paving stones vanished. Thus even an industry founded on bedrock could not withstand the force of technological change.

While all but one of the quarry pits on Cape Ann are idle and silent, many vestiges of their former activity still remain. Around several pits lie the rotting ruins of huge derricks. Here and there are coils and lengths of steel cable with which the derricks once were anchored to the ledges and in which not even a junk man now is interested. And in the ledges are huge bridles to which the lower ends of the cables formerly were fastened. Along the ridge back of Lanesville and Folly Cove, the bed of the old quarry railroad provides a smooth path for tramping, away from the busy highway. Then, too, there are the stone piers from Pigeon Cove to Bay View, which were built to facilitate the loading of the sloops on which the granite building stones and paving blocks were transported to their markets. And, here and there, especially at Halibut Point, are the huge grout piles, where waste stone from the quarries was dumped.

Some of the pits are as open and as bare as they were on the evening after the last workman picked up his drills and hammer and headed for a new job. In some instances the sides of the pits rise forty or fifty feet with straight variously tinted faces revealing the layers and faults in their geological structure.

151

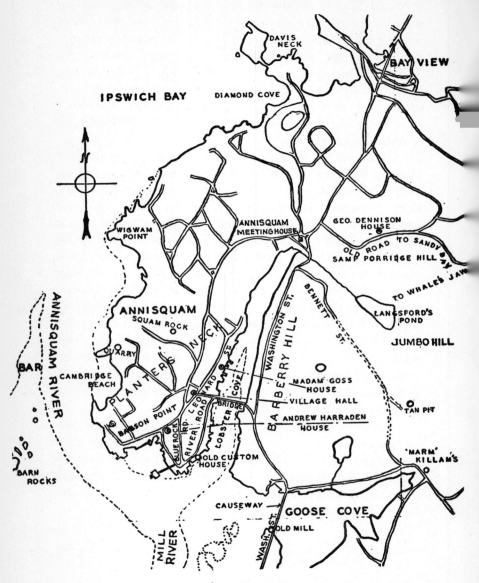

ANNISQUAM

Annisquam

ANNISQUAM, since the middle of the seventeenth century, has been one of the distinctive communities on Cape Ann. The village always has had an individuality of its own, an individuality which has not become blurred with age. It was at Planters Neck in Annisquam that a group of colonists are supposed to have set up a fishing stage in 1631, and they were among the first permanent settlers on the Cape. Just where they lived, however, and how long they stayed are facts that never were recorded. But the record is clear that Edward Harraden, presumably from Ipswich, established a residence on Planters Neck in 1657, and that he soon was joined by other settlers. Thereafter the village grew alongside the other settlements on the Cape, but with its own individual characteristics.

The Pilgrims called the place "Agassquam" but on a map of Massachusetts drawn in 1633 it was designated as "Wonasquam." The latter name appeared on a few other maps and records of voyages during the next few years. Then it became "Annis Squam" and before long "Annisquam." "Squam" was an Indian word, it is said, descriptive of the harbor inside the mouth of the river. Whether the forepart of the ultimate name of the village was adapted from the title of the Cape, or whether it derived from some other source or from a mere colloquialism is now entirely a matter of conjecture. From the early days down to the present time, the village commonly has been known among the people of Cape Ann as "Squam."

Most of the local place names in Annisquam, such as Lobster Cove, Goose Cove, Madam Goss Hill, Barberry Hill, Samp Porridge Hill, Jumbo Hill, Wigwam Point, and Diamond Cove, apparently originated from natural features, unrecorded episodes, local celebrities, or village folklore. Squam Rock, however, which stands high in the old pasture above Lighthouse Beach, and has been the climbing delight of generations of Annisquam children, got its present name by accident. It once was known as "Squaw Rock," since an Indian girl was said to have been fatally injured there by falling or by throwing herself despondently from its top. When the first picture postcards of this region were printed, one of them portrayed that famous landmark, but the printer assumed that an error had been made in the spelling so he changed "Squaw" to "Squam."

When the residents of Annisquam were authorized in 1728 to become a separate parish, that parish—the Third—extended from the neighborhood of Goose Cove to Halibut Point and Sandy Bay. When the Fifth Parish was carved out in 1754, the scope of the Third Parish was correspondingly reduced. As villages developed at Lanesville and Bay View in the nineteenth century, those districts also ceased to be part of Annisquam, and its area became limited to the region neighboring Lobster Cove and Goose Cove. That is its present status.

The individuality of Annisquam derives, in some measure, from its unique topographical features. In the glacial period, and perhaps for several centuries thereafter, the major part of what is now Annisquam consisted of two islands. From Diamond Cove the sea ran up to where the village church now stands and then divided. One arm ran in by Langsford's Pond and through the ravine between Barberry Hill and Jumbo Hill to Goose Cove and the river. Sand like that found on the seashore can still be seen in the bed of the brook which flows through the southern end of that ravine.

The second arm of the sea ran from the site of the village church through Lobster Cove to the river, and thus made Planters Neck a separate island.

On the Annisquam shore, from Diamond Cove to Mill River, rocky promontories alternate with coves and inlets, several of which have good beaches, and above the shore rise ledges and wooded uplands with several magnificent stands of pine, oak, and hemlock.

The contour of the Annisquam shore is such that it provides a great variety of vistas. From one point only a broad expanse of the ocean is seen. From another, the waters of the bay are framed by sand dunes and smooth beaches. From still another, the view is of the river, winding through hills and marshes. At other points various combinations of these vistas are to be had. And from a spot such as the top of Barberry Hill there is a broad view not only of the river but of the West Parish shore and its rugged terrain.

When a heavy sea is running outside, the foam-crested billows breaking on the bar at the mouth of the river, and along the Essex and Ipswich shores, provide a spectacle of nature's mighty force. Occasionally on a cold day in the winter, the inner sections of the bay and the river become filled with crunching masses of ice which glisten sparkling white against the blue water in the rays of a setting sun. And in the summer the waters of the bay vary their colors in shades of blue, gray, green, and brown, from day to day and sometimes from hour to hour, with changes in the tide, the wind, and the sky above.

The early settlers probably were less impressed by the picturesqueness of Annisquam, however, than by the strategic advantages of its location. It was, first of all, a harbor which provided good anchorage for seventeenth-century sailing craft. Although the bar at the mouth of the river was dangerous to cross at low tide in stormy weather, the harbor otherwise was easy of access and well protected. In fact it was the best harbor on the long stretch of coast between the northern shore of Cape Ann and Portsmouth, New Hampshire. Moreover, although the road to The Green by land was long and tiresome, the distances from Annisquam to The Green and to the Riverdale mills by water were short, and after the Cut was opened, boats could travel readily from Annisquam to Gloucester Harbor and thence up the coast to Salem and Boston. Thus Annisquam had the advantage of water transportation.

In the early eighteenth century a ferry for people and vehicles was put into operation between Annisquam and the West Parish shore of the river. The landing on the Annisquam side was at Babson's Point, at the end of Leonard Street. From the landing on the opposite shore (now Wingaersheek Beach) a county road was built to connect with the Essex Road. Since Leonard Street connected, at the head of Lobster Cove, with the old road through the woods to Sandy Bay, the opening of the 'Squam ferry provided a land route, much shorter than by way of the Cut, from all eastern and northern Cape Ann to Essex and Ipswich. The ferry thus gave Annisquam distinct advantages for land as well as water travel.

During the seventeenth century, from the time of the first settlement until about the end of the century, Annisquam, like the rest of Cape Ann, grew slowly in population. Farming, wood-coasting, and small-scale fishing provided the inhabitants with their livelihood. Then, at the turn of the century, when the village at Gloucester Harbor began to bustle with a new activity, and shortly before the settlement of nearby Dogtown took place, the port of Annisquam also became much more active, and for a period of ten years, at least, it actually rivaled Gloucester Harbor as a shipping and trading post. Although it subsequently was outstripped by Gloucester, Annisquam continued for nearly two hundred years to have an active overseas trade.

156

Annisquam occasionally suffered from disturbances by pirates, and during the Revolutionary War and the War of 1812 it was visited by British warships.

For about six months in the latter part of 1723 and early 1724, for instance, a gang of pirates headed by John Phillips had been terrorizing the New England coast and had seized thirty-four vessels, including four from Gloucester. In April 1724, the gang captured a new Annisquam sloop, the *Squirrel*, on its first voyage. The *Squirrel* was under the command of Captain Andrew Harraden of Annisquam. She had not been completely finished when she sailed, and after her capture, the pirates put Captain Harraden and his crew to work on completing the job. At an opportune moment, however, he and his men used their tools to overpower the pirates. Phillips and four of his men were killed; the other members of the pirate crew surrendered; and Captain Harraden thus regained control of his sloop.

When the *Squirrel* sailed back to Lobster Cove, the head of Phillips was hanging on her mast. The bodies of the other pirates who had been killed were strung up for display, it has been said, on Hangman's Island in the Annisquam River.

One of the notable British raids occurred on August 5, 1775. On that date the British sloop-of-war *Falcon*, which subsequently attempted to burn the village at Gloucester Harbor, came into Ipswich Bay and headed for Annisquam. The captain of the *Falcon* first sent a barge ashore at Coffin's Beach, across the river from Annisquam, to obtain a supply of fresh mutton from Major Coffin's pasture. Major Coffin, however, with the help of five or six neighbors, kept up such an active rifle fire from behind the sand dunes that the raiders were driven off without their mutton. The barge then was sent into Annisquam Harbor to seize a schooner which was supposed to have on board a cargo of West India merchandise. When the Britishers boarded the schooner, however, they found that the "merchandise" was a load of sand. After those frustrating experiences, it is understandable that Captain Lindsay of the *Falcon* was in such a bad temper when he sailed back to Gloucester Harbor.

During the War of 1812 British vessels again preyed on American shipping around Cape Ann, and Annisquam vessels were among those captured or destroyed. One of the families victimized was that of Gideon Lane, Jr.

On June 5, 1814, Gideon Lane III left Boston in the *Welcome Return,* a vessel owned by his father, with a cargo of groceries for Hallowell, Maine, on the Kennebec River. When he sailed from Boston, he had only his brother Oliver with him as crew. He needed a larger crew for working the vessel up the coast. Hence he headed for Annisquam to pick up two more men. When he arrived off Gloucester Harbor, he was informed by the captain of a fishing vessel that no British warship was in sight, although one was known to have been lurking recently around the Cape.

In the evening, soon after the fishing vessel had been spoken by young Lane, a heavy fog set in, and he decided to try to get around the Cape under its cover. He ran his ship close along shore, going inside Milk Island, through Straits-mouth Gap, and across Sandy Bay to Pigeon Cove. Shortly before daybreak, when the *Welcome Return* was off Andrews Point just beyond Pigeon Cove, a tender from a British frigate suddenly appeared alongside and took possession of the vessel. The tender, under the command of Lieutenant Napier, had been laying in wait for just such prey.

Young Lane's father learned of the capture immediately —there was a grapevine even in such primitive country—and obtained permission to go out to the frigate, the *Nymphe,* to negotiate for the release of his sons and the vessel. Captain Epworth, in command of the *Nymphe,* agreed to accept $3500 as a ransom price, and after a couple of trips to Boston, the Lanes succeeded in raising that amount and a release was effected. While the negotiations were in progress, how-

ever, either Gideon III or his father had to remain on the
Nymphe as hostage.

On June 13, before the negotiations for the ransom of the
Welcome Return had been concluded, the *Nymphe*'s tender
was sent into Annisquam Harbor to raid the shipping there.
During that raid, the Lane family had a second encounter
with Lieutenant Napier.

So many inaccurate statements have been circulated
about the episode that it seems advisable here to quote the
story as it was recorded by Lieutenant Napier himself in his
journal.

> Went into the harbour of Annisquam, burned two
> vessels, let one go because she belonged to an old man
> who had a wife and eight children and had lost $20,000
> within two years. Destroying this, his last, would have
> ruined him. Spared another, as I told them, because her
> name was the *Federalist* but the truth is she was aground
> and I could neither get her off or set fire to her there,
> without burning a number of poor people's houses.
> These little things, when constantly done, may cause
> distrust, or heighten that which already has broken out
> between parties. Saw a beautiful girl, sister to the people
> we took in the *Welcome Return;* assured her and her old
> mother of the safety of her brothers. Took out a beauti-
> ful sebaque [Chebacco] boat, called the *Rambler,* loaded
> with dry salt fish.[11]

The beautiful girl whom Lieutenant Napier saw was
Clara Lane, seventeen years old, and the *Federalist* was the
property of Captain Lane who also owned the *Welcome Re-
turn* which was being held for ransom. The wharf where the
Federalist was aground was on Lobster Cove in front of the
Lane residence on Leonard Street, the Madam Goss house.

---

11 *New England Blockaded in 1814,* The Journal of Henry Edward
Napier, Lieutenant in H. M. S. *Nymphe,* Walter Muir Whitehill,
ed. (Salem, Mass., Peabody Museum, 1939), p. 25.

The wharf was a couple of hundred yards above where the bridge now crosses Lobster Cove.

In telling the Lanes that he was sparing the *Federalist* because of her name, Lieutenant Napier was indulging in a sort of psychological warfare, as it nowadays would be called. The Federalist party in the United States and especially in New England had been against the declaration of war with England in 1812 and the British, as Lieutenant Napier indicated, liked to take advantage of opportunities to sow distrust and to aggravate the bitter feeling between the Federalists and the war-supporting Democrats. In this case the ruse worked, for in the *Essex Register*,[12] published two days after the raid, Lieutenant Napier's statement that he was sparing the *Federalist* because of her name was accepted at face value, with no mention of the fact that the vessel was aground.

The report in the *Essex Register* gave further details about the vessels burned and captured and concluded its item with the statement that after the raid the tender "steered in the direction of Ipswich Bay, and a considerable firing was afterwards heard." That firing apparently was from the muskets of Lieutenant Napier's men, for in his journal he recorded: "In passing down the coast saw some cattle grazing. Went on shore intending to take off as many as we could get. They run too fast, so we were obliged to make use of our muskets and brought one down to the boat. This kind of thing pleases sailors amazingly. A fine little girl, seeing what was going on at some distance and fearful for her flock, came and drove them away in the face of about eighteen armed men and a great gun.——Two fat sheep in addition to the above was the only fruit of our raid."[13]

Although the records on this point are not wholly clear, it appears to us that it was during the raid on Lobster Cove, when the *Federalist* was spared, that some of the British sea-

---

12 Napier, *op. cit.*, appendix, p. 60.
13 *Ibid.*, p. 25.

men went to Dogtown in search of Col. William Pearce.
They did not find him, but they did make off with a couple
of his sheep, and the "two fat sheep" to which Lt. Napier
referred in the quotation just cited probably were from Col.
Pearce's flock.

The Chebacco boat *Rambler*, captured by the British
in the raid on Annisquam Harbor, was fitted out as another
tender for the *Nymphe,* "the owner undertaking to pilot her
on the promise of her being restored."

Shortly after that raid, the residents of Annisquam built
a fort on Babson's Point, which commanded the entrance to
the river at its narrowest stretch, and mounted two six-pound
cannon there. That put an end to raids on Annisquam Harbor by British boats.

For about twenty years after the end of the War of 1812,
the port of Annisquam continued to be a busy place. Ships
were built at various yards on the shore of Lobster Cove, even
at the very head of the cove, where the water then was deep
enough at high tide to float the vessels when they were
launched. And Annisquam shipowners engaged extensively
in fishing and in foreign trade. Annisquam vessels carried
fish, grain, and flour to Dutch Guiana, for example, and
brought back sugar, molasses, coffee, and curios. Annisquam
vessels also carried cotton from New Orleans to France and
England and tobacco from Virginia to Germany.

At one time, during the height of the shipbuilding boom
in the 1829-32 period, seventy-five vessels of various sizes
made Annisquam their home port, two of the largest fleet
owners being George Norwood & Son and Gustavus Griffin.
That was a prosperous period for Annisquam and in the ten
years following 1828, the number of dwelling houses in the
village doubled, from thirty to about sixty. The prosperity
came to an end, however, with the Panic of 1837. Some of
the local shipowners and traders had been borrowing heavily
from the banks, and when they were unable to renew their

loans, they suffered losses from which their businesses never recovered.

After 1837 Annisquam declined as a commercial port, partly of course, because it could not accommodate the ships of larger size which by then were coming into general use.

In addition to these maritime undertakings, other industries also were started in Annisquam, some to supply local needs and others to cater to outside markets. In a swamp in the ravine which extends from Langsford's Pond to the neighborhood of Goose Cove, for example, was a tan pit, started in the early 1700's by Jesse Saville, who had a farm near the old road through the woods to Sandy Bay. One of the entrances to the tan pit was through the Saville pasture by a way now known as Hutchins Court. Another entrance to the tan pit was by means of a road from Goose Cove. An old stone culvert across the brook below the tan pit still marks that approach. A third means of reaching the tan pit was by way of a road which branched off from the road over the hill to 'Squam (Bennett Street) about halfway between Goose Cove and the head of Lobster Cove. That branch road was shown on the old maps as Saville Lane, but it came to be better known as the Tanyard Path. The hill along the side of which the Tanyard Path runs is very steep. It also is picturesque, with high ledges, big boulders, and magnificent trees.

The tan pit was dug in the center of the swamp, and white pine stakes were driven into the ground, with cross pieces on which the hides could be hung to be soaked and treated to convert them into leather. The brook flowing through the swamp supplied water for the tanning process, and bark from the oak and hemlock trees growing nearby furnished the tanning materials.

After the tan pit went out of use, the swamp filled in; the pine tanning frames were covered with peat and water; and for over a hundred years all the traces of the tan pit were obscured. Then in the fall of 1914, during an exceptionally dry period, a long-burning forest fire consumed the peat and loam in the swamp and brought the stakes of the old tanning frames again into view. Now the forest has grown up once more and again the remnants of that old industry have disappeared into the swamp.

Like other neighborhoods on the Cape where water power was available, the 'Squammers had a gristmill. It was located at the head of Goose Cove, where the old dam and sluiceway are still to be seen. The water for power was supplied by three brooks which merged above the millpond. One brook flowed alongside what is now Dennison Street from a Dogtown swamp. A second brook flowed westward from still another large Dogtown swamp, and the other brook was the one which flowed through the swamp where the tan pit was located. The mill was first known as the "Norwood Mill." After its operation was taken over by a Mr. Baker who married a Norwood daughter, it was called "Baker's Mill." Subsequently it became known as "Marm Killam's Sluiceway." We have no information, however, about Marm Killam or when she took over the mill.

When the dam and the causeway were built across the lower end of Goose Cove, where it joins Lobster Cove, Marm Killam's mill was superseded by a tide mill located on the causeway. The dam and causeway were built in 1834. The old mill on the causeway, which was both a gristmill and a sawmill, is still standing. Grain to be ground was brought to the mill not only by cart but also by small vessels which could tie up alongside the mill. The mill was built by Captain Gideon Lane III of Annisquam, James Babson of Newbury, and Addison Center of Gloucester. Captain Lane in his memoirs stated that the mill was a total loss to the builders, presumably as a result of the Panic of 1837. It then passed into the hands of the Hodgkins family who operated it for many years.

163

The construction of the dam and causeway at Goose Cove provided a substantially shorter and easier land route from Riverdale to Annisquam. Then in 1847 a bridge was built across Lobster Cove which made it possible to reach Planters Neck without going all the way around the head of the Cove. The state legislature had passed an act in 1832 which gave certain individuals the right to build a toll bridge across Lobster Cove, but the project was not carried through at that time. In 1847 a similar act was passed and the bridge was built. In the bridge there was a draw, twenty-two feet wide, which made it possible for vessels to pass through the bridge to the upper cove, and navigation for the full length of the cove was preserved.

The bridge was a toll bridge, but persons hauling coal, passing to or from a place of public worship, going to and from military duty or to and from funerals, and children going to and from school were exempted from paying tolls. Otherwise the tolls were: one cent for each foot passenger, five cents for each horse, chaise, chair or sulky; eight cents for each coach, phaeton, chariot, or other four-wheeled carriage drawn by two or more horses; twelve and a half cents for every wagon, cart, or other carriage drawn by not more than two horses; six cents for a cart drawn by more than four oxen; two cents each for horses, mules, and neat cattle; and four cents per dozen for sheep and swine. That schedule of tolls is indicative of some features of life in 'Squam a century ago.

The town of Gloucester took over the bridge in 1861 and made it a public way.

While shipbuilding was booming in Annisquam (1828-30) a quarry also was opened on the ocean side of the hill back of the Village Hall (Adams Hill). It was not a profitable venture and was operated for only a few years. It did, however, yield several landmarks.

The site of the quarry is still marked by scars in the side of the hill, and the stone pier which was built out from the shore for convenience in loading granite on the barges for shipment also remains as a landmark of the venture. But the most notable change resulting from the operation of the quarry took place around Lobster Cove.

When the quarry was opened, Leonard Street was the main street in the village. Another public way, Blue Rocks Road, led down over what is now Arlington Street to the rocks on the shore from which the road got its name. But there was no River Road; the westerly shore of the cove, from Babson's Point to the head of the cove, was mostly beach, with occasional ledges. A footpath ran along the shore, and of course there were lanes and paths leading from the houses on Leonard Street and Blue Rocks Road to the water front. After the quarry came into operation, grout, the quarry stone which was too irregular in shape for commercial purposes, was used to build the walls and piers which now line much of the shore of the cove. That made possible the construction of River Road, later called Curve Street, and eventually re-named River Road. Thus the present-day appearance of Annisquam was profoundly affected by the grout from the quarry on Adams Hill.

In addition to the foregoing industries, several other small-scale enterprises were operated in Annisquam during the shipbuilding era. There were several blacksmith shops, for example, which not only took care of the local farmers' needs but also furnished the iron work for the vessels being constructed on Lobster Cove.

For two hundred years after the settlement began at Planters Neck, the village of Annisquam grew in self-sufficiency. By 1830 it had its own industries and shops, its own church, its own school, its own doctor, its own post office, its own entertainment hall, and its own band. It was a well-rounded little community, in which many of the families were related by marriage. Then around 1840, at the time when the local shipbuilding industry was tapering off and the Adams

Hill quarry was petering out, newcomers began to infiltrate into the village. These were followed by others, in greater and greater numbers, and presently new means of local transportation also contributed to a social and economic transformation of the village.

At the time of the Civil War, Leonard Street was still the main residential and business street in the village. The business establishments located there, between Chester Square and the Village Hall, included a lumber shed, the village hay scales, the Deluge Fire Engine House, the "Mutton Shop," the post office and variety store where the village folk gathered each evening to receive their mail and pass along the local news, a cooper shop in which, during the winter, the owner made mackerel barrels, the coach-line stable, a fish market, and a grocery store. Between the Village Hall and the wharf opposite the Harraden houses, were more residences, the village schoolhouse, a blacksmith shop, and a couple of stables. On River Road there was another blacksmith shop and a store, the latter being located near the Blue Rocks.

The transformation of Annisquam from a self-sufficient little village into one which was primarily residential came about gradually and was caused chiefly by three major factors. One factor was the decline in shipbuilding and foreign trade at Lobster Cove, to which reference already has been made. A second factor was the opening up of easier means of travel to the shops and stores at Gloucester Harbor. And the third factor was the growing demand for summer residential accommodations in Annisquam.

The building of the causeway at Goose Cove was the first big improvement for land travel from 'Squam to Gloucester. As soon as the causeway was built, a short stretch of smooth road supplanted the long, rough, hilly route over Bennett Street and Pilgrim Hill. Soon after the causeway was constructed, furthermore, a stagecoach line began to provide regular service between the village and Gloucester Harbor, where it connected with the Boston and Salem coaches, the Boston steamer, and soon with the railroad trains. At the time of the Civil War the coach line was making three round trips a day to Gloucester. The coach line was operated by Annisquam men. At one time one of their neighbors undertook to operate a competing coach service, known as the "opposition line." Behind that competition there probably lies a spicy story of neighborhood conflict, but it seems never to have got on record. When the bridge was built across Lobster Cove, it further facilitated travel from Planters Neck to Gloucester.

Near the end of the nineteenth century, the trolley line was extended along Washington Street on the easterly side of Lobster Cove. That superseded the coach line and provided more rapid and more frequent transportation service. Then after World War I, automobiles and buses took the place of the trolley cars, with the result that a trip from 'Squam to Main Street in Gloucester could be made in fifteen or twenty minutes, whereas for two hundred years after Planters Neck was settled such a trip had required several hours.

Almost as soon as the causeway at Goose Cove was built and the coach line came into operation, summer visitors began to appear in Annisquam. The first of those visitors were accommodated in private dwellings as boarders. By the time of the Civil War, some of the visitors were beginning to purchase houses in the village for summer residences. As the invasion of the "furriners" continued, most of the buildings along Leonard Street which had been used for business purposes were converted into dwellings, and the village business district was almost eliminated. The next step of the invaders was to convert all the pastures along the shore of the bay, from Babson's Point to Diamond Cove, into sites for summer residences. The only pasture land not so converted was the 'Squam Rock pasture back of Light House Beach. Four small hotels were built, two of which later burned down. And thus Annisquam became one of the major centers of the summer business on the Cape. After World War II, however, more and more of the summer residences in Annisquam began to be converted into year-round homes, with the result that again the village seemed to be undergoing a major change. Descendants of the old families continued to reside in the village, but they were being outnumbered by the newcomers.

During all these changes in the village, some of the old landmarks have remained and several new ones have been added. One of the oldest landmarks in the village is the Andrew Harraden house at the corner of Leonard Street and River Road, built about 1700. It was there that the pirate vanquisher, Captain Andrew Harraden, lived. His daughter Betsy married Thomas Saville, a son of Jesse Saville, and the Thomas Savilles kept a tavern for many years in that old Harraden House. In fact, the house also is known as "Saville's Tavern."

The owners of the tavern at one time had two Negro slaves, Lem and Cato, who were especially fond of chicken. In one instance, Lem and Cato helped themselves surreptitiously to two fowls, which they hid under the attic floor until they might find an opportunity for feasting. Unfortunately, before that opportunity arose, their booty began to smell so strongly that it was discovered and the culprits exposed.

In the War of 1812 the Andrew Harraden house was used as a barracks for soldiers. Later, for many years it was a shoeshop, then a boardinghouse, and eventually again a private residence. James Jewett was the operator of the shoeshop. The footwear which he produced was known as "red-jack boots." The boots were nearly knee-high, made of fine, heavy leather, guaranteed watertight, and reddish brown in color. The leather was cut in the shop in Annisquam and then "put out" to local farmers' wives to be sewed. During the Civil War about sixty people were thus employed. The boots were distributed by a Boston wholesale firm and found a wide market among sailors, fishermen, and farmers. Like other "cow-hide boots," however, the red-jack boots of Annisquam were superseded about sixty years ago by rubber boots.

Diagonally across Leonard Street from the Andrew Harraden house is the Edward Harraden House (14 Leonard Street) which also seems to have been used for a tavern at one time. Both these houses were built at about the same date.

On one of the piers on River Road stands the so-called "Old Custom House." Actually it is only an old fishhouse, now converted into a summer residence. That pier also was the site of another small industry when the fish business was thriving in Annisquam. One Captain Wheeler had a large kettle and press there, in which he manufactured pogie oil for sale to tanneries.

Even though the Old Custom House did not figure in the episodes, Annisquam did have experience with customs collectors shortly before the Revolutionary War when all such agents of the Crown were especially unpopular. In September 1768, Samuel Fellows, who recently had been appointed local customs collector, was deemed by some of the people in Annisquam to be too assiduous in the performance of his duties. Consequently one evening a party of men from the village set out in search for him. He then was living in Jesse Saville's house, near Jumbo Hill, just off the old road through the woods to Sandy Bay. Mr. Fellows fled that place before the pursuing party arrived. In their efforts to persuade Mr. Saville to reveal the whereabouts of their quarry, they knocked him down and threatened him with more severe punishment, but they did not succeed in finding Mr. Fellows and never did apprehend him.

Mr. Fellows left town immediately and when Mr. Saville accepted an appointment as his replacement as customs collector, Mr. Saville's popularity with the townspeople became even lower. On the evening of March 23, 1770, a year and a half after the mob had threatened Mr. Saville in their search for Mr. Fellows, a party of men disguised as Negroes and Indians again visited Mr. Saville, seized him, and rode him on a rail to Gloucester Harbor, where he was further maltreated. The governor of the colony was highly incensed by this abuse of his tax collector and he addressed a protest to the General Court. The only member of the party who ever was identified, however, was Dr. Plummer's mulatto servant George, from the neighborhood of The Green, who was tried and convicted of having been a participant. George refused, however, to reveal the names of any other members of the Saville kidnapping party, and he persisted in his silence even when the officers of the law took him to Salem in March 1772, hung a halter around his neck, and stood him on the gallows for an hour. This episode, of course, was part of the prelude to the American Revolution, and it shows that the resistance which so irritated King George the Third and his minions was not confined solely to Boston and the Boston Tea Party. Gloucester and Annisquam also had their resistance affairs.

Despite the treatment accorded to Jesse Saville as customs collector, he was one of the most active men in the community. He ran his farm, coopered barrels, made ox-bows and scythe snaths, built walls and cellars, wrote deeds, administered estates, and operated the tan pit.

Another old landmark, on the point between Goose Cove and Lobster Cove, is the Hyatt House, said to have been built in 1664 by Francis Norwood. In 1878 the house was purchased by Professor Alpheus Hyatt for a summer residence, and there he started a marine biological laboratory. In 1881 the laboratory was moved across Lobster Cove to the Gustavus Griffin house (47 River Road) and still later to Woods Hole on Cape Cod. Thus the famed Woods Hole Marine Biological Laboratory had its beginnings in Annisquam.

Professor Hyatt had a 58-foot, two-masted schooner, the *Arethusa,* in which he made cruises for biological research.

He also owned a catboat with nearly square ends, bearing a name lettered in Chinese characters. By 'Squammers the catboat was nicknamed "Hyatt's Old Tea Chest."

The "Old Castle" on Leonard Street, about halfway between Chester Square and the bridge, was built in 1717 by Joseph Yorke. It was on the shore in front of the Old Castle that the first wharf and warehouse were built in the village.

The "Madam Goss House" also on Leonard Street (now No. 47) was built in 1728 by Captain Thomas Goss. A few years later Richard Goss became the proprietor and his wife, the former Elizabeth Harraden, was the "Madam Goss" whose name became permanently attached to the house and to the hill where it stands. Apparently it was because of the high esteem in which she was held by her neighbors that her name was thus perpetuated.

The Madam Goss House was bought about 1790 by Captain Gideon Lane Jr., whose family and ships figured in the raids by the British *Nymphe*'s tender. Captain Lane enlarged the house and operated a tavern in it for about twenty-five years. After 1815 it was solely a private residence until in the late years of the nineteenth century it became a clubhouse for the Regulator Club, a fun-loving local organization.[14] One of the diversions of the Regulator Club was to shoot sky-rockets up the chimney. Another was to initiate a member by blindfolding him and then running him up the front stairs and down the back stairs until he had become utterly bewildered.

The last meeting of the Regulator Club, it may be added, was held in the Village Hall, with admission-paying guests. On that occasion one of the members was lowered down an imitation chimney into a tub of water and then branded on his backsides with a hot iron. Before the stunt began, however, a thick piece of pigskin had been placed in the seat of his

---

14 Much of this information about the Madam Goss House was obtained from a memorandum written by S. Foster Damon, the current owner.

trousers, so that it was the leather rather than his hide which scorched and smoked and smelled when the branding iron was applied. The spectators were not aware of the pigskin and two women in the audience fainted. The commotion which resulted from that episode led to the disbanding of the Regulator Club. Several members of the club were artists.

The site where the Madam Goss House was located previously had been a summer camping ground for Indians, as evidenced by relics uncovered during later excavations. Those presumably were the same Indians who held clam and lobster picnics, so the legend goes, around the five springs on the top of Adams Hill which Dr. Isaac Adams had walled-in to make the "Gold Fish Pond" when he built the road to his summer residence close by.

George Dennison, who built a house on the old road through the woods to Sandy Bay, about a mile from the head of Lobster Cove, also operated a store there. It was opened in 1732 and Mr. Dennison sold groceries, woolen cloth, boots, fishing gear, and four brands of rum. No license was required in those days for selling liquor, and Mr. Dennison's store was only one of several retail establishments in 'Squam where rum could be bought.

In the eighteenth century the spot where the Dennison store was located was not so out of the way as it may seem to be today. It was on a main thoroughfare between Planters Neck and Sandy Bay. It also was only about a mile from Dogtown, by way of the Whale's Jaw path, and many men then living in Dogtown worked on the fishing vessels or in the shipyards at Lobster Cove. A road from Goose Cove (Dennison Street plus a section of road not now in use) also led into the Sandy Bay road near the Dennison store. Hence it was an eighteenth-century traffic center. The George Dennison house is still standing, in excellent repair.

The first schoolhouse in Annisquam was erected in 1798, on the Blue Rocks Road near Leonard Street. It was used as

172

a school for thirty-six years and then converted into a residence. For many years now it has been a summer place,
known as the "Bunny Cottage." The schoolhouse was replaced by a larger one, located on land near the Village Hall.

The Village Hall was built in 1828 for a Baptist meetinghouse. Captain Epes Davis was the preacher—on Sundays;
on weekdays he was a shipbuilder. Some years later the building was sold to Timothy Smith who renamed it "Mechanics
Hall," and made it into a hall for public gatherings. The
front part of the building was used for a variety store and
eventually the post office also was located there. To the rear
of the hall, Mr. Smith built an addition which was utilized
as a sail loft. When the sail-making business declined in the
village, the sail loft was converted into a clubroom and became the headquarters of the Blue Ribbon Reform Club.
Subsequently the main building was owned by John Davis,
who operated the post office and a restaurant there.

About 1900 the building was purchased by three women
who set up a perpetual trust under the terms of which the hall
was to be used in the public interest of the village. In addition
to housing the village library and post office, the Village Hall
also provides a place for the holding of the monthly suppers of
the Leonard Club (a local men's club) and a large hall for
village meetings, dinners, and entertainments. For more than
a hundred years the Village Hall has contributed substantially
to the maintenance of the individuality of Annisquam.

For several years just before the Civil War, there was a
bandstand in the schoolhouse yard, next to the Village Hall,
where the Mechanics Brass Band gave concerts in the summer.
The band had over fifteen members, all local talent. It was
disbanded in 1861 and never reassembled after the end of the
Civil War.

In addition to the landmarks already mentioned, there
are several other houses in Annisquam notable chiefly because some celebrity once "slept there."

In 1878 Winslow Homer, one of the great American artists, lived for about a year on Cape Ann, for a time on Ten Pound Island in Gloucester Harbor and then on Leonard Street (No. 4) in Annisquam. Gloucester vessels and Cape Ann fishermen thus became the subjects of some of his best-known paintings. One of the men who often posed as a model for Mr. Homer was a nearby Annisquam neighbor, Oliver W. Ingersoll, who lived in the cabin of a derelict schooner, the *Belle Gilmore*.

The *Belle Gilmore* was one of the last vessels which sailed out of Annisquam in the nineteenth century, and after her sailing days were over, she lay for some years tied up at a dock in the cove near the junction of Leonard Street and River Road. In fact, she was berthed so close to the street that her bowsprit extended out over River Road—a picturesque setting for a picturesque character, which obviously appealed to Mr. Homer.

In 1896, while Rudyard Kipling was in Gloucester to absorb Cape Ann atmosphere, to familiarize himself with Cape Ann fishermen and their lives, and to write *Captains Courageous*, he spent some of his time in Annisquam, living in the house at the corner of Leonard Street and Cambridge Avenue, next to the erstwhile residence of Winslow Homer. A small Annisquam boat, *I Am Here,* suggested the name *We're Here,* which Kipling gave to the fishing vessel in *Captains Courageous.*

Immediately after World War I, Mr. and Mrs. Walter Camp were guests for five summers in the house in which Kipling had lived. To his generation Mr. Camp was known as the Father of American football. He was most instrumental in the formulation of the code under which the game developed, and he also was the first and for many years the only selector of All-American teams.

Among the many other notable summer residents of Annisquam was General Sam Chamberlain, adventurer, sol-

174

dier, public servant, and artist. General Chamberlain lived for several summers in a house on Arlington Street (No. 20) and purchased two other houses on the opposite side of the street for his daughters.

The ell of the house occupied by General Chamberlain on Arlington Street was built about 1670 by a man who had been shipwrecked on the bar at the mouth of the river. He used timbers and other materials from the wreck for building the ell, and the old cabin doors from the wreck are still in the house.

Nowadays only a few lobster boats and other commercial fishing craft are tied up in Lobster Cove, but in the summer it is crowded almost beyond its capacity by pleasure craft. The Annisquam Yacht Club is one of the most active sailing organizations on the New England coast, and in years when the tuna are running in Ipswich Bay, Lobster Cove is a mecca for sports fishermen.

175

The River

THE ANNISQUAM RIVER is a predominant natural feature of Cape Ann, and like the sea around the Cape, the river constantly has affected the daily lives of the people who have lived near its shores. Even after the first rough, hilly roads were opened, the river provided the early settlers with a convenient means of travel and transportation from The Green to Gloucester Harbor and Planters Neck. And for fishing craft and coastwise transients it furnished a sheltered connection between Gloucester Harbor and Ipswich Bay. The river was a barrier, to be sure, to easy travel between the West Parish and the island section of the Cape, but that inconvenience was far more than offset by the other advantages it yielded.

The sand flats on the shores of the river, furthermore, supplied an abundance of clams for food and bait for fishermen. And the broad expanse of the marshes along the river and its estuaries afforded attractive spawning grounds for numerous varieties of fish and sanctuaries for water fowl.

During the last hundred years the river not only has continued to be an active route for commercial water traffic, but also has contributed notably to the attraction of summer visitors to the Cape. Its shores have become lined with summer homes. Its beaches and landing floats are populous with swimmers. And its waters in the summer are thronged with sailboats and motorboats in great variety, from tiny outboards to luxurious yachts and cabin cruisers. Indeed on a Sunday afternoon in midsummer, the traffic congestion on the river is beginning nowadays to rival that on the highways.

OLIVER INGERSOLL
Model for Winslow Homer, on the *Belle Gilmore*.

COASTAL FISHING BOAT

On marsh at head of Lobster Cove.

Perhaps it should be explained that the river actually is not an ordinary one. Although several small brooks flow into it, the river essentially is a salt-water estuary, open to the sea at both ends. The tide flows in and out at each end, with a rise and fall of eight to twelve feet.

When the first settlers came to Cape Ann, a marsh obstructed entrance to the river from Gloucester Harbor, but after the town was chartered, one of the first acts of the town meeting was to authorize the Reverend Richard Blynman to make a Cut through the marsh. Thereby the river was opened to navigation from The Green and Planters Neck to Gloucester Harbor. That action was taken May 26, 1643. As an inducement to the minister to open and maintain the Cut, he was granted three acres of upland and the privilege of collecting tolls from nonresidents who passed through the Cut. For inhabitants of the town, passage was to be free.

The Cut was just wide enough to permit the passage of small shallops, but it sufficed for the traffic of those days. A bridge was built over the Cut to enable land travelers to cross it. The bridge was pivoted at one end so that it could be swung open when a boat came along. Since a bridge-tender, of course, could not be afforded, persons taking boats through the Cut had to open and close the bridge themselves. Sometimes, however, they neglected to close it. Consequently in May 1704, the town voted that any person using the Cut who failed to close the bridge should be fined six shillings for each offense. The Cut was used frequently, not only by the townspeople but also by operators of vessels for the coastwise traffic who thereby avoided the loss of time and the risk involved in voyaging around the outside of the Cape.

In the winter of 1704 a heavy storm accompanied by an especially high tide filled the Cut with so much sand and gravel that it no longer was navigable. By that time, however, its maintenance had come to be of such wide concern that the legislature of the Massachusetts Bay Colony ordered the owner of the Cut to have it cleared and re-opened. By that date ownership had long since passed out of the hands of the Reverend Blynman. In fact, the privilege of operating the Cut had not been a perquisite sufficient to hold the reverend gentleman, and about 1650 he had departed with his small group of devoted adherents, to New London, Connecticut. The owner of the Cut in 1704 was Captain Nathaniel Coit and he was authorized to collect from nonresidents a toll of six shillings per vessel for each passage and from residents a fee of seven shillings a year for the privilege of using the Cut.

In February 1723, another heavy storm and high tide again filled the Cut with sand and then the authorities were unable to compel its owner, Samuel Stevens Jr., to re-open it. For the next hundred years, there was no navigation through the Cut. This experience with the Cut affords another example of the constant battle with the sea in which the people of Cape Ann were engaged.

In February 1822, another move was made to open the Cut to traffic. In that year the Gloucester Canal Corporation was formed with a capital of $13,500. Of that amount, $6,000 was subscribed by individuals, $6,000 by the federal government, and $1,500 by the Commonwealth of Massachusetts. The reconstruction of the Cut was completed in August 1822, and its opening was the occasion for a celebration. Col. William Pearce was the first to pass over the new bridge, in a chaise, and liquor, bread, and cheese were distributed at his expense to those who gathered to witness the ceremony.

The reconstruction of the Cut by the Gloucester Canal Company did not meet with financial success. The revenue from tolls proved to be insufficient to cover even the cost of maintenance, and on one occasion the tollkeeper absconded with the toll receipts. A main reason for the lack of patronage was the narrowness of the draw in the bridge. The Cut at that time was about two hundred feet long and twenty-five feet wide, but the passageway through the draw was considerably narrower. Consequently only small vessels could pass through. The river also was shoal at numerous places, so that the larger vessels, which by that time had come into common use, would have had difficulty in navigating it, dependent as they were upon sail power.

About 1830 the drawbridge began to decay and a new bridge, without a draw, was built. That remained for about ten years, but then the undertaking was abandoned. In 1848 the Cut was filled in by four citizens to whom the canal corporation granted land on both sides of the canal in payment for their labor. The bridge was replaced by a solid roadway.

In 1868 the Cut again was opened, primarily for the convenience of the Aberdeen Granite Company which was undertaking to operate a red-granite quarry at Wolf Hill. The quarry company paid the cost of re-opening the Cut and building a new drawbridge, but the quarry did not prosper and soon was closed down.

In an article in a Gloucester newspaper in 1888, in which some of the history of the Cut was reviewed, the following observation was made: "The chief use of the drawbridge now is for the purpose of letting yachters through and an occasional commercial vessel. In time, when the banks of the Annisquam shall have become built up with manufactories, the canal will be found to be an indispensable improvement." Thus in 1888, as in 1959 and in the years between, there were hopeful visions in Gloucester that the city might attract "manufactories." The river, however, has become lined not with industrial plants but with summer homes.

In 1910 the Cut was deepened and widened and a new, electrically operated drawbridge was installed. At the same time the channel of the river was dredged to make it navigable, even at low tide, for vessels of greater draught. Coincidentally with these improvements, changes were taking place in boat equipment which led to a heavy increase in

179

river traffic. More and more ships in the fishing fleets were being equipped with engines which enabled them to buck the tides and follow the channel of the river. Pleasure yachts were installing "kickers" which furnished propulsion when their sails were furled. And of course the motorboat era was beginning modestly to open. Hence more and more craft used the river as soon as its channel had been dredged and an adequate draw had been provided in the bridge over the Cut. Since 1910 the river has been dredged periodically to maintain the navigability of its channel.

While the Cut is primarily a travel convenience, it also has become the scene of a ceremony of simple beauty and great significance. Each year, on a Sunday afternoon in August, relatives and friends of the fishermen gather at the Cut to throw bouquets of flowers on the outgoing tide, in memory of those who have been lost in ocean tragedies. The flowers are carried out to sea by the tide and thus are spread over that one big grave.

From the Cut to the Annisquam Light, the river is replete with landmarks, old and new. We will note them in more or less navigable sequence.

Just to the north of the inner end of the Cut, where a ledge rises quite abruptly on the bank of the river, lies "Dunfudgin." When a boat was brought through the Cut three hundred years ago, the crew had to fudge it along with poles. As soon as they reached deeper water, however, with broader steerageway, they could ship their poles and hoist their sail; they were done fudging. Hence that became the name of the spot, a name which readily suggests welcome relief from tiresome struggles against tide and wind.

Diagonally across the river from Dunfudgin, where the western embankment of the railroad bridge now stands, was Hangman's Island. That was the islet on which the bodies of several members of the Phillips pirate crew were strung up in 1724.

Beyond the railroad bridge, on the eastern side, lies the site of The Green. If one pauses at this point for a moment to contrast the scene which lay before the settlers who erected their meetinghouse on The Green in 1642 and the scene which now greets the eye from the same spot, he has before him an epitome of some of the major changes which have transpired in the last three hundred-odd years. To the west there are still luxuriant growths of trees to be seen and on the hills back from the shore the forests are still dense. The tide still flows in the river and the clam flats are still muddy at low tide. The marshes, although traversed here and there by landing ways, are still green in summer and brown in winter. But now there is a railroad bridge across which passenger and freight trains chug. And around toward the northwest there is a modern high-level bridge for automobiles and trucks, well patronized. On the river, motor-driven fishing craft and pleasure boats are continually passing. And on the shores are numerous summer homes and a few factories.

One of the factories, near the western end of the approach to the railroad bridge, is where for many years the famous Le Page's glue was manufactured. It was produced from skins, bones, and gurry from the fish-curing plants at Gloucester Harbor, and the odor became a cause of considerable controversy. When the tide was low and the wind southwest, the odor from the sediment on the mud flat on the bank of the river below the factory was especially obnoxious to people living on the opposite shore. The only non-objectors were certain persons who owned stock in the company which operated the glue factory; to them the odor smelled like dividends.

Odors from the fish plants and related industries have been a perennial cause of complaint in Gloucester for upwards of fifty years, and in the case of the glue factory the owners were forced by public opinion and governmental action to find means of checking the emission of odorous fumes and

THE ANNISQUAM RIVER AND WEST PARISH

other noisome effluvia. The local supply of fish skins and gurry has become so inadequate in recent years, however, that the manufacture of fish glue has been discontinued in that plant.

As we proceed north from the railroad bridge to the point where the river starts to bend to the east around Wolf Hill, we reach the spot where the tides meet. The tide flows into the river both from Gloucester Harbor and from Ipswich Bay, and the currents meet slightly to the west of Wolf Hill, where the Little River joins the Annisquam. The mud flats and the marshes are so wide at that point, however, that the two tidal currents mingle almost imperceptibly—imperceptibly, that is, to anyone except a person rowing a boat from one tidal current into the other.

Trynall Cove, at the foot of Wolf Hill, was once the landing place for a ferry from the West Parish. The northern landing was on Rust Island, then called "Biskie," right where the embankment for the Route 128 bridge now rises. To shorten the trip to The Green and Gloucester Harbor from the west side of the river, a causeway was built in 1694 from the mainland across the marsh to Biskie—a causeway, incidentally, which is still passable and clearly visible from the westbound lane of Route 128 just beyond the new bridge. When, in July 1694, Samuel Hodgkins, who lived at Trynall Cove (Wolf Hill) was authorized to operate the ferry, it was stipulated that he should keep a good canoe with which to ferry single passengers over the river and a good boat which could carry two horses at a time in bad weather and three when the weather was favorable. The toll was a penny for a person and two pence for a horse; the ferry was operated by Mr. Hodgkins and his descendants for a hundred years.

Just beyond the Route 128 bridge on the southern side of the river, is one of the modern landmarks of the region— Montgomery's boat yard, a spot dear to many a youngster during the last fifty years. The yard was started by Nicholas

W. Montgomery in 1905. Eleven years later he began building sailboats especially designed for racing. The first racing boats which he built were of the "Bird" class. Then in 1921 he and Mr. Harry Friend designed the "Fish" boat, which immediately became the most popular class of small racing craft at Annisquam. All the Fish boats have been constructed around the same concrete mold. Many other sailboats, motorboats, and an occasional small fishing craft also have been built at this boat yard.

On the point to the north of Montgomery's yard is Riverview. On the old maps it is designated as "Whortleberry Hill," but when a summer colony was established there, about 1890, the name was changed to the less picturesque but, perhaps, more genteel one.

A majority of the people who built the first summer camps at Riverview were Gloucester families. The location was relatively cool in summer and it was a convenient horse-and-buggy drive from the downtown residential area. After World War I, as the automobile began to change summer living plans, more and more of the properties at Riverview passed into the hands of newcomers from outside Gloucester.

In the pasture back of Riverview rises Sunset Rock, from the top of which a magnificent view is obtained of Ipswich Bay, the western section of Gloucester Harbor, the river valley, and the surrounding terrain. Sunset Rock is the highest point in a large area of ledge which extends all the way to Washington Street, in the vicinity of the Riverdale millpond. In the old days the ledge near Washington Street was known, for some unrecorded reason, as The Poles.

Across the river from Riverview is one of the largest islands in the river. In the eighteenth century it was owned by Thomas Millet and it was designated as "Millet's Island." One account which we have found states that in 1790 Mr. Millet sold the island to Col. William Pearce, of Dogtown and Gloucester Harbor note. Another account states that Mr.

Millet sold it to Nathaniel Ellery, the fowler-merchant, who in turn sold it to Col. Pearce. Whoever the vendor may have been, Col. Pearce bought the island for a cartload of pickled fish, and for a long time it was known as Pearce's Island.

The island was heavily forested with oak, which was cut off in December 1821. The timber from the large trees on the northeastern section was sold to Messrs. Epes and George Davis of Annisquam, who floated it down the river to their shipyard on the inner side of Babson's Point. The rest of the wood was loaded on gondolas and shipped up the river to the Cut where it was sold, in quantities to suit purchasers, at five dollars a cord.

After the timber had been cleared off the island, the land was sold to Simeon Merchant, who established a farm there. The Merchant barn is still standing. Mr. Merchant kept one or more cows, of course, on his farm, but that was long before the days of artificial insemination, and when a cow was ready for "service," she had to be led across the marsh to Rust's Island at low tide and then over the causeway to some farm in the West Parish which maintained a bull. She was led back at the next low tide, the round trip being an all-day affair under those circumstances.

Pearce's Island is still owned by members of the Merchant family, but for the last half century it has not been a farm. In the early 1900's building lots were leased to tenants who built summer homes there. Before the river was dredged in 1910, persons could cross on foot at low tide over stepping stones from Thurston's Point to the bar in front of the island. Since the dredging took place the island has been accessible only by boat.

Below Pearce's Island is Jones Creek, by way of which the island can be circumnavigated at high tide in a small boat. On the old maps the creek was designated as "Long Cove." The main feature of Jones Creek, aside from the marshes through which it winds, is the long stone pier across the

185

marsh from the West Parish shore, constructed in the early quarry boom on the Cape to provide facilities for shipping granite which was to be quarried on the side of an adjacent hill. The owner used all his funds, however, in getting out the stone with which to build the pier and thus had no resources left for the commercial operation of the quarry. No one else saw fit to take over the enterprise.

Shortly after the end of World War I, a couple of barges which had been abandoned by a defunct dredging company in Lobster Cove were towed to Jones Creek, where they sank near the end of the stone pier. It was only through a great effort by the Leonard Club that the derelicts, which had become a serious menace to navigation in Lobster Cove, were removed.

During the Prohibition period of the 1920's, it generally was understood that the stone pier on Jones Creek was a spot occasionally used for the nighttime landing of smuggled liquor. The winding creek, the isolated pier, and the lonely roads leading to it, on which sentinels could strategically be posted, provided conditions favorable for smuggling.

Smuggling was not a novelty in the Annisquam River region in the 1920's. It went on there in the days preceding the American Revolution and again during the War of 1812. It also is reported that in 1868 a schooner—the *Echo*—was seized by revenue officers in Ipswich Bay with a cargo of thirteen hundred gallons of liquor brought from Nova Scotia. The operators of the schooner intended to smuggle the liquor ashore, landing it at some spot such as Jones Creek.

To digress for a moment, it may be in order to record an experience which one of the authors of this volume had during the late Prohibition era. He then had a summer residence at Riverview, and on a beautiful afternoon in August 1927, he took off in his small, secondhand motorboat for a little ride in the bay. When he was ready to return, he found that the boat would not steer back into the river against the wind and

186

the tide; the rudder was broken. Consequently he threw out an anchor, lit his pipe, and waited for help. It was Cape Ann Day, however, and all the boats usually coming through the river were attending the festivities at Gloucester Harbor.

Shortly after the sun went down, a sleek grey vessel came around Halibut Point and headed for the motorboat. It was a Coast Guard craft, commonly called a rum-chaser. The crew of the Coast Guard boat asked about the predicament and kindly offered to tow the motorboat back to Riverview, an offer which was gladly accepted. At the large summer house on Babson's Point a formal dinner party was in progress, and as the rum-chaser went by, the guests came out on the verandah to wave their napkins at the poor chap being hauled in. Other sympathizers also waved condolences as the boats proceeded up the river. And Charlie, the good-natured caretaker on Pearce's Island, exclaimed in amazement when he saw what was coming: "Gee, it's Dr. Copeland!" As the rum-chaser arrived off Riverview, a horde of children stampeded on to the float, with the victim's wife right behind them. Her greeting was "Well, they caught you this time, didn't they?" Every one was interested in the activities of the rum-chasers in those days.

To return to the landmarks on the river. On the easterly side nearly opposite the entrance to Jones Creek is the point, intimately associated with life at The Green, which originally was called Neck of the House Lots, then Meeting House Neck, then Gee's Point, and finally Wheeler's Point. At the time of the Revolutionary War, Captain Gee had a wharf near the outer end of the neck, from which he carried on fishing and shipping operations, and it was there that the British brig captured at Sandy Bay was tied up. Nowadays the area around the site of Captain's Gee's wharf is filled tightly with summer cottages.

Diagonally across Mill River from Captain's Gee's wharf, and somewhat farther inland, was Captain Rigg's wharf, and part of the foundations are still there. The wharf was built some time in the eighteenth century, and on the shore above it stood the flake yard, where fish were dried, and a warehouse for storage. Early in the nineteenth century, when shipbuilding, fishing, and foreign trade were booming around Lobster Cove, the wharf was owned by Samuel Riggs who then also owned three standing-room pinkies.

It is a far cry from Captain Riggs's pinkies and Captain Gee's sloops to the craft which now make Lobster Cove their home port, and one wonders how the old captains would fare if they were to try to handle some of the speedy little boats which sail these waters.

Sailboat racing became an organized sport at Annisquam in 1896, and for over sixty years it has been a major attraction for summer visitors. The river, opening out into the broad expanse of Ipswich Bay, has afforded especially favorable conditions for the sport, and Lobster Cove not only has provided a large mooring area for the boats but there the novices can learn to sail in safety.

The first racing organization was known as the "Squam Dory Club," which was formed in May 1896. It had quarters in a rented cottage on Babson's Point. Three years later the name was changed to the "Annisquam Yacht Club" and a new clubhouse was built. The first racing fleet was composed of clipper dories, fifteen feet long. In 1899 another class of "slippery little boats," called "half-raters," appeared. After World War I other classes were tried out—Cat boats, Fish boats, Dog boats, and Bird boats, but the Fish boats were the only one of those classes to survive at Annisquam.

During the early years of racing at Annisquam, in addition to the dory races, "open races" also were held. An open race was a handicap affair in which a variety of boats participated. Each boat which received a handicap was allowed a headstart of a specified number of minutes. Meanwhile all the boats which did not receive handicaps were lined up off Cambridge Beach, with anchors down and jibs up. At the starting signal, anchors were hoisted aboard and mainsails set. Then the race was under way. The tidal currents and the eddies, as well as the vagaries of the wind, added zest to the sport of seamanship in those races.

The entrance to the river from Ipswich Bay lies between a long bar which extends out from Wingaersheek Beach, on one side, and the Annisquam shore on the other. On the shore opposite the outer end of the bar is Wigwam Point, which got that name because it was a popular summer camping spot for Indians. In fact, one of the old memoranda which we have run across states that Indians from Maine came there as late as the summer of 1822 or 1823. Thus it appears that there was an interval of only a few years between the last of the Indian and the first of the white summer visitors to the Cape.

On Wigwam Point stands the Annisquam Lighthouse. For over 150 years that lighthouse has been a landmark for mariners sailing in Ipswich Bay. The first lighthouse was erected on Wigwam Point in 1800-01, eleven years before the first beacon light was placed on Eastern Point at the entrance to Gloucester Harbor. The original Annisquam Lighthouse was constructed of wood, octagonal in shape, forty feet high, and painted white. The keeper's house was painted red. The lamp in the lighthouse burned sperm oil until, nearly a century later, kerosene became available.

The original lighthouse was replaced in 1897 by a new structure built of brick, and in 1922 the oil lamp was superseded by an electric installation. The lamp is visible at sea in clear weather for a distance of fifteen miles.

On Davis Neck, which juts out into the bay about half a mile northeast of Wigwam Point, a watchhouse was built in 1705 to help guard against surprise by French and Indian raiders, and to give warning of any approaching pirates. In the nineteenth century a lifesaving station was located there

189

and one of the main tasks of the crew of that station was to rescue the vessels which occasionally ran aground on the Annisquam Bar. After the station was discontinued, the building in which the lifesaving crew had been housed became a summer cottage. Davis Neck, incidentally, was a defense post in both World Wars, and the machine gun nests of World War II are still to be seen in hollows between the ledges on the Neck.

While the river has been one of the picturesque features of Cape Ann and has provided useful facilities for travel and transportation and for summer recreational activities, it also has served another utilitarian purpose which has been almost completely overlooked in the various books and pamphlets that have been written on the history of the Cape. It also has been a handy source of food that must have been particularly helpful to the early settlers. Flounders, cunners, eels, and tautog have been quite plentiful in the river in recent years, and presumably they were even more abundant three hundred years ago. They could be caught from the shore or from small boats in any sort of weather. Hence it was not necessary to make a trip out in the bay to obtain a mess of fresh fish when other supplies of food ran short. Mackerel and herring still run occasionally in the river; in the 1700's and 1800's alewives were taken from the brook at Riverdale when they came in to spawn; lobsters still are caught in the river, and they, too, must have been available to the colonists.

But it was the lowly clam which probably contributed most abundantly to the food supply of the people who settled near the shores of the Annisquam. The flats across from The Green and those near Whortleberry Hill, Pearce's Island, Long Cove, Mill River, Babson's Point, and Wigwam Point were prolific breeding places for clams. In fact, the abundance of clams was one of the attractions which drew the Indians to Cape Ann in the summers before the white men came. That is evidenced by the piles of clamshells which have been un-

190

earthed from time to time in Annisquam, in the West Parish, and in 1956, on the southern side of Whortleberry Hill.

Clams were a self-propagating crop that seldom failed, and in the early days of the white men's settlement a family was in no danger of starvation when a pot full of clams could be obtained at any time of year from the nearby flats.

When the commercial fishing industry developed, clams came to be used extensively for bait by the Cape Ann fishermen. At the outset, when the boats were small and the trips were made chiefly to local fishing grounds, the fishermen themselves dug clams for bait. But eventually clam digging became a separate industry.

We have found two accounts of the clam industry as it throve on the flats of the Annisquam and Essex Rivers in the middle of the nineteenth century. One is in the story of Peter Gott,[15] the other in a history of Essex.[16] At that time commercial clam digging was carried on chiefly in the winter and spring by men and boys who were employed in farming and fishing in the summer. Gangs of ten, twenty, or fifty diggers went out on the flats at low tide and loaded their rowboats with clams dug from the mud. When the incoming tide forced them to suspend their digging, they took their loads to the shore where they had small huts heated with stoves. There they shucked the clams, that is, removed them from their shells with the aid of sharp knives, and placed the meats, with salt, in barrels. The barrels of shucked clams were picked up by the clam dealers, who made the rounds of the huts daily when the weather was favorable and at less frequent intervals when storms interrupted the diggers' work. The dealers stored the clams for sale to fishing vessels. Occasionally the salted clams were sold for export; they were sometimes shipped from Annisquam to France, for example, for use as bait.

15 J. Reynolds, M. D., *Peter Gott, The Cape Ann Fisherman* (Gloucester, Procter Brothers, 1856), pp. 264-69.
16 Reverend Robert Crowell, *History of the Town of Essex, from 1634-1868* (Essex, 1868), p. 352.

About twelve and one-half bushels of clams in the shell were required to yield the two and a half bushels of "meats" packed in each barrel. A bushel of salt also was used in packing one barrel of clams. Three men could dig a barrel of clams in one tide, provided of course, that they had good knees and rubbery backs.

In his account of the clam industry in Essex, Mr. Crowell stated that during the twenty-year period preceding the publication of his history (1868) about two thousand barrels of clams—twenty-five thousand bushels in the shell—had been dug on the Essex flats each year for sale to the Gloucester fishing fleet. Undoubtedly similar quantities were dug along the Annisquam River and its estuaries.

Within a few years after the foregoing account was written, however, the market for clams underwent a change. Fresh and frozen herring came to be used more extensively by the Gloucester fishermen for bait, and clams were sold more and more for human consumption. In November 1882, for example, a West Gloucester item in the local newspaper stated that there was an active demand for clams from buyers in Manchester, Salem, Peabody, and other towns, and that a large corps of diggers was busily employed on the flats.

About 1900 a new market for clams began to appear. They then became a popular recreational food item. On Cape Ann this new market started to grow when the streetcar lines were extended around the Cape and trolley excursions became popular. Then new eating places which featured "shore dinners" were opened at various recreation spots. Clam chowder, steamed clams, and fried clams were staple items on those menus. After World War I, the automobile and improved roads made the seashore accessible, especially on Sundays and holidays, to an ever-increasing number of patrons for the fried-clam emporia which sprang up along the highways. This was happening not only on Cape Ann, of course, but all along the New England coast.

DIGGING CLAMS ON THE ANNISQUAM FLATS

Sand Dunes at Wingaersheek

After 1930 the local supply of clams became greatly depleted, and to use a Yankee expression, clams on the river flats became nearly "as scarce as hen's teeth." The depletion of the clam flats cannot be attributed wholly to the digging of clams in such large quantities for the roadside stands, because the supply had continually replenished itself when great quantities were being dug for fishing bait. Other factors, some of which seem to be unknown, also contributed to the depletion. Horseshoe crabs and green crabs are charged with having destroyed many clams. At about the same time that clams became scarce, moreover, the eel grass also virtually disappeared from the river, and this simultaneous disappearance may have been more than coincidental. Perhaps the digging of the clams the year round, instead of mainly in the fall and winter, may have accelerated the depletion. But whatever the cause may have been, the supply of clams which had been a major resource of food and bait for nearly three hundred years was almost completely exhausted within a short period of time.

About 1860 herring came to be used more extensively by the Gloucester fishing fleet for bait. Part of the supply of herring was imported, frozen, from the Canadian Provinces, but some of it was obtained locally, especially by "torchers" operating out of 'Squam at night. A torcher carried a large torch of inflammable material in an iron frame on the bow. The torch attracted schools of herring to the surface around the boat so that they could be captured with large dip nets. At the outset the torchers were small boats, with sails and oars. Later a fleet of large four-oared dories operated out of 'Squam in the fall and often well into the winter.

Many of the torchers took their fish directly to Gloucester, but some trips were landed at 'Squam, usually at Capt. Wheeler's wharf where the old Custom House stands. Almost every night during the torching season there were at least two carts waiting on River Road for loads of herring to be taken to Gloucester.

One night a torcher with a full load of herring stopped at a wharf in Ipswich before returning to 'Squam. After the boat left Ipswich and was well out in the bay again, the crew discovered that they had a supercargo aboard. A large yellow cat was calmly sleeping on top of the load of fish. When the boat landed at 'Squam, the cat went ashore and quickly made himself at home. For some years thereafter that yellow cat reigned majestically over all the other cats on the 'Squam water front.

The yellow cat from Ipswich was not the only one of his breed to enjoy the torchers' herring. As the herring carts plodded along from Annisquam to Gloucester Harbor night after night, bright eyes were watching from the dark roadside, ready to pounce on the fish which occasionally slid off into the highway.

At a later date the crew of the boat on which the yellow cat took passage from Ipswich to Annisquam had another experience of quite a different sort. On this occasion they took their boat through the river to Gloucester Harbor. When they reached the wharf where they expected to sell their catch, no buyer was on hand. It was a bitterly cold night and the crew felt as though they were nearly frozen. Consequently, to obtain shelter, they broke into a small building on the wharf. There were no lights in the building but they found a stove there and material with which they tried to build a fire. The "wood," however, would not burn. While they were still trying to start a fire, another torcher arrived that had a lantern. Then it was discovered that the "wood" that would not burn was swordfish swords which some fisherman had been curing and polishing for sale.

As this brief account indicates, ever since the first white men came to Planters Neck and The Green, the Annisquam, with its manifold facilities, has played an intimate part in the daily lives of the people of Cape Ann and its summer visitors.

194

Magnolia and the West Parish

THE AREA COVERED in this chapter includes the section of Cape Ann which lies west of the Annisquam River. It is a large area, extending from Gloucester Harbor to the Essex River and from Kettle Cove to Coffin's Beach. It includes the Magnolia shore district, the expanse of wild country now transected by Route 128, and the peninsula between the Annisquam and Essex Rivers.

From several high points in this area broader views are to be obtained than from almost any other spots on Cape Ann. From the top of Tompson's Mountain, now generally known as Mount Ann, on a clear day, the scene to the northeast includes not only a bird's-eye picture of the Cape and Ipswich Bay, but also glimpses of the New Hampshire shore and Mount Agamenticus in Maine. To the southwest, from the same point, the taller buildings in Boston can be seen. Farther away there is a segment of the Massachusetts coast, stretching from Boston Harbor to Scituate and beyond. And to the south and east there is a broad expanse of ocean, usually with several sea-freighters crawling along the horizon. From some of the hills on the peninsula between the Annisquam and Essex Rivers, other views of the rivers, their marshes, and the surrounding country and ocean open up. Some of these views are quite charming.

Within this western section of Cape Ann there are occasional spots sufficiently fertile for farming, but rough, rocky hills, steep ledges, thick swamps, and ever-shifting sand dunes far exceed the tillable farm land in acreage. When the

195

pioneers settled in that area it was heavily wooded, and even today forests are still one of its main features, including some of the most magnificent pine, hemlock, oak, and maple trees on the Cape.

When the first colonists came to Cape Ann, some of them decided to locate their new homes on the west side of the river. Hence the settlement of that part of the Cape began simultaneously with the settlement in the immediate neighborhood of The Green. A few of those who settled on the west side of the river chose sites in the vicinity of Fresh Water Cove, on the western side of Gloucester Harbor, but a majority of them took up land between Little River and the Chebacco (Essex) River. As more settlers arrived, some of them also located west of the Annisquam River, with the result that in 1688 about one-third of the population of Gloucester was living in that region.

Since much of the land which was suitable for tillage was scattered in small acreages between nontillable areas, the farms of the early settlers were widely dispersed and travel was difficult. There were no deep harbors in West Gloucester, but Little River and Long Cove provided means of access to the Annisquam River for small boats, and Walker's Creek likewise gave access to the Chebacco River. At an early date roads were opened from the Cut to Salem and to Chebacco and Ipswich and those roads were readily accessible to some of the early settlers west of the river. Except for those thoroughfares, however, means of travel were meager for more than fifty years after the first settlement.

Then, during the last years of the seventeenth century and the first quarter of the next century, several new roads were opened and ferries came into operation which made it much easier to journey from the west side of the river to The Green, Gloucester Harbor, Annisquam, Sandy Bay, Chebacco, Ipswich, and Salem. The new facilities for travel were opened while the shipbuilding, fishing, and foreign trading enterprises were starting to thrive at Gloucester Harbor and Annisquam and at a time when the whole Cape and the surrounding towns were feeling new pulsations of economic activity. That also was when the settlement of Dogtown was taking place.

One of the first new facilities for travel was the ferry across the Annisquam River at Wolf Hill (Trynall Cove) to Biskie (Rust's Island) where the causeway built in 1694 ended. A road (Ferry Street) from Trynall Cove connected with the road from Wheeler's Point and Riverdale to The Green.

From the western end of the causeway a road extended through the woods to the vicinity of Walker's Creek, an estuary of the Chebacco River. That road through the woods came to be known as Tompson Street and on it the Second Parish Church was built. About halfway between the end of the causeway and Walker's Creek, Tompson Street crossed the road (Bray Street) from the Annisquam Ferry to Chebacco. The first half of Tompson Street now is passable only on foot, and not too easily at that. The stretch from Bray Street to Walker's Creek can be driven over in a jeep.

One of the earliest roads on the Cape was from the Cut to Chebacco. The original road did not follow the present Essex Avenue but ran from the Cut up what is now Bond Street and then turned to the left, running south of Mayo's Swamp (Fernwood Lake) across Wallace's Brook to the head of Little River, then on to Chebacco. In 1719 a road was opened eastward from the Chebacco Road along what is now a section of Concord Street. It crossed Tompson Street near the end of the causeway. In the same year Long Cove Way was opened to connect the other new road with Long Cove (Jones Creek) at a point where the creek was navigable. At that time Long Cove apparently was used more or less extensively for shipping by residents of the West Parish. Three years later a road was opened from what is now Wingaersheek Beach to Long Cove Way and thence through

197

what is now Bray Street to connect with the Chebacco Road. That was when the 'Squam ferry was put into operation.

The traffic over the new roads seems to have grown fairly rapidly, and thus the farms in the West Parish became less isolated. By 1759, in fact, the increase in travel led to a proposal that a bridge should be built across the river near the site of the Biskie ferry. The cost would have been so great, however, that nothing came of the proposal. If it had been built, that bridge would have been located where the Route 128 bridge now stands.

Although the Biskie ferry shortened the trip to The Green for the West Gloucester farmers, it still was a long distance for many of them to travel in going to church each Sunday. Consequently they petitioned for the privilege of setting up their own meetinghouse, and in 1716 the petition was granted. This soon came to be known as the West Parish, a name still in common use today even though the meetinghouse itself has long since disappeared.

The West Parish meetinghouse, which was built as soon as the petition was granted, was located on a hill on Tompson Street, three or four hundred yards south of where that street crosses Bray Street. A few foundation stones of the old meetinghouse are still to be seen, and a flat stone marks the location of the doorway. Just in front of the meetinghouse, when it was in use, was a granite horseblock, from which the good housewives mounted the pillions strapped behind their husband's saddles. The old horseblock, however, has now disappeared.

After the parish had built its new meetinghouse, Mr. Samuel Tompson was chosen to be its minister, but he died in 1724, when only thirty-three years old. His successor was a Mr. Jacques. When he was engaged to serve as pastor, the parish made an agreement with him whereby his salary was to be adjusted each year to fluctuations in the purchasing power of the local currency. Massachusetts had begun to issue paper money in 1690 and by 1724 inflation was in full swing. The arrangement between the parish and Mr. Jacques was essentially the same in principle as the one embodied in the wage agreements of General Motors and several other corporations some 225 years later. As might have been expected, controversy arose between Mr. Jacques and the parishioners over the adjustments to be made in the salary payments; they could not always agree on their cost-of-living index.

The original West Parish meetinghouse was kept in service for about a hundred years, and then, as the settlements along what is now Essex Avenue became more populous and as the parish split into several sects, it fell into disuse. On November 3, 1846, the old meetinghouse was sold at auction and material from its frame was used in the construction of Liberty Hall, located on Essex Avenue. Liberty Hall was used first for religious services by several denominations, then as a fire engine house, and finally for entertainments and a dancehall. How shocked the builders of the original meetinghouse would have been at those uses of their old timbers! When Essex Avenue was widened to accommodate automobile traffic, Liberty Hall was demolished.

Even before the first meetinghouse was built in the West Parish, permission was given to the families living in that area to have a local burying ground. Until 1698 all interments had been in the burying ground near Dunfudgin, east of the river, but in that year land was granted for a burying ground located on Tompson Street, about three-quarters of the distance from Bray Street to Walker's Creek. Some of the old gravestones have been stolen by vandals, and some have fallen down, but about twenty-five remain in place. Among those still standing is the one which marks the grave of the Reverend Samuel Tompson, "Pastour of ye Second Church of Christ, Glosester." It is a quiet, peaceful resting place, quite isolated from the hustle and bustle of twentieth-century life.

On Walker's Creek, not far from the old burying ground and in the general vicinity of the junction of Bray Street with the western section of Concord Street, is the site of an old gristmill, another of the landmarks of Cape Ann. It was a tide mill and its construction was authorized in 1690. It was built by William Haskell, Jr., and Mark Haskell. Hence it originally was known as "Haskell's Corn Mill." On Mason's map (1831) it was designated as "Burnham's Corn Mill." During the years when Annisquam vessels were carrying on their active trade with the West Indies, they often sailed up to the mill on Walker's Creek to load cargoes of corn meal. Hence meal ground in that mill was used for the purchase of molasses, rum, coffee, curios, and, perhaps occasionally, a slave.

That old mill was still standing at the time of the Civil War, when an infantry regiment was camped on a nearby hill for training. During drill on a warm summer day in 1861, the captain marched the regiment down to the old gristmill wharf. The tide in the creek was high, and when the soldiers reached the wharf the captain did not order them to halt. Consequently they marched right overboard into the water.

The old mill is gone now; only the remnants of the dam and some of the mill foundation remain to be seen.

The old gristmill was not the only landmark on Walker's Creek, but before following the creek inland, it may be well to take a look at the coastal section of the West Parish.

The largest farm in West Parish, in fact, one of the largest on all Cape Ann in the eighteenth century was owned by Peter Coffin. It was five hundred acres in extent, located on the shore of Ipswich Bay, directly across the river from Annisquam. The land originally was granted by the town of Gloucester to William Stevens, a shipwright. Title to the property subsequently was passed to Jonathan Willoughby of London, and in 1688 Tristam Coffin of Newbury purchased it from Willoughby. Peter Coffin, son of Tristam, took over

200

the land as soon as his father had purchased it and Peter further developed the farm that had been started by Stevens. When Tristam Coffin transferred the land to Peter, he entailed it to Peter's son, also named Peter, and in 1747 Peter II became the owner. Some years later his son, Peter the third, inherited the property.

The sand dunes on the Coffin farm, along the shores of Ipswich Bay and the Annisquam River, always have been one of the most notable landmarks on the Cape. The sand dunes also were a source of income to the Coffin family.

Early in the eighteenth century, sand from the dunes along the river began to be sold for covering the floors of dwelling houses. That was before floor paint or carpets had come into use. The sand also was used for scrubbing unpainted kitchen floors long after carpets were put down in the "front rooms." The sand from the Coffin dunes was the finest available in this region and a premium price was obtained for it. The market included all the towns from Portsmouth to Boston.

When the land which became the Coffin farm was granted originally to William Stevens, the boundaries were not clearly fixed. Consequently, as the market for the sale of sand from the dunes expanded and became lucrative, a controversy arose between Mr. Coffin and his neighbors, who owned rights in the adjoining common land, as to who was entitled to the income from the sale of the sand. In 1722 an agreement was reached under the terms of which the income was to be shared equally by Peter Coffin and those who held rights to the common land. That agreement continued in effect until 1799, when the full title to the sand dunes in question was sold to Peter Coffin III for four hundred dollars. The price at which the sand was marketed in 1725, it may be noted incidentally, was a halfpenny per bushel. The marketing of sand from the Coffin dunes is another example of the ingenuity and resourcefulness shown by the early residents of Cape Ann in finding means of making a living.

The sand dunes along the shore of the bay also provided a means of defense. It was from behind those dunes that Major Coffin and four or five assistants drove off the raiders from the British warship *Falcon* in August 1775, when they sought to seize sheep in his pasture. The accounts differ as to whether Major Coffin was assisted in that encounter by his neighbors or his slaves, but they agree that a half-dozen men kept up such an active rifle fire by running back and forth behind the dunes that they gave the raiders the impression that the defending force was much larger than it actually was. The raiders withdrew without capturing any sheep.

The building in which Major Coffin's slaves were housed was located in a grove of poplar trees beside the present road to Wingaersheek Beach, at the entrance to a wide point of land which juts out into the marshes toward Annisquam; and that land probably was the most fertile part of the Coffin farm. From the top of a rocky knoll on that point a unique and beautiful view is to be had of the lower stretches of the Annisquam River, Mill River, Lobster Cove, the village of Annisquam, and Wigwam Point.

There is a legend that Peter Coffin the first warned his son and his grandson against cutting off the trees behind the sand dunes, lest the sand blow in and cover the farm. Peter III did have a quantity of wood cut on the farm, but whether that accelerated the spread of the dunes is a moot question. The sand around the dunes is continually shifting, whether or not there are trees nearby. This legend may merely have reflected neighborly gossip about Peter III. After graduating from Harvard in the class of 1769, he read law in a judge's office in Haverhill, then returned to Gloucester where he engaged in trade and failed. After that, he decided to move back to the farm in the West Parish and lived there only so long as he could support himself by the sale of wood. Such a career may have given occasion for neighborhood gossip.

The Coffin name has been preserved in "Coffin's Beach," the mile-long stretch of smooth, sandy shore between the mouth of the Annisquam River and the entrance to the Essex River. In 1882 the land along the northern end of the beach was divided into building lots and the first summer house was built there. From those beginnings Coffin's Beach and the section of it now called Wingaersheek developed into one of the chief summer resort areas on Cape Ann. In the next sixty years after 1882 about twenty or twenty-five summer homes were built along the beach and then, after the end of World War II, a large colony of summer and year-round residences sprang up near the southern end of the beach.

On maps of Cape Ann published between 1630 and 1670, the beach was designated "Wyngaerts Hoeck."[17] Then, after Peter Coffin cleared the hinterland for his farm, it became known as "Coffin's Beach." When the summer settlement began in 1882, it apparently was thought necessary by those developing the property to have a new name. Consequently Wyngaerts Hoeck was revived, with a new spelling "Wingaersheek." That name presently came to be applied only to the southern end of the beach, at the mouth of the Annisquam River, and since 1920, when automobiles began to put America on wheels, Wingaersheek Beach has become an increasingly popular spot for transient bathers and picnickers during the summer months.

The source of the name "Wingaersheek" has long been a topic of discussion on Cape Ann. Sometimes it has been ascribed to an Indian origin, but it probably goes back to Wyngaerts Hoeck. The meaning of that also has been debated, and some persons have attempted to link it to the Norsemen's Vineland, since Wyngaert could have been a cor-

---

17   James R. Pringle, *History of the Town and City of Gloucester* (Gloucester, 1892), p. 17.

ruption of the German *weingarten* or vineyard. We are convinced, however, that there is a far simpler and more plausible interpretation of Wyngaerts Hoeck.

The latter part of that odd name probably is the more significant one. The Dutch have a term "hoek" and the English a word "hook" which is applied to a certain type of coastal area. In *Webster's Unabridged Dictionary* one of the definitions of "hook" is as follows: "A sharp bend or curve, as in a stream, or a spit or narrow cape of sand or gravel turned landward at the outer end, as Sandy Hook." That definition is a very good description of Coffin's Beach, with its outer end hooking into the Essex River.

Before coming to the New World, the Pilgrims who settled Plymouth, it is to be recalled, had lived for some years in Holland, not far from the Hoek van Holland. Consequently they must have known well the shape of a "hook." After their arrival in the new land, they explored the whole coastal area to the northward, as evidenced by their trips to Cape Ann, their trading activities with Indians on the northern coast, and eventually their founding of settlements in Maine. Under those circumstances it would have been natural for them to give the designation of "hook" to the spit of sand across the river from Planters Neck. It also would have been easy for the early mapmakers to spell it "Hoeck" instead of "Hoek" or "Hook."

There is no evidence regarding the origin of Wyngaerts but the hook well may have been so named for Wyngart, or Wingart, or Wingard. Many a strange spelling appeared on seventeenth and eighteenth-century maps. It also may be worth mentioning in this connection that on the map published by Captain John Smith in his *Advertisements for the New England Planters* in 1631, the point on the northeastern corner of "Cape Anna," a few miles across the bay from the there unnamed beach, was designated as "P. Wynthorp." That name has a partial similarity to Wyngaerts

204

Hoeck, and suggests some possible relationship, especially when one remembers the prevalency in those days of confusion in names and spellings. The source of the name, however, matters little to the thousands of persons who now enjoy the bathing and the beach parties at Wingaersheek every summer.

Let us return now to Walker's Creek and its neighborhood. On a peaceful, quiet glade near the head of the creek, at 11 Lincoln Street, stands the old Haskell house, one of the oldest dwellings on Cape Ann. The house was built in the middle of the seventeenth century by Richard Windrow who sold it in 1656 to William Haskell. The Haskell family, of which William was the pioneer, was one of the foremost families in the West Parish, and the old Haskell house was their ancestral home.

Members of the Haskell family were not only enterprising and prolific, but also notable for longevity. Aaron Haskell, who died in 1834 at the age of eighty-three, had seven children who lived to be over eighty years old, one of them reaching the age of ninety-six.

Such instances of longevity seem to us to be worth more than passing note. The climate of Cape Ann was rigorous; the facilities for living were primitive; the food was coarse and rough; the medical facilities for many years were extremely meager; and some of the occupations were hazardous. Despite these conditions, however, a considerable number of the early inhabitants and their descendents lived to ripe old ages. The Haskells were notable examples, but there were also several others.

In his history of Gloucester, John J. Babson has over 160 pages on the genealogy of the early settlers and their descendents. In many instances he gives the dates of death and the ages of the decedents, the dates ranging from 1684 to 1858. That list includes 191 persons aged 70 or older at time of death. Of the 191, 65 were 70-79 years old when they

205

died; 90 were 80-89 years old; 29 were 90-99 years old; and seven lived to be over 100. Several others on the list, for whom age at time of death was not specified, were referred to as having lived to "an advanced age," or "a very advanced age." For the period since 1860, moreover, we have noted, from fragmentary records, numerous other instances in which residents of Cape Ann have lived upwards of 80 years.

During the first two hundred years or more after the settlement of the Cape, infant mortality may have been high and children's diseases ravaging, so that any person who survived his childhood may well have possessed such a strong constitution that he had a good chance of reaching a notable old age. Nevertheless, it appears that Cape Ann, despite its rigorous climate, was a healthy place in which to live, and the record of the Haskell family helps to support that conclusion.

On a brook flowing from an inland swamp, where the brook crossed the Chebacco Road, a sawmill was built in the early days by one of the Haskells. The millpond was on the site now occupied by a winter hockey rink. This is still another illustration of the way in which the early settlers utilized every little brook to provide water power for sawing lumber and grinding grain. The Haskell mill burned down in 1883.

When a municipal water supply system was established for Gloucester, a large storage basin was created on the site of the swamp from which the brook flowed to the Haskell sawmill and thence to Walker's Creek. The muck was dug out of the swamp; a dam was built across the lower end, and the excavated area became a beautiful pond—Haskell's Pond —which is still one of the largest storage basins for the Gloucester water supply.

Farther to the east on the Chebacco Road, in 1682 another sawmill was built on a brook which flowed into Little River. That brook had its origin in Dyke's Meadow, which also became in later years a storage basin for the city's water

206

supply. Both Haskell's Pond and Dyke's Meadow lie in the heavily wooded area around Mt. Ann and can be reached by paths from that point or by paths from Essex Avenue.

Also near the head of Little River stands the Old Freeman House, another famous landmark of Cape Ann. The house was built in 1709 by Jacob Davis, who operated a tavern there. In 1730 it was purchased by Robert Freeman, the son of a Gloucester Negro slave who had acquired his freedom. For two hundred years the property continued to be owned by Robert Freeman and his descendents. Then in 1932 it was sold to new owners, who renovated it and operated it as the Stage Coach Inn for eleven years, before reselling it to another family for a private residence.

Magnolia Avenue, which connects Essex Avenue from the vicinity of the Old Freeman House with Western Avenue in Magnolia, was known to Gloucester people half a century ago as the "Little Heater." It received that name from its frequent use for warming up trotting horses. Amateur trotting races were a popular sport in those days. There also was a "Big Heater" for stiffer workouts. The Big Heater was the road from Manchester to Essex. The road which became Magnolia Avenue was laid out in 1724, presumably for the convenience of residents of the West Parish who might have occasion to travel to Salem.

As we approach the end of our geographical tour of the Cape, we proceed next to Fresh Water Cove, on the southwestern side of Gloucester Harbor. The cove was given that name by Champlain when he landed there in 1606 to obtain a supply of fresh water from a spring on or near the shore. There are two springs near the cove—one on the shore, which is covered with salt water at high tide but flows fresh when the tide is out, and another on higher land. In the account of his voyage Champlain did not indicate which spring he patronized, but the name which he gave to the cove was perpetuated.

207

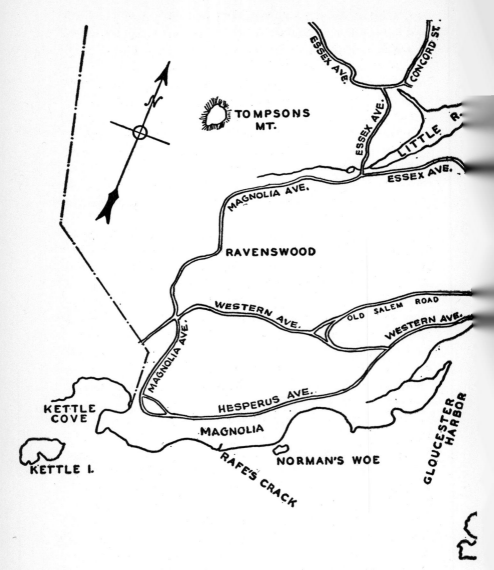

MAGNOLIA AND WEST GLOUCESTER

One of the old houses near Fresh Water Cove deserves special mention. That is the Master Moore House, which stands on a hill on Hesperus Avenue overlooking the Coast Guard Station. It was built in 1752 by William Moore. In 1775, while he and his twelve-year-old son Joseph were fishing in a small boat near the shore, Mr. Moore was seized by the crew of a British warship. The boy was permitted to row ashore at Kettle Cove, but the father was detained aboard the warship where attempts were made to force him to act as a pilot. He refused to be a traitor, however, and was sent to a prison ship in New York Bay where he died.

Joseph Moore had a bent for mathematics and as a young man he developed a new method of teaching navigation. He had a textbook printed in which problems in navigation were worked out. And for over sixty years he conducted a school in his home for young men who desired to study navigation. His students, of course, were chiefly from Gloucester. The tuition was eight dollars per quarter, and it often was paid in produce instead of cash. He was known as "Master Moore" and that name naturally came to be associated with the house where he lived and taught. When he died in 1845, he was eighty-two years old, another instance of longevity.

On the outer shore beyond Fresh Water Cove are two natural landmarks—Norman's Woe and Rafe's Chasm. Norman's Woe is the reef made famous by Longfellow in the "Wreck of the Hesperus." Whenever there are swells in the sea thereabouts, the surf breaks high on the reef.

A short distance to the west of Norman's Woe is Rafe's Chasm, once known as Rafe's Crack. The chasm is a crevice in the ledge, extending in from the shore line at right angles for a distance of about two hundred feet. It is sixty feet deep and from three to ten feet wide.

As waves from the ocean roll up on the shore, they thunder into the chasm. The surf in the chasm at the time of a storm is spectacular. It also is dangerous at such a time unless the spectator remains at a distance; if a person is swept into the chasm by a heavy swell, there is little hope of his being rescued.

When the weather is calm, however, the cliff above the churning waters affords a scenic view which belies the thunder below. To the northeast Niles Beach, Eastern Point, and the breakwater provide a background for the scene. To the southwest the Manchester shore line, Marblehead, and the Half-Way Rock in the distance furnish a different sort of background. To the southeast lies the open ocean. And in the foreground lobster men, in their seemingly tiny boats, are peacefully pulling their traps just offshore.

The rugged shore to the west of Norman's Woe and Rafe's Chasm has been the scene of numerous wrecks and also has had its wartime experiences. During the War of 1812, for example, a minor battle took place there for possession of a French privateer—the *Invincible Napoleon.* The vessel had been captured by a British warship which in turn had been forced to surrender it to a Salem privateer. While the prize was on its way to Boston, two British frigates appeared and gave chase to the vessel. To escape capture, the prize crew ran the ship ashore near Norman's Woe. An alarm was sounded in Gloucester, and over a hundred men and boys gathered in the pine woods on the shore near where the vessel had been grounded. When boats from one of the British frigates attempted to board the *Invincible Napoleon,* the Gloucester sharpshooters forced them to withdraw. Then the frigate came in near enough to fire broadsides into the woods and under that cover the British succeeded in gaining possession of the ship. That was not the end of the matter, however, for while the *Invincible Napoleon* was being taken to Halifax by the British, she was recaptured by another American privateer and taken to Portsmouth.

Kettle Cove got its name, according to tradition, from

the fact that Kettle Island was once connected with the mainland by a sand bar in such a way as to give the shore line the shape of a kettle, and for over two hundred years following the first settlement the adjoining mainland, as well as the cove itself, was known as Kettle Cove.

Until 1867 the point between Fresh Water Cove and Kettle Cove was forest land. There was a small fishing hamlet on the shore, and on the road which later was named Western Avenue there was a farmhouse which was one of the stopping places for the Gloucester-Salem stagecoach. Early in the nineteenth century the farmhouse was converted into a tavern, with a bar, a ninepin alley, and accommodations for dancing, and it became a popular resort for hay-ride parties in summer and sleigh parties in winter.

In 1867 the land on the point at Kettle Cove was purchased by Daniel W. Fuller of Swampscott. The forest was cleared off. Roads were constructed. Building lots were laid out. Several summer cottages were built. And the whole area was given the name "Magnolia," from the swamp magnolias which then grew abundantly thereabouts. In 1877 a hotel was built on Hesperus Avenue and by 1885 there were four other hotels established nearby. In 1886 a rink was built at Stanwood's Grove where roller-skating and dancing parties were held.

The first hotels in Magnolia were rather modest establishments, but they were superseded by much more luxurious hostelries, and presently sumptuous summer homes were built. People came to Magnolia not only from Boston and New York but also from numerous other cities, such as St. Louis and Cincinnati, to spend the summer. Wealthy summer residents kept four-in-hand coaches for riding around the countryside and their yachts were moored in the harbor. New York and Boston stores of the exclusive type opened summer shops in Magnolia where the prices placed on the merchandise led people residing elsewhere on Cape Ann to refer irreverently

211

to the main street in Magnolia as "Robber's Alley." Thus, for a period of about forty years Magnolia was a highly fashionable summer resort.

World War I marked the beginning of a change. Heavy federal income taxes, economic depressions, dependable automobiles, and new roads forced or led to new living habits and tastes and caused Magnolia to undergo the same sort of transition that was experienced by numerous other fashionable summer resorts in New England and elsewhere. Some of the big summer houses were converted into guest houses; numerous smaller dwellings were built; and the swanky shops were replaced by more modest stores. Despite the change in the clientele, however, Magnolia continued to attract a large number of summer visitors, and of course, it lost none of its natural beauty.

On the northern side of Western Avenue in Magnolia lies Ravenswood Park, which is another one of the natural beauty spots on Cape Ann. It was founded through the munificence of Samuel E. Sawyer, a native of Gloucester who entered business in Boston and amassed a fortune. Mr. Sawyer's ancestral home was at Fresh Water Cove and he had a fondness for the surrounding country. Before his death in 1882 he had bought numerous wood lots between Western Avenue and Bond's Hill. In his will he directed that they were to be retained by a self-perpetuating board of trustees, which he named, "for the protection and beauty of Cove Village, now so-called, but some time in the future to be laid out handsomely with driveways and pleasant rural walks and then dedicated in the name of Ravenswood Park." He also set up a trust fund of sixty thousand dollars, the income of which was to be used in developing and beautifying the park.

The park has an area of more than five hundred acres, and it has been developed in accordance with Mr. Sawyer's directions, with beautiful driveways and paths. Although relatively few people nowadays seem to have the time or the inclination to visit Ravenswood, it is a delightful place through which to walk or drive at any season of the year. In several sections of the park there are stands of majestic pine and hemlock trees. Elsewhere there are birches, beeches, and numerous other varieties of trees and shrubs. In one of the swamps, swamp magnolias are growing wild, the most northern point at which that species is found in a wild habitat. In the years before the park was created, when the magnolias were much more plentiful, they were dug out of the swamp and sold for landscape gardening around homes in more or less distant cities. Fortunately the creation of the park prevented the extinction of the local growth.

Beside one of the paths leading to the magnolia swamp is a "rocking stone," a boulder which is so neatly balanced on a pivoted bottom that it rocks back and forth when several men push against its side. It is not the only rocking stone on Cape Ann, but is the most accessible one. Two others are located in the woods back of Lanesville. One of them, which lies beside the old quarry-workers' path from Bay View to Pigeon Cove, weighs about seventy tons and can be rocked by one man. Still another formerly lay on the shore at Bass Rocks but was wedged up some years ago to guard against accident, and it no longer rocks. It is an interesting natural phenomenon that each of those rocking stones should be so precisely balanced that it can sway back and forth and yet remain on the spot where it was deposited by a glacier thousands of years ago.

Another landmark in Ravenswood Park is the Old Salem Road, now only a narrow path in some sections. It runs through the northern end of the park and winds around to Western Avenue, about a quarter of a mile west of the main entrance to the park. The Old Salem Road was the first land route from Gloucester to Salem and it continued to be the main land route for about 150 years. Then around 1800 it

213

was superseded by the road nearer the shore, now called Western Avenue.

Near the section of the Old Salem Road which crosses the northern end of Ravenswood are the cellars of houses which were located there when the road was a thoroughfare. One of those cellars marks the site of the Pest House, which was erected by the town in 1777 for the isolation of people ill with smallpox. After that house was built the road often was called the Old Pest House Road and was so designated on Mason's map of Cape Ann published in 1831.

Perhaps the most interesting landmark on the Old Salem Road in Ravenswood Park, however, is the site of the hermit's cabin. The hermit's name was Walton and about 1884, according to his own account[18] he was suffering from aggravated dyspepsia, malignant catarrh, a severe cough, and sore lungs. He then was living in Boston and he was advised by the doctors whom he consulted to leave the city and live somewhere in the country. He took a steamer from Boston to Gloucester, where for three days he tried to find a job on a fishing vessel. But he was so emaciated that the skippers were apprehensive that he would be a Jonah; hence they would not hire him.

Having been unable to go to sea, Walton turned to the pine woods on the Old Salem Road beyond Bond's Hill. There he put up a tent in which he lived for five months, from August to December. Within two weeks after he entered upon that outdoor life, his cough was gone; in two months the catarrh had disappeared; and the dyspepsia presently also ceased to trouble him. Consequently he built himself a cabin there, in which he continued to live for eighteen years, without any return of his ailments.

For companionship he made pets of wild animals and birds—"Satan," a raccoon; "Bismarck," a red squirrel; and "Wabbles," a song sparrow.

---

18 Mason A. Walton, *A Hermit's Wild Friends* (Boston, Dana Estes & Co., 1903), pp. 11-12.

The hermit, in commenting on Satan, said: "A coon can reason as well as the average human being. My captive proved to be as artful and wicked as Beelzebub himself."[19] Satan also had "a bristling battery of claws and teeth operated by chain lightning."[20] He whipped all the dogs that ventured within his range. In the winter Satan lived with the hermit inside the cabin and was perfectly at home there.

Bismarck took over the hermit's dooryard as his domain and savagely fought off other squirrels, gray or red, who ventured to intrude on his precinct. He gathered and stored not only nuts but also mushrooms.

Wabbles was found by the hermit after the sparrow had been wounded by four buckshot in the muscle of a wing joint. The hermit removed the shot and fed the bird who thereupon made the hermit's neighborhood his summer home. He was able to fly again when the wound healed, but in a somewhat wabbly fashion, hence his name.

When Wabbles returned from his first winter migration, he took unto himself a spouse, but Mrs. Wabbles would not live in the woods. She had to have her nest built in a field some distance from the hermit's cabin. Wabbles took the hermit to see the nest, and after the young birds were hatched brought them to visit the hermit, who fed them with cookie crumbs. They liked the cookies so well that they refused to obey their mother when she came to take them home. After his first wife had been killed in some accident, Wabbles married again, only to be henpecked. He returned to Ravenswood, however, every summer, for fourteen years, and while there he regularly woke the hermit at daylight each morning by coming up to his hammock and chirping or singing loudly.

Ravenswood is so secluded that it still is a favorite haunt for many birds and wild animals.

---

19 *Ibid.*, p. 32.
20 *Ibid.*, p. 41.

Ledges, Swamps, Moors, and Marshes

OLD CAPE ANN is a rocky place, as evidenced by such out-croppings as the terminal moraine on the eastern side of the Cape; the ledges and boulders in Dogtown; the Poles, near the Green; Squam Rock and Adams Hill in Annisquam; the quarry ledges in Bay View, Lanesville, and Pigeon Cove; Mt. Ann and numerous other hills in the West Parish; the rocky shores of Lanesville, Halibut Point, Pigeon Cove, Straits-mouth, Thachers, Salt Island, Bass Rocks, Eastern Point, and Magnolia; and the old stone walls that still zigzag through fields and brush and forest. In fact, it sometimes seems as though the Cape were almost wholly ledge and boulders. Nevertheless, there is some fertile land and a considerable acreage of marshes, beaches, sand dunes, and swamps, and all those topographical features, as well as the river, have had real significance for the people of Cape Ann.

The tidal marshes along the Annisquam River and its estuaries and on the West Parish flank of the Essex River, the sand dunes, and the beaches on the Cape have an aggregate area, we estimate, of approximately 3,500 acres. The area of swamp land, furthermore, now is about 2,800 acres; and three hundred years ago, before certain swamps had been drained or filled in and before other swamps had been converted into reservoirs, the aggregate area of the fresh-water swamps on the Cape exceeded 4,000 acres. The total area of the Cape is somewhat under fifty square miles, or 32,000 acres. Hence, when the first settlers came, the aggregate area of the marshes, sand dunes, beaches, and swamps was about one fourth of the total area of the Cape.

One of the largest swamps in the seventeenth century was the Harbor Swamp, with an area of approximately one thousand acres. Its upper edge was near the high land, along the crest of which the road ran from The Green to the old mill on Wine Brook. From that ridge the swamp extended to the neighorbood of what is now Prospect Street, and from it a brook flowed to Gloucester Harbor at Pavilion Beach. After the settlement developed at the Harbor, the swamp was drained and converted into fertile farm land. Then, as the town expanded in the late nineteenth century, the former swamp land became a residential and industrial district.

Numerous smaller swamps here and there on the Cape also have been filled in to facilitate road construction or to satisfy the convenience of private owners.

While some swamps thus disappeared by being drained or filled in, others were dammed and flooded. The water reservoirs at Haskell's Pond, Dykes Meadow, Fernwood Lake, Wallace's Pond, and Babson's Reservoir once were swamps. A swamp above the site of the old mill on Wine Brook was converted into a millpond when the mill was built, but it has long since reverted to its original state.

The largest swamps that are now in existence on the Cape include Brier Swamp in Dogtown, where Wine Brook has its source; the Maple Swamp nearby, through which Wine Brook flows toward the gap in the terminal moraine; the Rifle Range swamp, between Dogtown and Goose Cove; the swamp in Ravenswood Park; and Long Swamp in the wild country to the south of Dykes Meadow. Numerous smaller swamps are spotted at frequent, though irregular, intervals all over the Cape. These are in pockets which were gouged out of the bedrock by glacial action, the pockets in some instances having been at least eighteen feet in depth. Over the centuries since the last glacier receded toward the polar regions, the pockets gradually have been filled with decayed

217

vegetable matter and hence have become particularly rich habitats for wild life.

All these topographical features of Cape Ann—rocks, ledges, moors, marshes, and swamps—provide conditions which are favorable to the growth of a wide variety of trees, shrubs, and flowers, and they afford breeding grounds, food, and protection for many sorts of birds, animals, and marine creatures. The location and the contour of Cape Ann are such that winds and breezes off the ocean moderate somewhat the extremes of the New England temperatures, both in summer and in winter. Since the winds and breezes usually are moisture laden, furthermore, they nourish the growth of vegetation, even among the rocks and ledges of the Cape.

This wildlife adds greatly to the picturesqueness of the Cape, but in the early days it was not the beauty of the forests but rather their usefulness which primarily interested the local colonists. When the first settlers came to Cape Ann, its forests provided timber for building houses and ships and wood for making furniture and farm and household implements. The roots, bark, and juices of various trees and shrubs also furnished native medicines, materials for tanning leather, and dyes for coloring homespun fabrics. In the seventeenth century and in the first years of the eighteenth century, moreover, the local forests supplied the inhabitants of Cape Ann with their chief merchantable products—timber, lumber, and cordwood—which could be sold in Salem, Boston, and neighboring coastal towns.

White pine, oak, and hemlock constituted much of the merchantable timber produced on the Cape in the days of its forest economy. Other sorts of trees which furnished materials for special uses or which could be converted into cordwood included red maple, black walnut, white ash, beech, cherry, yellow birch, black birch, black locust, American elm, slippery elm, linden, hornbeam, tupelo, and black mulberry. That is not a complete list, of course, but it serves to indicate the wide variety of trees growing within the confines of this rocky and swampy promontory.

Very few trees are still standing which were here when the first settlers arrived, but descendents of practically all the old species are to be found, and some of them afford a good indication of the size of the trees in the virgin forests which existed here three hundred years ago.

The largest white pine that we have found on the Cape stands beside the road to the abandoned Magnolia railroad station. It is 11 feet, 11 inches in circumference at a height of three feet from the ground.[21] Near the old tan-pit path, in the ravine which extends from the head of Lobster Cove in Annisquam to the vicinity of Goose Cove, there is another white pine 10 feet, 1 inch in circumference, and also one 9 feet, 3 inches in girth. Each of these pines is 90 to 100 feet tall, with a straight, clear trunk. The primeval trees were larger, of course, than these latter-day specimens, but even so, these and others which are still standing would have made splendid masts for Gloucester fishing schooners. It was from such trees as these, furthermore, that material was obtained for the beams, planks, and pine-paneling used in the construction of colonial houses and pine furniture.

Hemlocks grow profusely on the hills beside some of the swamps and brooks of Cape Ann, where there is moist subsoil into which they can send down their deep roots and where at the same time there is an abundance of rocks and boulders around which they can tightly clasp their shallow roots. In Ravenswood Park and on the slopes of Mt. Ann there are especially fine stands of hemlock. There the thick boughs of the trees provide cool shade in summer and sound-deadened solitude in winter. The largest hemlock which we have noted stands near the northern edge of the swamp in Ravenswood. It has a girth of 8 feet, 10 inches and probably is over two

---

21 All the tree measurements cited in the following pages were taken at that height.

hundred years old. On the opposite side of the swamp is another hemlock which is 8 feet, 6 inches in circumference. Both these trees are about 90 feet tall. Numerous other hemlocks on the Cape are nearly as large as those two.

Because of its coarse, splintery texture, hemlock was not used extensively for the interior finish of colonial homes or for furniture making, but it did provide boards and timbers for dwellings and for other structures. Hemlock, moreover, is particularly resistant to deterioration in salt water. Hence it was used for building wharves. Hemlock bark has a high tannin content, and in colonial days it was used for tanning leather, for dyeing sails and nets, and for medicinal purposes. Thus the hemlocks were very useful to the colonists.

Another evergreen that flourishes on Cape Ann is known locally as "red cedar," but actually is a juniper. The trees have little commercial value—their berries, so far as we know, never have been used here for making gin—but they do add significantly to the scenery of the Cape. Although the junipers grow everywhere in the open country, it is on the Dogtown moors that the most picturesque specimens are to be found. On the crisp Dogtown landscape, those "cedars," like the boulders alongside which they stand, often seem to belong to some biblical setting.

White oaks also grow plentifully on Cape Ann, many of those in the virgin forests having reached a height of one hundred feet. They furnished the colonists with sturdy timbers for the construction of ships, houses, barns, churches, and mills. Staves of white oak made the best tight cooperage for barrels to hold water, rum, and other liquids. White oak also was used for making clam baskets when clam digging became an active enterprise. Men from 'Squam, for example, regularly crossed over to the West Parish in the fall, cut a straight white oak butt, and brought it home. The butt then was soaked in water and pounded until the annual growth layers

220

could be peeled off in strips. From those tough strips clam baskets were fashioned.

The largest white oaks that we have found still standing are located on Concord Street, near the southern corner of Bray Street, in the West Parish—one 8 feet in circumference and another 7 feet, 10 inches. They probably are about three hundred years old.

Another old tree, which probably dates back at least to the arrival of the first settlers at The Green and Planters Neck, is a red oak measuring 14 feet, 11 inches in circumference that stands on Riggs Point, between Mill River and Lobster Cove. It has witnessed all the stirring events that have taken place around Annisquam Harbor during the last three centuries.

Another old red oak, measuring 12 feet, 3 inches in circumference, stands on Poplar Street, not far from the site of The Green. By it for many decades passed the ox teams of the villagers on their way to the mill on Wine Brook and to Fox Hill where old "Luce" George and Tammy Younger lived.

Several other red oaks and scarlet oaks only slightly smaller than the ones which have been mentioned are standing at various points on the Cape. These old oak trees which still survive are another indication of the wealth of forest materials that the early settlers found awaiting them here. The climate of Cape Ann obviously was one which oak trees liked, and the rocks of the Cape provided firm anchorage for their tough roots.

In addition to furnishing sturdy timbers for construction work, the oaks of Cape Ann also had other uses. Oak bark was used for tanning leather, and the acorns could be used for food.

John Josselyn, whose *New England Rarities* was published in 1672, also recorded uses of acorns which may be of current interest. He made his observations while living in

221

Scarborough, Maine, but at that time there already was enough migration of people back and forth between Cape Ann and southern Maine for the residents of both districts to have had common knowledge of the subjects covered in his report.

Josselyn stated that the Indians took the rottenest maple wood that they could find, burnt it to ashes, and then from the ashes made a strong lye. White-oak acorns were boiled in the lye until the oil rose to the surface. The acorn oil thus obtained was used as a sauce for meat and especially as a lotion with which the Indians anointed their naked limbs and the heads of their papooses, to protect them from the sun.[22] Whether the white settlers on Cape Ann utilized white-oak acorns for those purposes is of course problematical, but so much sunburn lotion is now used on the Cape every summer that it has seemed to us worth while to note that a similar concoction was made by the Indians three hundred years ago and probably for centuries before then.

Although its wood has not been nearly so useful as the wood of several other varieties of trees, the beech is the predominating hard wood on Cape Ann. In his very interesting and authoritative book on trees, Peattie states that the beech "loves what the farmer loves—rich limestone overlain by deep, level, dark loam."[23] If one can judge from the forests of Cape Ann, however, the beech also loves thin, gravelly, acid soil devoid of limestone and dark loam.

The beeches now standing on Cape Ann are greatly varied in contour. Some of them are tall and straight, with no low branches. Others have branches starting a foot or two from the ground and radiating out at least fifty feet on all sides of the trunk. The beech forests of Cape Ann provided firewood, of course, for the settlers, and their nuts were tasty

---

22 *Opus cit.*, p. 94. This book was first published in England, but a reprint was put out by Edward Veazie of Boston in 1865. The references here are to the 1865 reprint.
23 Donald C. Peattie, *A Natural History of Trees, Eastern North America* (Boston, Houghton, Mifflin Co., 1950), p. 180.

tidbits for the children and also for vast numbers of birds and small animals.

In addition to the common American beech trees on the Cape, there also are several copper beeches, the largest of which, so far as we know, stands on the point between Goose Cove and Lobster Cove in Annisquam, near the old house supposedly built by Francis Norwood. The tree measures 14 feet, 8 inches in circumference. Since copper beeches are not native trees, the seed or seedling from which the old tree grew must have been brought from England and planted there about the time that the Norwood house was built in 1664.

The climatic and soil conditions on Cape Ann also are favorable for the growth of black walnut trees. Because of the demand for the wood of those trees for making gun stocks and especially for cabinet work in the nineteenth century, they became scarce. There is at least one old veteran left, however. It stands on Vine Street, just off Washington Street in Riverdale, near the Riggs house, one of the oldest houses on the Cape. The trunk measures 15 feet, 6 inches, and probably is more than two hundred years old. Its location is only a few hundred yards from the big old red oak mentioned above. Captain Riggs and his family apparently cherished fine trees.

In addition to the foregoing varieties of trees, the Cape Ann farmers and fishermen found many others readily available here to serve a multitude of purposes: white ash, for example, for making such items as sled runners, axe handles, spade and shovel handles, oars, and keels for small boats; hornbeam, for making handles for heavy tools such as sledges and mauls; locust, for the production of tree nails, the wooden pegs with which timbers and planks were fastened together in the construction of buildings and ships; red maple, especially abundant in the large swamps, for excellent firewood; black cherry, the fruit of which was used so commonly for flavoring rum that it came to be generally known as the rum-

223

cherry tree; black birch, from the sap of which birch beer was brewed; and sassafras, from the leaves of which tea was steeped and from the oil of which a flavoring extract for foods was prepared. Still other trees served other needs, and big elms furnished welcome shade around colonial homes.

The rather unique topographical and climatic conditions which favor the growth of such a great variety of trees within the confines of this rocky, swampy promotory also enable many shrubs and flowers to grow here.

Among the shrubs, the blueberry bushes must be given first place. The soil and climate of Cape Ann are especially suited to the growth of blueberries—low-bush on the uplands, and high-bush on both the uplands and the lowlands. On the lowlands they are found along the edges of the swamps, particularly in the Dogtown area and around Long Swamp. Blueberries were so abundant here that they provided a substantial portion of the much-needed fruit in the diet of the early settlers, and during the picking season were the chief sustenance, it has been said, of some of the last residents of Dogtown. Even today, in the summer months, Dogtown is thronged with blueberry pickers.

Blackberries also grow on the Cape, but in nothing like the profusion of blueberries. Beach plums, from which delicious jelly can be made, once were so abundant that a cove in the Lanesville district was named "Plum Cove." Now they are scarce on the Cape. Elderberry bushes still grow here in numerous spots. Elderberries formerly were used for jelly-making and for producing a tasty wine; nowadays, however, the birds are about the only ones to make use of them.

Barberries originally were a European shrub, but they were brought over by the colonists at an early date. They then propagated themselves so rapidly that they soon seemed to be wholly at home here. Although the barberry bushes were full of despicable thorns, as every gardener knows, the berries and the foliage were colorful, and the berries were used for mak-

224

ing jelly, pickles, wine, and a milder beverage called "shrub." From the bark and wood, furthermore, a fast yellow dye was produced. Perhaps the former popularity of barberries in this vicinity is best attested by the fact that beside practically every old cellar hole in Dogtown there stands a clump of these bushes.

With blueberries, blackberries, beach plums, elderberries, barberries, and also cranberries to be had for the picking, the colonial housewives, even on salty old Cape Ann, did not lack for appetizing and healthful fresh fruit in summer or for dried and preserved fruit and jelly in winter.

Bayberries also throve on the moors of Cape Ann, and for the colonial women they furnished material for making candles. The wax was extracted from the hard, gray berries by boiling, and although the light from a bayberry candle was not so bright as that from a tallow candle, the bayberry wax was a heartily welcome addition to the supply of candle-making material. After kerosene lamps replaced candles for lighting homes in the late nineteenth century, some of the housewives of Cape Ann continued to make bayberry candles, for the sake of the sweet aroma they give off when burning.

Bayberry wax also had other uses. It was mixed with tallow, for example, to make a salve to be applied to sores and inflamed spots. In the early nineteenth century, moreover, wax from bayberries gathered on Cape Ann was sold for use in the manufacture of shoe blacking and other polishing substances. Thus, over the years, the bayberry bushes furnished both light and pin-money to the womenfolk who lived on the Cape.

By giving color to its rugged landscape, the shrubs growing on Cape Ann also must have helped to brighten the lives of the fisherfolk in the olden days, just as they have enhanced its attractiveness for present-day residents and visitors in all seasons of the year. At the same time that the blueberry bushes are in bloom, many of the open moors and hillsides are tinged a delicate pink and white by the flowers of the shadbush. In an earlier era wild flowering dogwood, which grew chiefly on the outer edges of the upland forests, also contributed to the springtime coloring.

In the swamps in springtime the flowering shrubs include the spice bush, hobble bush, laurel, white azalea or swamp honeysuckle, rhodora, and magnolia. The spice bush is not a showy shrub, but its tiny yellow blossoms are one of the harbingers of spring, and its bark, berries, and wood are aromatic. The hobble bush, with its clusters of white flowers, and the white azalea, like the spice bush, are to be found in many of the swamps of Cape Ann. The laurel, with its evergreen leaves and masses of pink flowers, likewise grows luxuriantly in the swamps and on the hillsides, from one end of the Cape to the other. The rhodora, which has delicate purplish-pink blossoms, is a much more reticent shrub; it hides away in rather inaccessible spots in the deep swamps. The magnolia, unlike the other shrubs just mentioned, grows only in one place on Cape Ann, in the swamps in the Ravenswood Park area.

In the southern states the swamp magnolia attains tree size, but on Cape Ann it has only a slender trunk. Deep in Ravenswood swamp it grows amid tall maples and in the shadow of big hemlocks. Its ivory-tinted flowers have a haunting fragrance, and in the autumn its bright red seeds, as they dangle temptingly on gossamer threads from the light green cones where they have ripened, provide tidbits for the birds.

Among the shrubs which bloom in the summer on Cape Ann, the sweet pepper bush also deserves mention. This small shrub, with its showy spikes of white, fragrant flowers, finds the soil and climatic conditions of the Cape very much to its liking. It thrives in the moist ground along the edges of open swamps and it grows also, in larger clumps, on the uplands, particularly beside the old roads in Dogtown, and thus contributes to the beauty of that landscape.

In autumn, Cape Ann does not have so much bright gold and crimson foliage as northern New England, but the sumac, the shadbush, the tupelo, and the blueberry and huckleberry bushes cloak many of its hills and moors in deep scarlet. At the same time the maple-leaf viburnum patches the undergrowth along the forest paths with a rich burgundy.

In the autumn and early winter additional touches of color are furnished, especially in the swamps, by the red berries of the hobble bush and by those of the black alder or winterberry.

Several of these shrubs, in addition to beautifying the landscape, served utilitarian purposes for the Indians and the early settlers. The mildly acid, delicately flavored berries of the sumac were used by the Indians for making a healthy, cooling beverage, and the Indians even dried and stored sumac berries for winter use. The beverage not only had a pleasant taste but it also served as a remedy for colds. The English settlers soon learned these virtues of sumac berries and continued to use them for many years.

The Indians applied the bark of the black alder, after it had been chewed to a pulp, as their chief remedy for cuts and bruises. A brew made from alder bark also was used to alleviate the pain of burns and scalds. The English, of course, soon began to make use of that Indian remedy also, and on Cape Ann they had a supply of alder bark close at hand. From the swamp magnolia a concoction was prepared for treating chronic rheumatism and intermittent fever. From the leaves and bark of witch hazel, a bush with popping black seeds and small wry flowers that appear on the bare branches in late autumn, an extract was derived which had a soothing odor and was used by the Indians and the colonists as a remedy for numerous ailments.

The berries of the shrubs which have been mentioned and many others that grow on the Cape, and the nuts and berries of the beech, oak, cherry, and other trees provide food for a multitude of birds. In the spring and summer more than fifty varieties build their nests in the forests and swamps and on the moors of Cape Ann. In the autumn, the Cape is a way station for scores of other varieties of birds as they migrate southward. Its geographical location, jutting out into the ocean, makes it a convenient stopover point.

One variety of bird which formerly visited the Cape in great numbers on their southward flights but no longer appears is the passenger pigeon. The topography of Cape Ann made it a natural resting place for them and the local supplies of beech nuts, acorns, and other nuts and berries enabled them to eat heartily at this stage of their flight.

Unfortunately for the pigeons, however, it was discovered in various localities in New England that their flesh was a food delicacy, one for which there was a good demand in the cities when markets for luxuries grew up there. This led to wholesale trapping of the birds and their virtual extinction.

On a fairly level spot below the tan pit in the ravine in Annisquam, is a line of stones, most of them about the size of a ten-quart pail, arranged in the shape of a rough quadrangle about twenty-five feet long and fifteen feet wide. The purpose for which those stones had been placed there was a mystery to us until Miss Dorothy E. Snyder published an article in 1955 with an illustration of a pigeon trap in Boxford, Massachusetts, and a statement that such traps at one time had been built in numerous other locations.[24]

The trap operated as follows: The bed inside the border of rocks was raked smooth and then baited with nuts, wheat, and cracked corn. A net was laid along the rocks at one side of the bed and covered with leaves and brush. A stiff sapling was bent over the bed and attached to a stick along one edge

---

24 Dorothy E. Snyder, "The Passenger Pigeon of New England," *Bulletin of the Society for the Preservation of New England Antiquities*, XLV, 3 (Winter, 1955), p. 70.

of the net. The sapling was held in position by a rope which was connected to a trigger in a blind nearby where the operator was concealed. When the trap was full of pigeons eating the bait, the trigger was pulled and the sapling sprang up so quickly that it spread the net over the bed before the pigeons could fly away. The border of rocks served, of course, to keep the pigeons from escaping around the edges of the bed and also to prevent their being crushed by the net. As many as five hundred pigeons sometimes were caught in a trap at one time.

We have no doubt that the stones in the Annisquam ravine were once the walls of a pigeon trap, and there well may have been others on Cape Ann, for beech nuts and acorns were plentiful, and in primitive days the number of pigeons stopping off here was large.

Cape Ann's supplies of nuts and berries help support our year-round bird residents, such as the blue jays and chickadees, and they also attract flocks of late fall and winter visitors—myrtle warblers, purple finches, gold finches, pine grosbeaks, evening grosbeaks, cedar waxwings, fox sparrows, white-throated sparrows and others, and thus make Cape Ann a mecca for birdwatchers.

The soil and climatic conditions of Cape Ann also foster the growth of a great variety of flowers and plants, ranging from lowly lichens to lovely orchids. Within a few hundred yards of each other, in this rather limited geographical area, are to be found plants which grow only on lean, arid land, plants that flourish in the lush peat of swamps, and plants that like the deep shade of a forest. And not far away, on some sections of the Cape, are plants that grow only on salt marshes, sand dunes, and beaches. Altogether, at least five thousand varieties of plants, it is estimated, grow on Cape Ann.

Some of the scarcest flowers growing on the Cape are to be found in the swamps, especially in their deep, boggy jungles. Arethusa, or Indian pink, which blooms about the middle of June, and the pogonia, or "snake-mouth," and the calapogan, or "grass pink"—two other orchids—which bloom somewhat later than the arethusa, are among these. Still other quite rare flowers growing in the swamps are the white fringed orchid, buckbean, pitcher plant, sundew, and cardinal flower. The cardinal flower, with its bright scarlet color, is the most brilliant flower growing on the Cape.

In view of the diligence with which many colonial housewives cultivated the flower gardens around their homes, it is reasonable to suppose that they also enjoyed the wild flowers, including these rare ones which nowadays attract botanists to Cape Ann.

The list of the more common plants and flowers growing here is far too long to enumerate, much less to comment on. Consequently we mention only a few, to illustrate their great variety and some of their primitive uses.

Cattails furnished leaves which were used for making rush-bottomed chair seats, durable, and also far more comfortable than wooden seats. The leaves also were used for making baskets and the dry stalks for candle wicks.

The horse tail, a very elementary little plant, with a rough stem containing a considerable quantity of mineral matter, was used extensively by the colonists for scrubbing pots and pans and for various abrasive purposes.

The marsh marigold, with a bright yellow flower, provided leaves which once were widely used in the spring season as a pot herb. It is supposed to taste like spinach and was only one of a large number of wild plants which were available to the settlers on Cape Ann for food.

The horned bladderwort serves no utilitarian purpose, but its yellow flowers are especially fragrant. It grows in some of the sphagnum swamps on the Cape, alongside the pogonia and calapogan.

The floating bladderwort, with tiny yellow flowers, is one of the especially interesting plants growing on the Cape. Like the pitcher plant, it is carnivorous. It is supported in the shallow water where it grows by tiny air bladders on its roots and branches, which also serve as traps that catch small aquatic creatures to feed the plant.

In midsummer fragrant white water lilies bloom in great numbers in several Cape Ann ponds, especially in the Lily Pond, the long, narrow strip of shallow water beside the railroad tracks between West Gloucester and Magnolia, and in Langsford's Pond in Annisquam. In the latter pond there are also beautiful pink pond lilies, an exotic plant introduced from abroad but now thoroughly acclimatized here. Such flowers as these lend color to the rugged landscape of old Cape Ann.

The forests of the Cape, furthermore, like many of those elsewhere in New England, are carpeted with delicate mosses and the evergreen leaves of the wintergreen, bearberry, and gold thread. There, too, are clumps of feathery ferns, including the evergreen Christmas fern, and numerous other wild plants and flowers. In the spring the beautiful pink lady-slipper blooms profusely in some of the wooded areas, and later in the season the rattlesnake plantain, another orchid, with rosettes of evergreen leaves, puts forth its less conspicuous whitish flowers.

On the moors in the springtime there are acres of tiny bluets and small patches of dogtooth violets. And in the autumn, just when the foliage of the shrubs is beginning to turn scarlet, many a hillside in Dogtown and elsewhere is covered with the bright blue flowers of the dwarf, rough-leaved aster. Interspersed with the asters are clumps of brilliantly yellow goldenrod.

The brightness of the color of the goldenrod and of several other flowers growing on the Cape sometimes has been attributed to the nearness of the sea; but of that we have no proof.

231

Cape Ann, as has been pointed out, offers many contrasts, and that fact is exemplified again when we leave the swamps, the forests, and the moors, to take a look at the plant life on the nearby marshes, sand dunes, and beaches. The flora of the salt-water lands are altogether different from those of the swamps, forests, and uplands.

In the early spring, for instance, the Hudsonia, heathlike in appearance, puts forth its bright yellow flowers on the sand dunes, and later the seeds of those flowers provide an abundance of food for the birds and little animals which live on or near the sand hills.

In the summer, the sea rocket, a fleshy little plant which grows in the dry beach sand, shows its purplish flowers. Throughout the spring, summer, and autumn, moreover, the dusty miller covers large patches of beach sand with its silvery gray foliage.

The marram grass waves its gray-green blades atop the dunes and keeps on growing even though the sand around it is ever-shifting. It has tough roots, often ten or twelve feet long, which go down through the dunes to a point below high-tide level. Thereby the plant obtains its nourishment. Those long roots, furthermore, become matted and interwoven, especially at their lower extremities, and thus secure a firm mooring for protection as the sand in the dunes is shifted by winds and waves. The roots of the marram grass also serve as a binder to protect the dunes against devastation when raging storms attack them. Without the marram grass in the dunes, many of the summer cottages which have been built along Coffin's Beach would be at the mercy of nearly every heavy northeaster which rolls upon that shore.

The grass which covers the marshes along the river is of a different species, of course, from the marram grass, and it has served other purposes. For one thing, it provides protection for the little fish which are hatched in the myriad of

salt-water pools among the marshes. In former times, furthermore, it was used for hay.

During the latter part of the nineteenth century, and
probably long before that, the grass was cut in the summer-
time and piled in great stacks on the marshes. Poles were
driven into the marsh to provide foundations high enough to
raise the bottoms of the stacks above the high-tide range. In
the fall and winter the hay was removed from the stacks and
transported in "gundalows" to landings on the river, whence
it was carted to local farms. The "gundalows," a Cape cor-
ruption of gondolas, were heavy flat-bottomed boats, with high
prows and stems. They were either poled or rowed with long
sweeps and steered by means of an oar in the stern. Although
the salt-marsh hay was not highly nutritious, it served as a
useful supplement to the local hay crops, especially for feeding
young cattle.

Amidst the grass on the marshes grows the marsh samphire, or glasswort, as well as other plants especially adapted
to that habitat. The marsh samphire is a dwarf saline plant
with succulent stems that turn a brilliant red in the autumn.
The samphire is edible, and it was widely used by the colonists
as a salad. The supply available from the Annisquam marshes
was ample for their needs.

Another plant growing in the marshes is the marsh rosemary, which bears spikelets of lavender colored little flowers
for two or three months during the summer. The roots of the
rosemary are thick, woody, and astringent. Josselyn, in his
seventeenth century book to which reference has been made,
refers to a plant which we have not been able to identify, but
which just possibly may have been the rosemary. He called
it "Dogstones" or "Satyrion," and he stated that it grew on
salt marshes. Dogstones and Satyrion are obsolete names for
orchids, but orchids do not grow on salt marshes. Hence the
plant either was not an orchid or it did not grow on salt

marshes. The identity of this plant might be of some consequence because Josselyn stated that it was used "to procure
love . . . . I once took notice," he said, "of a wanton woman's
compounding the solid roots of this Plant with Wine, for an
Amorous Cup; which wrought the desired effect."[25] That
was in Puritan New England in 1672! If Dogstones grew on
the salt marshes near Scarborough, Maine, they almost cer-
tainly grew on the Annisquam marshes too, and one wonders
whether any of the witches used them hereabouts.

Just as the plant life of the beaches and salt marshes
differs from the flora of the swamps, forests, and uplands of
the Cape, so too does the birdlife differ, and in the late summer, autumn, and winter, especially, birdwatchers are attracted there. On one morning in August 1958, for example,
on the beach at the mouth of the Essex River, there were at
least ten thousand shore birds, perhaps twenty thousand. They
were too numerous to count. That was at the height of the
migration of those birds southward. Among them were cur-
lews, plovers, turnstones, dowitchers, sanderlings, knots, willets,
and several varieties of sandpipers. On the same beach, also,
were hundreds of terns, herring gulls, and great black-backed
gulls.

Shortly after the shore birds pass through on their annual
journey to the south, grebes, scoters, ducks, loons, and geese
appear. And offshore phalaropes, gannets, and other sea fowl
join the flocks of gulls on the dragger grounds. When winter
comes, more visitors from the arctic regions appear, to spend a
few weeks or months on the shores of Cape Ann—snowy owls,
horned larks, snow buntings, dovekies, Canadian geese, and
several varieties of ducks. The seeds of the plants on the
beaches and in the marshes, the vegetable and marine matter
on the clam flats and in the open coves and creeks, and the
small creatures living in the forest and brush provide food
for these winter visitors, each according to his taste. Some of

---

25 Josselyn, *op. cit.*, p. 81.

the sea fowl thus attracted to Cape Ann undoubtedly were a welcome addition to the food supply of the colonists.

The sea around the Cape also teems with plant and animal life. Some of the fish, such as mackerel, striped bass, tuna, sharks, and dogfish are migratory creatures, but far less regular than the birds in their seasonal travels. Many other sorts of fish, however, as well as small marine creatures, are constant residents of the waters around the Cape. And in the sea also a great variety of plants grow.

One of the marine plants growing most abundantly on the rocky shores of Cape Ann is the rockweed, a bushy plant, with stems often two or three feet long. Rockweed has air bladders on its branches which enable them to float when submerged by the tide. The leaves and stems of the rockweed are rich in nitrogen and other elements which are valuable for enriching the soil, and it often was used by Cape Ann farmers in earlier days for that purpose. Since rockweed is covered with a slippery, gelatinous secretion, it remains moist long after it has been removed from the sea. Consequently nowadays it is used by some Cape Ann lobstermen for packing live lobsters to be shipped to more or less distant markets.

Irish moss is another seaweed which flourishes in Cape Ann waters. It grows below the tide line, in water deeper than that where rockweed appears. Large quantities of this moss, however, often are wrenched loose by heavy storms and washed ashore. In earlier times the moss thus accumulated on the beaches was gathered on Cape Ann, as well as elsewhere, for use in the preparation of jellied puddings and medicinal compounds. Nowadays Irish moss often piles up, during a storm, in thick windrows on beaches such as those at Brace Cove and Kettle Cove, where it produces a stench if left to rot. When the decayed particles are washed into the sea again, they become a fertilizer for marine growth just as the decayed leaves in a forest provide leafmold which enriches

235

the soil for trees, shrubs, and plants. It is one of Nature's fertilizers.

Thus, wherever one turns on Cape Ann, whether it be in the fields or in the forests, on the ledges or in the swamps, on the moors or in the marshes, on the river or on the sea, he always is face to face with Nature.

A Chronological Summary

THE SAGA OF CAPE ANN, as related in the preceding chapters, covers upwards of three hundred years, and it falls into five fairly distinct chronological periods.

The first period extended from 1623 to about 1700. Although Champlain and Captain John Smith had visited this region at earlier dates, the white man's story really began with the arrival of the Dorchester fishermen in Gloucester Harbor in 1623. Following closely in their wake came the Pilgrims from Plymouth across the bay, and the clash occurred between Captain Myles Standish and John Oldham, Roger Conant, and the Reverend Lyford. In 1628 the Puritans from England began to settle in Salem and thence to spread out and establish the Massachusetts Bay Colony. The strategic location of Cape Ann led to the planting of a settlement on this promontory by the Puritans in 1642. At that time a town was chartered, a meetinghouse was built, and a canal was cut through the marsh to provide a navigable waterway from Gloucester Harbor to the neighborhood of The Green and to Planters Neck and Ipswich Bay. A mill also was erected on Wine Brook, the first of a dozen mills to be built to take advantage of every little brook and creek on the Cape. The founding of the settlement at Gloucester was a particularly enlightening example of the careful and diligent planning which the Puritans exercised in establishing themselves in the New World.

For the next half century after the town of Gloucester was chartered, the settlers on Cape Ann were clearing their farms and cutting cordwood and timbers to be shipped to Salem and Boston. The food that was grown on the farms was supplemented by fish, clams, and lobsters from the river and neighboring ocean waters, by sea fowl, and by no means least, by the abundant blueberries and other native fruit. The moors and forests and swamps, as well as the fields and the seashore, helped the settlers to supply their primitive needs.

The second period extended, roughly, from about 1700 to 1783. Around the opening of the eighteenth century commercial fishing, foreign trade, and shipbuilding began to thrive on Cape Ann. The cessation of warfare with the French encouraged Cape Ann fishermen to venture more frequently to the banks off Nova Scotia and Newfoundland. The schooner rig was invented. The first schoolhouse was built on The Green. The center of the town began to shift from The Green to the vicinity of Gloucester Harbor. Annisquam became an active shipbuilding and trading community. Dogtown was settled. The West Parish was set off as a separate community with its own meetinghouse and burying ground. Settlements were started at Pigeon Cove and Sandy Bay. And pirates came to prey on Cape Ann ships.

By the middle of the eighteenth century, several of the merchants and foreign traders were enjoying a prosperity which enabled them to build fine homes. Taverns became more numerous. Witches were active. And the Reverend John Murray arrived to found the first Universalist Church in America and to start a bitter local feud, which resulted in a breaking down of basic religious regulations. Finally, as the restrictions imposed on their trade by King George the Third became more oppressive and obnoxious, the inhabitants of Cape Ann, as well as those of Boston, began to indulge in resistance to the tax collectors.

The Revolutionary War, with its interference with shipping and foreign trade, brought great hardships to Cape Ann. That was the end of the second period.

The third period covered the years from the end of the Revolutionary War to about 1840. For thirty years after the end of that war, recovery on Cape Ann was slow. Fishing and foreign trade improved gradually, only to be harassed again by the British. Local trade increased, however, and a stagecoach line to Boston was inaugurated which brought Gloucester into closer relations with that metropolis. Then came the War of 1812, and the British raids on Cape Ann afforded significant examples of how that war was waged.

After the end of the War of 1812, the Cape Ann fishing industry took on new life. In addition to cod, the old standby, the local fishermen began to catch mackerel and halibut on a large scale. Trips were made to the dreaded Georges as well as to the Grand Bank. Shipbuilding was revived at Annisquam and Essex, as well as at Gloucester Harbor. In 1823 the quarry industry was started at Pigeon Cove and presently spread to Lanesville. Dogtown became a deserted village.

Then came the Panic of 1837, and the boom collapsed.

The fourth period, which covered the years from 1840 to 1914, was marked by the adoption of mass-production methods in fishing—the use of trawls in cod fishing and of purse seines in mackerel fishing; by the introduction of the clipper-bow design in schooner construction; and by the influx of Irish and Finnish workers, to be followed by Portuguese and Italians.

The most notable feature of this period, however, was the start of the business of catering to summer visitors, first at East Gloucester, Bass Rocks, Pigeon Cove, and Annisquam, then somewhat later at Magnolia.

The railroad line to Boston was opened. Thereby the marketing of the products of the local fisheries was facilitated, and travel was stimulated. The causeway at Goose Cove and the bridge across Lobster Cove were built. Then presently came the horsecars and the electric cars which provided more rapid means for travel around the Cape. These developments contributed to a growth of the summer business as well as to the opportunities for recreation for the local residents.

The final period includes the years since 1914. Even before World War I broke out, revolutionary changes were under way in the local shipbuilding industry. Auxiliary motors were being installed in fishing schooners and experiments were being tried with all-power driven ships for fishing. World War I marked the end of the shipbuilding industry on Cape Ann, except for a few racing craft. The diesel engine took the place of sails. The catches of cod, halibut, and mackerel by Gloucester fishermen declined and were replaced only in part by whiting and redfish (ocean perch). Fish processing continued to be one of the main local industries, but more and more of the fish used has been imported, in the form of frozen slabs, from Canada, Greenland, and Iceland.

In 1910 a new bridge was installed at the Cut and the river was dredged to accommodate larger vessels. After the end of World War I, these improvements encouraged the use of the river by fishing craft and especially by pleasure boats.

At the same time that the fishing vessels were being equipped with engines, land travel also was becoming motorized, and new highways were built which made Cape Ann more and more accessible to people living elsewhere.

The influx of summer visitors went on apace, and the Cape Ann beaches, especially the one near where Major Coffin's farm once was situated, became heavily congested with transient patrons on Sundays and holidays. The new facilities for motor travel, furthermore, attracted more and more year-round residents to the Cape.

Thus life on Cape Ann has undergone many changes during the last three hundred years. Despite all those changes, however, the Cape has retained its picturesque terrain, its colorful wildlife, and its unique scenic views. Around the Cape, furthermore, there are still many landmarks which date back to its primitive days.

INDEX

INDEX

Aberdeen Granite Co., the, 179
Abigail, the: fishing records of, 101
acorn oil, 221-22
Adams, Dr. Isaac, 172
Adolph, the: story of, 60
Agassquam. *See* Annisquam
Alcott, Louisa May, 66
Alden, John, 5
alder bark: uses of, 227
alewives, 29, 190
Alice M. Jacobs, the, 92
Allen, Joseph, 27
Alley, John B., 144
Ames, Major General Adelbert, 143-44
Ames Estate, the, 143
Andrew, A. Piatt, 73
Andrew Harraden house, the, 168
Andrew's Point, 124
Annisquam: clam-shell mounds at, 16, 190-91; shipbuilding at, 88, 161-62; naming of, 153; individuality of, 153, 154-55; early topography of, 154-55; trading post, 156, 161; transportation in, 156, 166-67; ferry, 156, 198; *Falcon* raid on, 157-58; tan pit, 162; brooks in, 163; industry at, 165-66; transformation of, 166-68; landmarks in, 168-75; first schoolhouse, 172-73; sailboat racing at, 188-89. *See also* Goose Cove; Lobster Cove; Planter's Neck
Annisquam Harbor, 155-56, 158-61
Annisquam River, the: for commuting, 19; traffic on, 176, 180; description of, 177; landmarks on, 180-86, 187-90; a source of food, 190-94

A

Annisquam Yacht Club, the, 175, 188
Arethusa, the: research boat, 170
Arethusa: rare plant, 230
Arlington Street, 165, 175
artists' colony, 67, 135
Atalanta, the, 95, 108
Atlantic cable, the, 131
"Aunt Rachel," 35
auxiliary engines, 92, 93
Avery, Reverend John, 128-29
Avery's Ledge, 129

B

Babson, James, 163
Babson, John, 124, 134
Babson, John J., 13-14, 23, 45, 142, 205-06
Babson, Roger W., 38
Babson's Point: ferry landing, 156; fort at, 161
Babson's Reservoir, 20, 21, 38, 217
Back Road, the: Dogtown, 24, 31, 32
back shore area: extent of, 62
Back Street, Gloucester, 44
bait, 102-03, 191-92, 193-94
bait mill invented, 113
Baker's Mill. *See* Marm Killam's Sluiceway
barberries, 224-25
Barberry Hill, 154
bayberries, 225
bayberry wax, 225
Bartlett, Capt. Bob, 91
Bass Rocks, summer resort, 68. *See also* East Gloucester
Bay View: granite quarries at, 142-46; naming of, 143; lobsters shipped from, 145
beach plums, 224
Bearskin Neck: attacked by frigate, 134; naming of, 134; artists' colony, 135

243

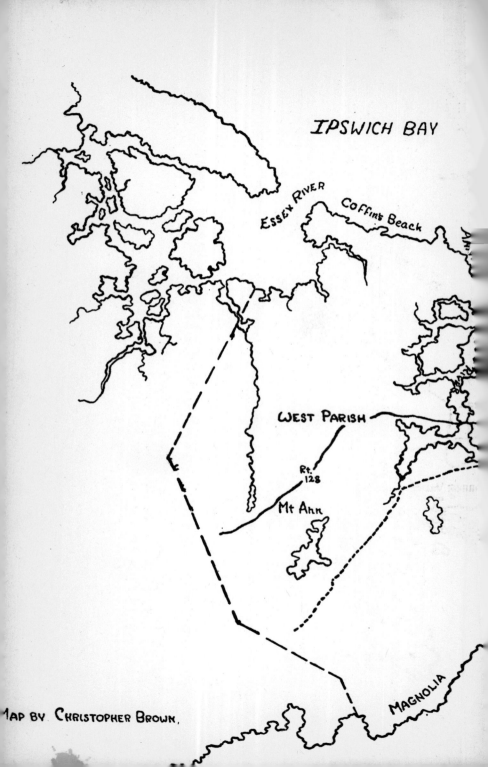

IPSWICH BAY

ESSEX RIVER

Coffin's Beach

WEST PARISH

Rt. 128

Mt Ann

MAGNOLIA

MAP BY CHRISTOPHER BROWN.